D0078506

Satire in Colonial Spanish America

The Texas Pan American Series

Satire in Colonial Spanish America
Turning the New World Upside Down

Julie Greer Johnson

Foreword by Daniel R. Reedy

 University of Texas Press, Austin

Publication of this work has been made possible in part by a
grant from the Program for Cultural Cooperation between
Spain's Ministry of Culture and United States Universities.

Copyright © 1993 by the University of Texas Press
All rights reserved
Printed in the United States of America

First edition, 1993

Requests for permission to reproduce material from this work
should be sent to Permissions, University of Texas Press,
Box 7819, Austin, TX 78713-7819.

⊗ The paper used in this publication meets the minimum
requirements of American National Standard for Information
Sciences—Permanence of Paper for Printed Library Materials,
ANSI Z39.48-1984.

Library of Congress Cataloging-in-Publication Data

Johnson, Julie Greer.
    Satire in colonial Spanish American : turning the New World
upside down / by Julie Greer Johnson ; foreword by Daniel R.
Reedy. — 1st ed.
      p.   cm. — (The Texas Pan American series)
    Includes bibliographical references and index.
    ISBN 0-292-77654-3 (alk. paper)
    1. Satire, Spanish American—History and criticism.
2. Spanish American literature—To 1800—History and
criticism. I. Title. II. Series.
PQ7082.S26J64 1993
867.009'98—dc20   92-42849

DISCARDED
WIDENER UNIVERSITY

WIDENER UNIVERSITY
WOLFGRAM
LIBRARY
CHESTER, PA.

To Merle E. Simmons and Dana D. Johnson

Contents

Foreword

Toward the end of the seventeenth century, Peruvian poet and satirist Juan del Valle y Caviedes penned a prescription for laughter as a means by which society could cure itself of its ills. He advised the readers of his clandestine verses, "Ríate de ti el primero . . . , ríate de ellos después . . . , ríate de todo, puesto que, aunque de todo te rías, tienes razón" ("Laugh first at yourself . . . , laugh at others afterwards . . . , laugh at everything, for even if you laugh at everything, you have the right to do so") ("Prólogo al que leyere este tratado" "Prologue to the One Who Reads This Treatise"). Caviedes' focus on laughter highlights but one component of the multiple ingredients which distinguish and identify the satirical mode of expression during the colonial period in Spanish America. Sarcasm, invective, parody, burlesque, censure, irony, and paradox all found a fertile environment for implementation as tools which satirists, in prose or verse, employed to criticize, provoke, censor, and titillate.

No subject was deemed to be sacred, nor was any individual of high or low station exempted as an object of the satirist's condemning view, acerbic wit, or sarcastic invective. From the *pasquines* with which Hernán Cortés' comrades lampooned their leader to the satires of protest published by Santa Cruz y Espejo at the close of the colonial era, government institutions, rulers, church fathers, specific individuals, and societal groups such as blacks, mestizos, mulattoes, women, doctors, and other professionals were all fair targets for the satirist's barbs.

Because satire often deals with human frailty, there tends to be a moral and didactic focus that in its caustic tone and degree of censure goes beyond normal disapproval and extends to extremes of exaggerated proportion in its condemnation of institutions, persons, or societal values. Such is especially true during the dominance of the baroque style and aesthetic in the seventeenth and early eighteenth centuries. In her *Satire in Colonial Spanish America,* Julie Greer

Johnson explores how this mode of expression flourished as a genre of New World writing from the earliest times of the discovery and conquest, throughout the colonial period, to the present day. Hers is the first comprehensive examination of the subject of satire in the colonial era, building on her own segmental studies as well as those done by others, enlarging our understanding of satire's many practitioners over three centuries, defining the various manifestations and concepts of this mode of expression, and filling the gaps in our knowledge through a well-constructed framework of theoretical concepts and actual practice.

Satirical wit is the pivotal topic on which the author focuses her attention, and justifiably so, since humor and the provocation of laughter are often the most identifiable external characteristics of the genre. As well, her primary thesis that Spanish America's satirists were individually, and collectively, intent on dismantling Spain as a symbol of political and religious power which dominated society and culture during the colonial period is borne out by her observations. On the one hand, they were opposed to cultural and political hegemony, while on the other, their writings suggest a growing self-awareness, leading ultimately to an awakening consciousness of national identity as a people in the eighteenth and nineteenth centuries. This process should not be construed necessarily as the product of a conscious political stance by writers from diverse periods of time and different regions of the viceregal world. Rather, their attitudes seem to be the result of an unconscious and individual orientation away from the cultural, political, and intellectual dominion of Spain and toward a sense of personal freedom as individuals and as societal groups.

The projection of utopian images on the New World by Spanish conquerors was clearly at odds with the realities which native Americans, Creoles, transplanted Spaniards, and others were able to see around them. The illusion of the Spanish vision was contrasted with the perception of those who were experiencing realities which were clearly nonutopian. Thus, a number of major figures can be identified among Spanish America's satirists who offered perspectives that run counter to those projected by Spain. Chief among these writers are Mateo Rosas de Oquendo, Juan del Valle y Caviedes, Sor Juana Inés de la Cruz, Juan Rodríguez Freile, Esteban Terralla y Landa, Alonso Carrió de la Vandera, and Eugenio de Santa Cruz y Espejo, whose collective works extend from the late sixteenth through the end of the eighteenth centuries.

What accounts, then, for the fact that many of these authors have been so little known or read until the second half of the twentieth century? Why, only now at the close of the century, is the first comprehensive examination of colonial Spanish American satire appearing? A number of reasons could be posited, but one dominant factor is common to most of these figures. As persons who often wrote provocatively about political repression, religious control, and artistic censorship, occasionally with specific reference to powerful figures in Church, state, and society, their works were frequently not published during the lifetime of the author but were circulated clandestinely in manuscript form. As Irving A. Leonard has pointed out in his *Books of the Brave,* government and Church were instrumental in controlling the flow of printed materials from Spain to the New World, and without the favorable imprimatur of Church and Crown, few works of a provocative nature were printed either in America or on the Peninsula. Even those that made their way into print were not easily circulated under the rigid controls of the time.

A single case in point will illustrate how numerous New World writers were relegated to obscurity beyond their lifetime as the result of relying on circulation of manuscript copies of their works when avenues for publication were not readily available. The author of some 350 poems whose themes and topics left few strata of Peruvian society unscathed, Juan del Valle y Caviedes saw only 3 of them in print during his lifetime as occasional verse in texts on other subjects. Yet, on the basis of various manuscript versions of his poetry which are extant in libraries and archives today, we can assert that his texts were reasonably well known during his time, and were imitated and bowdlerized after his death. At the close of the eighteenth century, his works were rediscovered and brief selections published for the first time in Lima's *Mercurio Peruano.* Attempts to edit more complete versions of his texts were not to come until the last three decades of the nineteenth century, and not until 1984 was an edition of his works available in a reliable, annotated edition without the expurgation of selected verses and poems which had often been seen as too bawdy or obscene by earlier editors. This same sketch, with variations, could be drawn for the works of most of the major figures treated in this study with the exception of Sor Juana Inés de la Cruz, Mexico's Tenth Muse, despite the fact that some of her writings aroused the criticism of the church hierarchy, resulting in her silence as an obedient nun during the last years of her life.

The central concept posited by Professor Johnson's study is that satire was the chief vehicle of expression whereby marginalized sectors of New World society could challenge the facade and misrepresentation of the colonizer. It was a kind of subversive discourse which sought to provide a countervailing and more authentic view of aspects of the New World, particularly as they dealt with political, social, cultural, and artistic hierarchies. In so doing, satirists offered an alternative vision of life in colonial Spanish America from that of the colonizer, by providing divergent, corrective, and reformational viewpoints for their readers in open opposition to the more utopian views of officialdom.

In terms of their satirical art, many of these writers followed the literary models which they knew from Spain but with a reconceptualization of this art appropriate to the environment in which they wrote. Such was particularly true of their acceptance and emulation of such writers as Spain's Francisco de Quevedo y Villegas whose works challenged his country's idealism from within. Others chose to invert traditional models by creating parodies or inversions of standard modes which would reflect negatively on commonly accepted and authorized forms of expression.

In their pursuit of self-expression in the context of a regulated and often oppressive environment, colonial Spanish American satirists utilized popular humor and a full arsenal of rhetorical devices and imaginative language in their expression of ideas which would reflect their own environment and the realities which distinguished them as emerging national groups. By offering views counter to those of the colonial empire, they were, de facto, defining themselves as a people through their own creativity and originality. Thus, their self-reflection and rhetorical experimentation became an important aspect of the redefinition and rediscovery of the New World—a process which progressed and expanded from the sixteenth through the eighteenth centuries as the Spanish Empire diminished in strength and influence and as the dominance of Creole points of view increased.

Julie Greer Johnson's study of the satiric mode in Spanish America offers a comprehensive and cohesive view of the development and role of satire in the colonial era through her examination of many of its most important writers and her commentary on their literary artistry. She aptly points out that satire was a vital force in the process of metamorphosis of colonial society struggling to free itself of Spanish hegemony as it moved resolutely toward a new sense of independence and of cultural and political identity.

Daniel R. Reedy
University of Kentucky

Acknowledgments

Several institutions have provided financial assistance for my study of satire, and I wish to thank them for their generosity. Research was funded primarily by the John Carter Brown Library of Providence, Rhode Island, and the University of Georgia Foundation. A Columbian Quincentennial Fellowship and a National Endowment for the Humanities Travel Grant also enabled me to complete particular stages of my investigation at the Newberry Library in Chicago and the Benson Latin American Collection at the University of Texas in Austin. The publication of this book was graciously supported by the Spanish Ministry of Culture.

Throughout the various stages of my work, many colleagues have read preliminary manuscripts, written letters of recommendation for grant proposals, and offered advice on specific aspects of colonial satire. I am especially indebted to Rolena Adorno, Raquel Chang-Rodríguez, Aníbal González, Djelal Kadir, Pedro Lasarte, Asunción Lavrin, W. Michael Mathes, Jan Pendergrass, Enrique Pupo-Walker, Daniel R. Reedy, Hildebrando Ruiz, Georgina Sabat de Rivers, and Joseph T. Snow for their consideration and encouragement. I am also grateful to Sharon Reed for her skill and patience in preparing the typescript. The final production of the book would not have been possible without the time and care taken by Theresa J. May, the executive editor of the University of Texas Press, and the assistance of her talented and diligent staff.

Earlier versions of portions of this book have previously appeared in print, and I wish to thank the editors of these publications for publishing my work initially and for granting me permission to reproduce it in this present volume. These articles and essays are the following: "A Satiric View of Colonization: Rodríguez Freile's History of New Granada," *North Dakota Quarterly* 55.3 (1987): 166–174; "A Comical Lesson in Creativity from Sor Juana Inés de la Cruz," *Hispania* 71.2 (1988): 442–444; "Lo grotesco en Terralla y

Landa," *Revista de Crítica Literaria Latinoamericana* 14.28 (1988): 317–325; "Cristóbal de Llerena and His Satiric *Entremés*," *Latin American Theatre Review* (Fall 1988): 39–45; "Traveling in Eighteenth-Century Spanish America: The Evaluation of a Disgruntled Spaniard," *SECOLAS Annals* 20 (March 1989): 40–47; "*El Nuevo Luciano* and the Satiric Art of Eugenio Espejo," *Revista de Estudios Hispánicos* 23.3 (1989): 67–85; "Rosas de Oquendo and *La victoria naval peruntina*," *Studies in Honor of Merle E. Simmons*, ed. Heitor Martins and Darlene J. Sadlier (Bloomington: Hispanic Literary Studies of the Department of Spanish and Portuguese, Indiana University, 1990), pp. 233–247; "New World Chronicles: A Self-Evaluation," *Ideas '92*, no. 6 (January–April 1990): 7–16; "Satire and Eighteenth-Century Colonial Spanish American Society," *Coded Encounters: Race, Gender, and Ethnicity in Colonial Latin America* (Amherst: University of Massachusetts Press, 1992), the selected proceedings of the Symposium honoring Lewis U. Hanke; "La obra satírica de sor Juana Inés de la Cruz," to appear in *Relecturas del barroco de Indias*, ed. Mabel Moraña (Madrid: Ediciones del Norte, 1992); "La risa como medicina en el Perú del siglo XVII: El remedio de Juan del Valle y Caviedes," to appear in *Literatura latinoamericana del período colonial*, ed. Lúcia Helena Costigan and Beatriz González Stephan (Caracas: Ministerio de la Cultura de Venezuela, 1992).

J.G.J.

Introduction

An artistic blend of wit and criticism distinguishes the satire of any period as a stimulating and, indeed, challenging form of expression. Literary historians attest to its long tradition from Aristophanes to Huxley, Orwell, and Ionesco, and contemporary writers continue to explore its potential. While critics have renewed their efforts to define it more precisely over the past twenty years, initial credit must be given to Northrop Frye for delineating satire's uniqueness as a form of discourse and for placing it within a comprehensive theory of literature in his *Anatomy of Criticism*. Historical and theoretical studies that have appeared since its publication support his initiative and have traced satire's development from the literary mode back to magic ritual, outlined critical approaches to satiric writings, and examined their structure and character portrayal. Among the important contributions to research are Robert C. Elliott's *Power of Satire*, Ronald Paulson's collection *Satire: Modern Essays in Criticism*, Alvin B. Kernan's *Plot of Satire*, and Maynard Mack's article "The Muse of Satire."

This expression of enthusiasm by a number of critics, while having its greatest impact on scholars studying satire written in English, has not been without recognition by those of other modern languages. Satire has especially influenced the works of such Spanish American writers as Bioy Casares, Borges, Cabrera Infante, Cortázar, Donoso, Fuentes, García Márquez, Lezama Lima, Onetti, Puig, Rulfo, and Vargas Llosa, and the application of newly proposed critical concepts to their novels and short stories has barely gotten under way. Alfred MacAdam, for example, provides a model for extensive study of many of these contemporary authors in his seminal work *Modern Latin American Narratives: The Dreams of Reason*, and Ardis Nelson's *Cabrera Infante in the Menippean Tradition*, Jonathan Tittler's *Narrative Irony in the Contemporary Spanish-American Novel*, and Emir Rodríguez Monegal's "Carnaval/antropofagia/parodia" contribute to the development of specialized aspects of this critical mode. More recent studies, such as *Chicano Satire* by Guillermo E. Hernández and *La parodia en la nueva novela hispanoamericana* by Elżbieta Skłodowska, have added to the momentum of this scholarly reconsideration, and several comparative works, such as Linda Hutcheon's *Theory of Parody* and Frank Palmeri's *Satire in Narrative*, place contemporary Spanish American writers among those currently at the forefront of satiric and parodic expression.

Pioneering studies on satire similar to those just mentioned, however, are absent for the colonial era, and as the discourse of this period is brought into the mainstream of Spanish American literature with the success of contemporary writers, such an undertaking seems appropriate and should lay vital groundwork for future investigations. Although previous research on viceregal authors of satiric writings has brought recognition and esteem to the more prominent practitioners of the art, the body of articles and books that comprise it is relatively small. Such studies have also traditionally focused on individual satirists and have generally contained analyses of their works as contributions to the development of poetry or prose fiction in the New World rather than to the history of satire. This study, then, is designed to present a reinterpretation of works by several of the colonial period's major figures as well as an analysis of those by some lesser-known writers who contributed to this critical mode in the Indies.

Apart from the basic need to uncover satire's development in early Spanish America, additional resources have recently become accessible through the publication of editions and translations of works by colonial satirists, which make a general study particularly fitting at this time. In 1990 Pedro Lasarte's critical edition of *Sátira hecha por Mateo Rosas de Oquendo a las cosas que pasan en el Pirú, año de 1598* appeared, and plans are being made by the same editor to publish another of this satirist's works. The complete works of Juan del Valle y Caviedes, the period's most outstanding writer of satire, were edited by Daniel R. Reedy in 1984, and this volume was preceded by Philip L. Astuto's 1981 edition of *Obra educativa* by Eugenio de Santa Cruz y Espejo and by Alan Soons' 1978 edition of *Lima por dentro y fuera* by Esteban Terralla y Landa. Emilio Carilla's 1973 publication of *El lazarillo de ciegos caminantes* continues to be the most valuable presentation of Alonso Carrió de la Vandera's travelogue, and Juan Rodríguez Freile's *El Carnero* has been edited numerous times, notably by Miguel Aguilera in 1963 and by Darío Achury Valenzuela in 1979. While these editions have stimulated the interest of Latin Americanists in colonial authors, translations of the latter two works by Walter D. Kline and William C. Atkinson, respectively, have made them available to comparatists studying both narrative and satire.

Given the present state of scholarship, I propose to fill existing lacunae by examining the works of early Spanish America's major satirists and by presenting them as a cohesive body of discourse indicative of the transculturation then taking place in the New World, yet one that runs counter to the dominant ideology and rhetoric of colonial expression. Their literary dismantling of imperial Spain as the indisputable symbol of political and religious power and as the primary source of social and cultural dynamics in the New World is the focus of my study. Chapter 1 contains a general description of colonial satire and a discussion of the more important factors that shaped its development. In order to show that it was not an isolated phenomenon and that it did indeed flourish at the close of the colonial period, each of the next three chapters is dedicated to the principal satirists of a single century. Works are analyzed as separate entities to demonstrate the interaction and reliance of satirical devices on one another and their overall effectiveness in fulfilling the author's purpose and design. After reviewing the first three hundred years of satire's development in colonial Spanish America, my investigation concludes in Chapter 5 with a reappraisal of its importance within colonial discourse and an assessment of its influence on modern Spanish American literature.

The chronological presentation of Spanish American satire's development highlights its continuity over three centuries and reveals its evolutionary pattern of ideas and literary techniques. Topics that persisted and intensified with time manifest the existence of irreconcilable differences between Spain and its possessions and confirm the presence of a growing self-awareness among Americans that would eventually lead to the emergence of a collective national consciousness. Because of the satirists' desire for liberation, which was not limited to social, political, economic, or religious issues but extended into the realm of artistic creation as well, satiric writings, more than any other kind, capture the mounting turbulence within early Spanish American society and anticipate the birth of its unique cultural identity as it embarks upon the national experience.

Satire in Colonial Spanish America

1. Origins of Satire in the Old World and the New

For many Europeans the discovery of America was the fulfillment of ancient prophecy and the herald of the long-awaited revival of a golden age. Inspired by such wondrous descriptions as the enchanted Hesperides, the utopian Atlantis, the biblical terrestrial paradise, and other marvellous settings, they had embarked on voyages in search of an alternate route to Asia and not unpredictably thought that they had found the marvels they were seeking.[1] For others, however, their heightened expectations only led to greater disillusionment as discrepancies between the glowing visions of the New World and its strikingly distinct reality became apparent, and it is from this group that the earliest writers of Spanish American satire emerged. Relying more on their own New World experience to shape their perceptions than on the resurrection of Old World fantasies, they reacted against the euphoria of the time, and they did so by refusing to accept Spain's illusory image of America as well as the rhetoric that conveyed it and projected it throughout the years of Spanish domination. By bending inversely the magical lens through which Europeans at first generally perceived America, satirists reoriented traditional elements to create an entirely new configuration and one that portrayed the New World trying to break with the Old. Although this inversion initially appears to be destructive in nature, it provides a new artistic dimension that enhances the potential of the original conception and compounds its previous possibilities. Because these Spanish American satirists called for a redefinition and restructuring of reality as well as its literary representation, their works provide an informative and creative alternative to the general body of early New World writings, and they represent a significant countercurrent within colonial discourse. In order to understand the precise form the inverted image would take, it is essential to consider briefly the nature of the original one by reviewing the unusual circumstances surrounding America's discovery and the spirit in which the first descriptions of it were conceived.

The sighting of one of the Bahama Islands on October 12, 1492, convinced Christopher Columbus that he had indeed been chosen by God to begin the conversion of the world's remaining heathen races, thought by the ancients to be the last phase of human history, and a prelude to the world's destruction.[2] Reflecting on the Admiral's assessment of his role in the discovery, Bartolomé de las Casas remarked, "Cosa maravillosa cómo lo que el hombre mucho desea y asienta una vez con firmeza en su imaginación, todo lo que oye y ve, ser en su favor a cada paso se le antoja" ("How marvellous a thing it is how whatever a man strongly desires and has firmly set in his imagination, all that he hears and sees at each step he fancies to be in its favor").[3] After having arrived at this unspoiled, gardenlike spot in which human beings appeared to live in complete harmony with nature, Columbus thus concluded that he was approaching a paradise on earth, a belief he expressed in a letter to the Spanish monarchs. His initial impressions, which reflect the classical *locus amoenus* of Virgilian tradition, were intended to describe his findings in optimum terms, a measure that he hoped would assure Spain's expansion into the area and confirm his function as the instrument of divine prophecy.

> Esta isla es bien grāde y mȳ llana y de arboles mȳ verdes y mūchas aguas y vna laguna en medio mūy grāde sin ninguᵃ montaña y toda ella verde q̃s plazer de mirarla.

> (This island is quite big and very flat and with very green trees and with much water and a very large lake in the middle and without any mountains; and all of it so green that it is a pleasure to look at it.)[4]

This idyllic setting was inhabited by exceptional physical specimens of humanity, who lived in a state of innocence and were naturally amenable.

> Mȳ biē hechos de mūy fermosos cuerpos y mūy buenas caras. . . . Ellos dever ser buenos s[er]uidores y de buē ingenio q̃ veo q̃ mūy presto dizē todo lo q̃ les dezia: y creo q̃ ligeramēte se harian xp̄ianos q̃ me pareçio q̃ ninguᵃ secta tenian.

> (They are very well formed, with handsome bodies and good faces. . . . They should be good and intelligent servants, for I see that they say very quickly everything that is said to them; and I believe that they would become Christians very easily, for it seemed to me that they had no religion.)[5]

Although Columbus' illusion was somewhat diminished on his second voyage in which he learned about the existence of cannibalistic tribes, the destructive force of hurricanes, and the scarcity of gold, he continued to affirm the political and eschatological importance of his discovery. The Admiral's idealistic vision was enthusiastically accepted by the Spanish Crown and embraced by Spaniards who interpreted the New World as being a part of the old order and described it by drawing comparisons between Europe and America. Proof of the perpetuation of this utopian spirit may be found in the verses of Alonso de Ercilla's description of the Chilean landscape in *La Araucana*[6] and Bernardo de Balbuena's presentation of New Spain's capital in a constant state of springtime in his *Grandeza mexicana.*[7] The primitive native as well, as an integral part of this setting, continued to capture the imagination and became the "noble savage" of Las Casas' *Historia de las Indias* and the creator of a great civilization in the *Comentarios reales* by the Inca Garcilaso de la Vega.[8]

New World idealism also spawned other manifestations of the fantastic and the mythical, as Columbus himself became somewhat of an archetype as he played out his role as a valiant figure on a quest in unknown lands. Writers of chivalric novels like Garci-Rodríguez de Montalvo were inspired by the singularity of his endeavors, and early chroniclers tended to envision the exploits of the conquerors, who followed in his footsteps, as knightly adventures. Bernal Díaz del Castillo, who was one of those influenced by this way of thinking, remarked in his *Historia verdadera de la conquista de la Nueva España* on seeing the city of Tenochtitlan for the first time that it is similar to one described in *Amadís de Gaula.*[9] Fray Gaspar de Carvajal, who was also enticed by the caballeresque, characterized some fighting tribeswomen along South America's principal river system as resembling the Amazons of *Amadís'* sequel, *Sergas de Esplandián*, and reports of the New World location of their elusive matriarchal realm proliferated.[10]

The impact that the discovery of America had on Europe's intellectual community was profound, as the new land was thought to be the realization of dreams. Just twenty-four years after Columbus' first voyage, Sir Thomas More's *Utopia* appeared asserting that the New World was not simply another place but the symbol of a new beginning and a fresh start for a civilization that now viewed itself as tired and worn. This was an opportunity to return to a glorious past that was unaffected and much less complicated and a chance either to locate a perfect society or to create one through careful supervision and planning. Optimism was running high and appeared to be unflagging, and the enthusiasm it engendered served well Spain's ambitious plans for imperial expansion. Enticed by promises of prosperity and happiness, many Spaniards eagerly enlisted in the countless expeditions to explore the New World, and real efforts were made by zealous colonists to establish ideal societies in several parts of the Americas. In New Spain More's influence is evident in the catechistic *Doctrinas* penned by Mexico's first bishop, Fray Juan de Zumárraga, and in the governance of Indian settlements by some religious orders. The Franciscans under the direction of Fray Toribio de Benavente, who was also known as Motolinía, endeavored to establish Indo-Christian colonies, and Vasco de Quiroga, the bishop of Michoacán who translated *Utopia* into Spanish, used the work in guiding his relations with the natives under his jurisdiction. South America was not without its experiments in utopian living either, as carefully regulated mission villages, organized among the Guarani in the Paraguayan jungle, stood as a monument to the Society of Jesus in the New World.[11]

Although the Spaniards embarked upon a number of striking ventures of utopian design, their most immediate task, indeed the most important one after the conquest, was to communicate a specific set of beliefs and values to American residents at large and in essence to impose Old World culture upon them. This would ensure the creation of orderly and harmonious territorial divisions to be added to the world's then most powerful empire. Colonization, therefore, was not simply a matter of establishing a physical presence in the region but of transmitting a conceptualization of the New World's subjugation in which the Peninsular-born male Spaniard was the dominant force within a society that, while being patriarchal, was equitable and all-encompassing. Although other groups, such as Indians, blacks, mestizos, women, and even American-born Spaniards, or Creoles, were accorded positions inferior to him, his relationship to these lower echelons was protective and paternalistic. Spain had achieved complete military dominance over native Americans, and it, therefore, deemed its culture to be superior to theirs as well.

Confirmed by the conquerors and propagated by friars during the conversion, this hegemonic vision became the most pervasive ideology of colonial thought, and its literary manifestations made utopia a principal theme of colonial discourse. The signs and codes that accompanied this utopian perception were appropriated and conventionalized, either consciously or unconsciously, by early New World writers, who, while not excluding criticism and controversy from their works, usually acknowledged Spain's preeminence on the premise that it governed its citizens in a reasonable manner and provided for the growth of a stable society.[12] At a time when fact and fiction blended to form a concept of history, New World chroniclers and historians drew upon a number of creative literary devices in the process of composing persuasive and eloquent accounts that were morally instructive, and they did so in accordance with the principles of Renaissance historiography. These writings generally provided paradigms of identity for New World inhabitants to follow, and in this respect, they were designed to play a role in the positive formation of society and to create within it a certain homogeneity as colonization progressed. Aided by the resultant atmosphere of confidence and optimism, Spain, therefore, would become further ensconced as a power in the New World and would subsequently establish itself as the absolute authority in the newly formed American viceroyalties.

Some members of colonial society, however, for reasons of place of birth, race, sex, or ill fortune, were unable to participate in Spain's utopian dream and enjoy its benefits. They found the solemnity and sanctity of the image of the New World that the colonizer projected to be an elaborate facade and an intolerable deception, and in protesting its misrepresentation, they virtually turned the New World upside down. Contending that utopianism ignored the current sociopolitical realities of the New World and, above all, underestimated the extraordinary impact of its distinctive landscape, they sought a mode of expression that would convey their ideas, concerns, and expectations, and so present the point of view of the Other.[13] The use of subversive discourse, some members of these marginalized sectors of society hoped, would enable them to arrive at a more authentic and comprehensive view of the New World, and with this goal in mind, they endeavored to shorten the distance between the word and the object it represented by separating illusion from reality and myth from history. In order to expose the mythological foundations upon which Spanish American culture had supposedly been validated, therefore, they responded by inverting or reversing a number of traditional literary strategies, which would, in turn, cast doubt upon the prevailing authority and the ideology it espoused. This was their only recourse in the absence of a totally new language to describe and interpret their unique surroundings, and they successfully obstructed the integrity of a number of conventional models by widening their associative possibilities or by changing completely their points of referentiality.

Although all writers of subversive discourse shared the same basic objectives—to create a place for the members of their respective groups in early Spanish American society and culture and to improve their lot—satirists stand apart from other advocates of subversion in the colonies. Creoles and other like-minded individuals were satire's chief practitioners, and their works differ significantly from those by writers from indigenous backgrounds and from those by some religious women. Indians and mestizos, who were educated by the Spaniards, occasionally used subversive discourse to accommodate native American signs and codes within the mainstream of traditional Western culture, and nuns and other religiously devout females frequently couched controversial self-expression within the accounts of their mystical experiences in an effort to create interior space free from ecclesiastical censure.[14] While all writers of subversive discourse were acutely aware of the social inequities and injustices affecting their particular group, it was the satirists who chose to identify these imperfections by exposing to ridicule certain persons, customs, or institutions. Particular works, discursive strategies, and styles that overlooked the so-called flaws in these aspects of society often became targets as well, and common among satirists' complaints were their excessiveness, obsolescence, or lack of veracity.[15]

In order to address the most pressing social issues that concerned them as well as to point out the moral implications of these matters, colonial satirists sought not to replace one view of society with another but to reorient their readers by changing the way they saw and understood people and events and thus enable them to formulate their own ideas about the world in which they lived. By juxtaposing a satirically fashioned profile of society with the idealized version of life in the colonies espoused by both Church and state, writers of satire endeavored to initiate a dialogue between these two sharply contrasting viewpoints that would provide a new dimension for readers and a third possibility for their consideration. This middle ground between two opposing visions was not clearly delineated by the satirists, and its openness and ambiguity were meant to provoke conscious deliberation on the part of their readers and to urge them to arrive at their own interpretation.[16]

Colonial satirists chiefly accomplished their main objective by completely leveling utopian aspirations, a process that resulted in a negative and often grotesque configuration of the New World. Political, social, cultural, and rhetorical hierarchies were consequently lowered, and idealism and spirituality were reduced to the realm of the material and the physical as human nature triumphed over civilization. Although writers of satire focused on the extreme opposite of the prevailing view of the viceroyalties in their efforts to unravel this systematic and authoritative perception, their purpose in devising a double-directed discourse was to guide their readers away from any singular understanding of their environment and to arouse within them a consciousness capable of searching for a rational and constructive alternative of their own.[17]

Language was of great importance to satirists just as it was to other writers of subversive discourse. Instead of correcting any misunderstanding or misinterpretation of it, however, they often demonstrated its vulnerability to manipulation by carrying it to the opposite extreme, a measure that underscored the ability of language to blind as well as illuminate. Leveling procedures deflated metaphorical imagery by insisting upon its literal interpretation, and this, in turn, reduced allegory to irony. Colloquialisms, obscenities, and cacophony were familiar items in the satirists' lexicon, and when all manner of terminology was thought to have failed, they delighted in devising neologisms to disrupt and violate traditional rhetorical patterns. With an air of spontaneity but the resolve of deliberate calculation, they frequently mixed various forms of communication that appeared to contradict each other. They also interspersed the classical with the popular, the formal with the impromptu, and the erudite with the ordinary in a further effort to disconcert their readers and to suspend them between two opposite poles of understanding.[18]

Although colonial satirists rarely lost sight of the seriousness and the urgency of their corrective and reformational mission, they seldom missed an opportunity to demonstrate their wit and humor either. Laughter was usually the most immediate response elicited by the satirists' presentation, and it served both as a weapon and as a safety valve for the public at large against the rigidity and insensitivity of the colonial establishment. However, the lack of resolution of these two antagonistic approaches to understanding the world, which pitted the utopian against the satiric, proved to be a sobering element of the satirist's art and one that was ultimately disquieting to the readership. In a society whose discourse was centered around the viceregal court and the convent, colonial satire was an important indicator of an emerging popular culture and a growing national consciousness in early Spanish America.

The vision of the New World projected by colonial satirists is not dissimilar to the worldviews of other writers of satire. An allegedly utopian society was destined to fail, and it often precipitated the presentation of life as devoid of idealism, characterized by disunity and disorder, and based upon corruption and vice. Temporal or spacial journeys were especially suitable for dismantling the official version of political and cultural history in the early Americas because they structurally paralleled their more serious counterparts. This structural resemblance also permitted satirists to include themselves among the cast of characters and provided them with a format in which they could interpolate numerous brief portraits and vignettes. The broad scope and flexibility of the trip, or tour, additionally enabled writers to implement a wide range of techniques in the fulfillment of their satiric designs as well as to demonstrate the circular or meaningless progression of time or history.

Most of the characters who appear in satiric works generally represent recognizable New World types, and their diversity reveals the full extent of American subalternity. Whether hated or feared, they were frequently portrayed either as fools or as opportunists waiting to prey upon innocent victims. Very few details are used in describing these individuals, and the satirist customarily focuses on their unfavorable qualities that are targeted for exposure and on those that emphasize social and cultural differences. Such cursory portraits are designed to discourage readers from becoming emotionally attached to these personages. This detachment, therefore, predisposes them to reject the point of view projected by the satirist that is as distorted as the one under interrogation. Many of these characters remain nameless and are referred to only by their sex, race, profession, nationality, or some other distinguishing feature. Colonial satirists regularly assailed Indians, mestizos, blacks, and women, and they especially drew attention to the growing division between the *peninsulares* (Spaniards born in Spain) and the *criollos* (those of Spanish descent born in the New World). Self-interest rather than concern for the common good is generally portrayed as the guiding force behind the characters' actions, and arrogance, greed, hypocrisy, incompetence, and ugliness characterize their behavior. The particular manifestations of these traits, however, were often dictated by the historical circumstances under scrutiny.

Satirists themselves may also become characters in their own works, a measure that may either emulate or undermine the eyewitness reporting of the chronicler in New World *relaciones,* or they may speak through one of their literary personages. Although in some instances actions and sentiments are ostensibly autobiographical, this can be deceptive, since these figures are often used simply as technical devices to create subterfuge or controversy. Some writers of satire appear to be structurally separated from the events they narrate in order to demonstrate their isolation from the mainstream of society, while others purport to experience life to its fullest and to voice the plight afflicting ordinary people. The satirists' portrayal of themselves, in the latter instance, may destine them to be targets of their own attack when they admit to their own indulgences and seem to suffer the consequences of vice and folly along with everyone else. In any case, the satirists' purpose is to create skepticism and doubt in the mind of the reader, and their apparent self-contradiction and ambivalence are essential to the success of their satire.

Although the satirists' worldview may be distorted to the extent of using the grotesque, it must bear some semblance to reality in order to convey a set of concepts that may be applied to an understanding of actual circumstances. Once writers have established a critical relationship between their satiric view and the one that is traditionally presented, and indicated the challenge that the resultant interpretive space poses, the individual reader must then consider what ramifications the resolution of the two perspectives has for him or her. As the satirists disassemble tradition, therefore, readers are encouraged to think constructively about themselves and their current situation.[19] A meticulously detailed backdrop, complete with names, dates, and places, may accompany the authors' satiric projection and so make their observations and suppositions appear to be not only relevant but truthful as well, or the setting may be merely suggested to the readers, who must then devise their own imaginative context. Daily life and current issues that are not dealt with elsewhere because of their sensitive or controversial nature frequently become the focal point of satiric works, and the bold, direct treatment that they receive is rarely matched in any other form of literature.

As a result of the extratextual concerns of society and morality, colonial satirists addressed discursive issues that they felt had directly contributed to the misrepresentation of the New World in early Spanish American writings. In an effort to halt the perpetuation of a hegemonic ideology at its rhetorical foundations, therefore, they both sought and devised models of discourse that countered the officially sanctioned ones and that also accommodated their own satiric projections. The course of action taken by colonial satirists generally follows two basic strategies: one concerns the inversion of traditional models employed by New World writers in order that they might serve a satiric purpose, and the other regards the transfer from the Peninsula of previous models that were already capable of fulfilling a satiric design and could be easily reconceptualized within the historical and geographical setting of the New World. Although both of these strategies created numerous possibilities for colonial satirists, they also endeavored to formulate other alternatives by compounding and combining the two in a single rhetorical structure, thus imposing multiple coding rather than the requisite double coding on their texts.

In her recent study *A Theory of Parody*, Linda Hutcheon concludes that parody is a form of repetition with a critical distance that enables the reader or receiver to reassess the initial or backgrounded text in light of its remodeling. Because it provides an appropriate framework for a double-directed discourse whose dialogic is open-ended, colonial satirists found parody to be their most effective rhetorical means of questioning authority as well as of depicting the tension and conflict that surrounded them. It is important to note here that only those parodies that interact with satire will be examined in this study, since parody, according to Hutcheon's definition, may include a number of works that range in tone and intent from admiration to derision.[20] Also of importance is the fact that the inversion of conceptual and rhetorical models previously introduced into the New World was used by other colonial writers of subversive discourse as well. It must be reiterated, however, that satirists used the resultant critical dialogue, which had been established between the backgrounded text and the newly created metatext, in order to expose or discredit aspects of officially approved communication or to reflect derisively on officialdom itself.

The strategy of inversion was particularly effective in targeting colonial works that, it was thought by discerning observers of the time, were inappropriately or unconvincingly encoded with aspects of the New World environment. Heroic literature, whether written in prose or poetry, was an outstanding example of this misappropriation, and it quickly became a frequent target of colonial satirists. By reversing nonsatiric discourse through parody, therefore, they created a sharp contrast between what was stated and what was actually meant, and in devising this ironic distance they successfully separated the reader from the text to review its form and content analytically. Since satirists who employ parody must decode the initial work and encode it in a distorted form within their own literary creation, the task before the reader consequently involves the decoding of both texts rather than only one and an assessment of the discrepancies between them. The failure of the reader to identify a work as a parody and to have some knowledge of the parodied text nullifies the key given by writers to decipher their work. Such an oversight not only results in neutralizing the ironic dimension of the work but may even result in making the reader the object of the satire.[21] Critics as well who have not fully understood the ironic role of previous discursive models in the creation of subversive discourse have at times mistakenly classified some parodies as belonging to the traditional textual arrangements that were in fact their mark. This misunderstanding has subjected a number of these works to inappropriate judgmental criteria, and thus to unnecessary criticism. Many early nonsatiric colonial writings did not follow a single generic matrix and therefore facilitated the encoding of multiple parodies. These parodic constructs could then function simultaneously and penetrate one another.

Apart from inverting the most commonly accepted forms of officially sanctioned discourse, colonial satirists also employed easily recognizable Spanish models that had proven effective for satirists on the Peninsula but were generally excluded from the colonies. Since these constructs had already opposed Spain's idealism and attempted to dispel the nation's illusory image of itself, they were not among those approved by the Council of the Indies to document the dramatic expansion of the Spanish Empire into the New World and to provide paragons of behavior for its colonists. These models, some of which were already the result of discursive inversion in Europe, were inherently ironic in their perspective and were predisposed to the infiltration of burlesque, mockery, and other tools of the satirists' art. Picaresque and dreamlike frameworks, for example, violated existing literary conventions by definition and served as well as an instrument of social evaluation and criticism.

Because the intertextual relationship between the previous rhetorical models and the newly constructed ones is similar to the first inversive strategy used by colonial satirists, this second procedure may also be referred to as parodic, according to Hutcheon. In this case, however, the discursive restructuring is respectfully done, and the critical distance between the text and the metatext, created by the acclimatization or historicizing of the established textual arrangement, suggests revisionary rather than revolutionary change. The parodied text, therefore, is not the target of the satirists but one of the weapons in their satiric arsenal.[22]

The use of previous models in this second strategy, although it is also equally evident in the implementation of inversion, clearly reveals a basic paradox of parody in general, which, in turn, often becomes a characteristic of colonial satire as well. While questioning traditional discourse, satirists and parodists alike affirmed and reinforced it in their challenge and typically looked to the past to provide them with something new. A striking example from Spanish literature, in which satire and parody interact to produce such innovation, is *Don Quijote.* Michel Foucault has referred to it as "a negative of the Renaissance world," and its pivotal function in the development of narrative has long been recognized by both critics and scholars.[23] In creating a critical difference, therefore, Cervantes liberated his work to such an extent from the backgrounded text that the result was the inception of a unique, autonomous form.[24]

Although colonial satirists transgressed social, moral, and textual norms with artistic creativity and human perceptivity, their real effectiveness at challenging both officially codified discourse and the administrative system in the Spanish American viceroyalties ultimately rested on the competency of their readers. Their task was a complex one and more demanding than the reading required of a nonironic text, for example. In composing their works, satirists have not simply devised a metatext, or a reinterpretation of a previous text that may be accepted or rejected by the reader, but a mock metatext that compels its readers to formulate their own interpretation. Although satirists are adamant about the need for reform, they rarely provide the alternative means to achieve it. This open-endedness or atmosphere of ambivalence permits the participation of the readers in the hermeneutic process to a considerable extent, and thus enables them to become one of the text's creators. Such ambiguity in the construction of the work also allows for the malleability of cultural identity in the New World. This entire cognitive procedure, however, is contingent upon the reader's knowledge and ability to relate the past to the present in terms of both social order and the structure of official means of communication. If readers fail to detect a work's irony, a crucial component of both satire and parody, then they are not prepared to evaluate the critical dimension created by a double-directed text, and the satirists' carefully constructed critical space is lost. Under these circumstances the audience best prepared to understand colonial satire was composed principally of male Creoles. While attempting to gain greater support among this growing segment of the New World's population, however, satirists also created cause for concern elsewhere, and indeed an alarm was sounded in official circles on both sides of the Atlantic.

Two opposing views of the New World, one of the victor and the other of the frustrated malcontent, coexisted almost from the Spaniards' arrival in the Caribbean area. The Spanish Crown, however, was intent upon maintaining an impression of the empire that exuded confidence and exemplified solidarity, and it routinely suppressed any opposition to it. Spain had gone to great lengths to unify itself politically and religiously by 1492, and it would not tolerate dissension in its overseas possessions. Officials of both Church and state believed satiric writings fostered skepticism and cynicism, and they feared that the very principles on which their institutions rested could ultimately be challenged.

The responsibility for the censorship of literary works in colonial Spanish America was assumed by both civil and ecclesiastical authorities. The Inquisition, established in Lima in 1570 and in Mexico City in 1571, was the principal body to judge the acceptability of manuscripts and books and a tribunal to decide cases in which laws had allegedly been broken. The Church sought primarily to protect the welfare of its Indian charges as well as to maintain its own dignity and that of the clergy, but it was also charged with overseeing the interests of the state.[25] The printing press had been brought to the New World in 1538 at the behest of Mexico's bishop, Fray Juan de Zumárraga, and it was instrumental in the religious conversion of native Americans.[26] Materials used in the teaching of the Indians, therefore, comprised the vast majority of works produced in the colonies, and government documents needed by colonial administrators were the next priority. Because of the severe limitations placed on works considered for publication as well as the strict censorship imposed upon those that were actually published, books printed in the New World became associated with colonial authority and Spanish hegemony.[27] For this reason, colonial satire circulated principally in manuscript form during the sixteenth and seventeenth centuries. With the founding of newspapers in the viceroyalties, however, satirists discovered an important outlet for some of their previously prohibited discourse, and they were also able to present their views to a wider audience much more immediately.[28]

Methods for controlling the introduction and circulation of inappropriate or objectionable printed matter were both preventative and punitive. As early as 1506, Ferdinand imposed an official restriction on the shipment of fiction to the New World. This prohibition was reiterated in 1531 by Juana la Loca in a decree addressed to Seville's House of Trade, and the document specifically mentions works of fantasy such as *Amadís de Gaula*. In 1556 the first *Index* was published in Spain, and important additions were made to the list in succeeding years. Among the outstanding volumes either banned or expurgated were Rojas' *La Celestina*, works by Francisco de Quevedo, and Cervantes' *Don Quijote*. The circulation of printed matter was further curtailed by 1560 when the Council of the Indies made it necessary for printers and vendors of books about America to secure a license. Punishment meted out by Inquisitors was the penalty for violating any of these regulations, and it varied from torture and imprisonment to exile from the New World.[29]

This elaborate system proved successful against foreign ideological threats such as Protestantism and, to a lesser degree, the Enlightenment but was relatively ineffective in censoring the internal flow of information. Countless ship manifests are evidence that literary works arrived in the Indies and circulated freely and that chivalric novels, *Don Quijote, La Celestina*, and picaresque literature were popular among colonists.[30] A number of prominent individuals, nevertheless, were painfully aware of the consequences of violating censorship laws. In 1572 the son-in-law of Juan Pablos, Mexico's first printer, became one of the initial victims of the Inquisition. Pedro Ocharte, who had taken over the printing business after his father-in-law's death, was accused of promoting a book that denied the importance of the intervention of saints. This matter came to the attention of Pedro Moya de Contreras, who was appointed as Mexico City's first Inquisitor by Philip II, and his strict orthodoxy resulted in Ocharte's interrogation by torture.[31] Several years later, this same Church official, who had then become archbishop, was again involved in issues of censorship. This time, however, the Inquisition had inadvertently sanctioned two short dramatic pieces that criticized New Spain's viceroy, Martín Henríquez de Almansa, and challenged the implementation of the *alcabala*, or sales tax. Caught up in this controversy between Church and state were Fernán González de Eslava, whose theatrical *coloquios* combining secular and religious elements later became famous, and the well-known poet Francisco de Terrazas. Both were jailed, although the identities of the real authors of the *entremeses* were never disclosed, and Juan Pérez Ramírez, who wrote *Desposorio espiritual* appeared as a witness in the case.[32] Also among the first victims was Pedro de Trejo, who suffered the consequences of writing verse and was forced to give up poetry altogether after a judgment by Mexico's newly established Holy Office condemned him to public penance and a period of service on the royal galleys.[33]

Throughout both the seventeenth and eighteenth centuries, isolated incidents of censorship continued to touch the lives of prominent literary figures. Mateo Alemán's arrival in Veracruz in 1608 was marred by the confiscation of his copy of *Don Quijote*, though it was later returned to him. Toward the end of the century, the great poet Sor Juana Inés de la Cruz expressed concern over the power of the Inquisition in her *Respuesta a Sor Filotea de la Cruz* and used its threatening posture to justify the presentation of secular subject matter in her works.[34] Even light, Golden Age *comedias* were occasionally banned, as was the case of the 1682 performance of Juan Pérez de Montalbán's *El valor perseguido y traición vengada* scheduled in Mexico City's Coliseo,[35] and the eighteenth-century Colombian abbess Madre Castillo was warned by her confessor that readers of such frivolous works could not secure salvation.[36] Although more drastic methods of control were taken by the government as dissidence spread in the colonies, its efforts to eradicate opposing views became less effective. The atmosphere of repression, nevertheless, forced Alonso Carrió de la Vandera to have one of his manuscripts published surreptitiously and prompted the burning of copies of Esteban Terralla y Landa's poem describing Lima at the end of the eighteenth century. The satirist to suffer most from censorship was probably Eugenio Espejo, who had numerous works of his banned by officials in New Granada and who died as a result of frequent encarceration for expressing opinions regarded as dangerous to the state.[37]

Although relatively speaking only a few writers, printers, or book dealers suffered personally as a result of colonial censorship or had their books destroyed on a large scale, its potential power undoubtedly served as a deterrent to certain types of criticism. For this reason, only a few satirists emerged from Spanish America's early literary history, and those who did took careful measures to conceal their identity by providing sketchy or false biographical information about themselves. Artistically, however, they met the threat of suppression with considerable resilience, and cloaking their combativeness with creativity, they produced works of artistic merit and documentary relevance. By the time the Crown took decisive steps to block political satire during the latter half of the eighteenth century, it was too late to stop its spread. Anticipating the empire's demise, satirical writing flourished as discontent increased, and it ultimately helped to fan the flames of revolution.

Colonial satire, while growing out of an extraordinary set of circumstances, bears some resemblance, nevertheless, to ancient forms of discourse that challenged tradition and officialdom. In exploring the origins of the modern novel in his *Problems of Dostoevsky's Poetics,* Mikhail Bakhtin identifies a distinctive literary typology, which he refers to as the serio-comic. Types of literature contained in this classification were derived from a form of popular response that, he contends, inherently questions authority and draws its inspiration from the carnivalesque.[38] In recent years, however, certain inadequacies in his theories have been uncovered, especially with regard to his limited view of parody and the grotesque and his overstatement of the actual role of carnival in the process of literary transformation. Despite these observations, critics still agree, based upon their own studies of discursive self-reflexivity and polyphony, that a reconsideration of the Russian Formalists' criticism is in order and that Bakhtin's ideas may provide an important point of departure on which to formulate a new, more precise theoretical approach to narrative.[39] Given some inexactitudes in Bakhtin's theory, nonetheless—and in the absence of any other more convincing theoretical framework at this time—his description of the serio-comic and the isolation of several of its components have particular relevance for the appearance and expansion of satire in the New World and for a positive assessment of its potential role in the evolution of Spanish American letters.

Originating in oral folk traditions and in the observance of pre-Lenten festivities, according to Bakhtin, the carnival attitude toward the world has little regard for sociohierarchical barriers and advocates equality among people. Freedom and frankness characterize its expression, and it strives for the unusual through the complete reversal of normality. Because of the flexibility and versatility of carnival elements, they can easily infiltrate any literary mode and are capable of instigating change for the purpose of its renewal. The resultant discourse, therefore, is shaped by experience and imagination and focuses on the present. Characters may be drawn from myth or legend, but their contemporization strips their image of its original significance and places them in a critical light.[40] While the concept of the carnivalesque as described by Bakhtin no longer holds currency, the spirit of carnival is still a vital part of Spanish American life, a trait that inevitably emerged with the fusion of cultures at the time of the Spanish conquest and colonization of the New World.[41]

Within the realm of discursive strategies designated as the serio-comic, Bakhtin focuses on Menippean satire, a special form of literary work first written by Menippus and Varro and generally regarded as an ancient precursor of present-day satire. Although it was initially distinguished from other forms of the serio-comic because of its predominance of comedy and its greater freedom and potential for the creation of fantasy,[42] Menippean satire eventually incorporated such forms as the Socratic dialogue, a type of ideological debate begun by Plato and Socrates, and the simple parody. *Menippea* thus contains a more obvious blend of diverse styles and structures than other serio-comical expression, and its penetration into a variety of literary paradigms generally fostered the development of multiple parodies. As Bakhtin points out, the encroachment of this early form of satire upon other types of literature "serves . . . not in the positive embodiment of the truth, but in the search after the truth, its provocation and, most importantly, its testing." While the influence of carnival logic on literary works is indicative of the erosion of national tradition and the obliteration of time-honored ideals, it is also characteristic of a preparatory period in which new images and innovative ideas are formulated.[43]

In the case of Spanish America, colonial satire reflects the search for a different and original set of ideas that would place Americans at the forefront of their own destiny historically and artistically and enable them to relate directly to their own environment and all aspects of its distinctiveness. By consistently combining elements of popular humor with an aggressive spirit, colonial satirists gradually established satire as a means of self-definition and a form of political resistance, and thus confirmed its use as an effective vehicle of subversion for a marginalized group. In the process of nullifying traditional signs and contradicting certain conventional codes of rhetoric, satirists were compelled to rely more extensively on literary mechanisms than the early chroniclers and historians, and as a result of their heightened desire for creativity and originality, they explored the vast potential of fiction heretofore untapped by colonial authors.

Satire expressed in Spanish first emerged during the Middle Ages as a mode of communication for the Spaniards' critical nature.[44] It was probably derived from the Latin theater and was influenced by native Peninsular forms of entertainment. From the *Reconquista* and the forging of the world's most powerful nation to the accession of Joseph Bonaparte to the Spanish throne, Spain's turbulent history provided innumerable matters of controversy, which found their way into its literary tradition. Challenged by the problems of contemporary life, anonymous authors of popular sayings as well as artistic geniuses of the Golden Age took the opportunity to speak out, and the creativity with which they did so undoubtedly attracted a number of colonial writers to satire as a creative means of making their opinions known. Encouraged by the general success of satiric works on the Peninsula, satirists writing in the colonies often used similar structure, language, tone, themes, and character types as the immediate point of departure for criticism of the hegemonic conceptualization of the New World being imposed upon them.

The first notable reference to Spanish works conceived in a satiric vein is found in the condemnation of them in the thirteenth-century *Siete partidas* of Alfonso X. According to this source, popular plays, or *juegos de escarnio*, were banned by the state because they frequently mocked the Church, its members, and its doctrines, and they often bordered on the obscene as well. Unfortunately, these skits no longer exist, if, indeed, they were ever in written form, but their scrutinizing tenor and anticlerical theme continued long after the medieval period.

Although the earliest documentation of satiric elements was confined to drama, they eventually found their way into other genres as well. Two distinguished Spanish satirists emerged during the fourteenth century, and the tone and point of view of their works represent opposite extremes of the art in much the same way that Juvenal's satires contrast with those of Horace. In his *Libro de buen amor* Juan Ruiz, the archpriest of Hita, portrays the life and society of his time, which was characterized by a relaxed moral climate. With candor and freshness, he humorously recounts his own numerous love affairs and warns of the dangers of such indulgence. Apart from the author's profile of his own personality and his inclusion of many conversational elements in his poetry, *Libro de buen amor* also marks the debut of two literary types, which will become models for characters in other masterpieces of Spanish literature. Trotaconventos, the churchman's go-between in his many amorous encounters, is a precursor of Rojas' Celestina, and Don Furón, who later takes her place, is a forerunner of the Spanish *pícaro*.

Pero López de Ayala, another outstanding satirist of the fourteenth century, saw the many weaknesses in society just as his predecessor Juan Ruiz had, but his condemnatory attitude and position of superiority toward human frailty in his *Rimado del palacio* are strikingly different from the latter's benevolent advice. As a royal official at the court of five monarchs, López de Ayala was witness to many important affairs of state and dealt with diverse types of people of varying stations who presented themselves before the king. Poetically documenting this era of political upheaval in his work, he serves as the supreme judge for both men and events, and the unbridled indignation and outrage with which he expresses himself are a hallmark of his criticism. López de Ayala is the first writer to give significant direction to satire in Spain through his distinctive style, and his bitter attacks on vice and corruption at all levels of society were unmatched until Quevedo's rise to prominence in the seventeenth century.

Satiric poetry was also written during the fifteenth century, but the best examples that have been preserved remain anonymous. They continue to document the social deterioration and governmental misconduct of the times, and the concealment of the poets' names is, no doubt, a sign of the increased pressure of censorship. The "Dance of Death" was a popular theme of medieval poets throughout Europe, and the first Spanish version of it appeared in the early 1400's. The structure of the composition is ideal for the rapid review and criticism of a series of societal components, and the poem's principal character serves as a unifying and equalizing force among them. In the *Danza de la muerte*, representatives of all walks of life present themselves before the Grim Reaper, who holds them accountable for their sins and coldly passes judgment on them without regard to their status.

A number of stanzas of popular origin also circulated at this time, which comprise the first satiric works in Spanish dedicated solely to a political theme. Attesting to the deplorable state of the monarchy during the reigns of John II and Henry IV, verses such as those of *Coplas de ¡Ay, panadera!* and *Coplas del Provincial* degenerate into sheer invective with their violent accusations and flurry of name-calling. The *Coplas de Mingo Revulgo*, on the other hand, with its allegorical framework and symbolic characters, was more artfully conceived. In this poem the shepherd Mingo Revulgo, who represents Spain and its people, complains about the lack of protection for his flock from an overseer, King Henry IV, and cites the danger posed by a pack of wolves, who are the influential members of the court led by Beltrán de la Cueva.

Satire was also well represented in the fifteenth century by the prose writers Alfonso Martínez de Toledo, the archpriest of Talavera, and Fernando de Rojas, who both made important contributions to its development. The former is especially noted for his portrayal of female characters, and his scathing attack on women in *El corbacho* is a prime example of misogyny in Spanish literature. The archpriest of Talavera's critical perspective will be repeated in the picaresque, and the theme of antifeminism will surface again at the end of the century in Rojas' *La Celestina*.

Drawing generally upon literary tradition for inspiration, but especially from the works of Juan Ruiz and the archpriest of Talavera for his description of women and the portrait of his female protagonist, Fernando de Rojas composed a genuine masterpiece of Spanish literature distinguished by its expression of realism and its contributions to the modern novel. The author of the famous *tragicomedia* endowed his characters with exceptional human qualities from their speech and manners to their inevitable shortcomings. He, too, like those before him, points out the startling weaknesses in humanity and dramatizes, from a highly moralistic standpoint, the harsh consequences of sin.

During the sixteenth century, the interest in satire continued to grow, and new literary vehicles for its expression were explored. Criticism of the Church intensified with the spread of Erasmism, and in 1554 the first important picaresque work was published.

Rome was the center of both religious and political activity for many Spaniards and the object of their satire as well. Bartolomé de Torres Naharro, a Spanish priest who won the favor of Leo X, was well aware of ecclesiastical corruption, and he clearly depicts it in his *Comedia tinelaria*, a play involving the intrigues at a high papal official's residence.

Alfonso de Valdés also assailed Roman society, albeit on a much broader scale. He used Rome's moral degeneration as the justification for its sacking by the troops of his patron, Charles V, in his prose work *Diálogo de Lactancio y un arcediano*. His other important satire, *Diálogo de Mercurio y Carón*, continues his wide-ranging attack, especially on people in high places, and it follows, to some extent, the structure of the *Danza de la muerte*. Passengers representing people of superior station board a craft to carry them across the river Styx, and each is judged by the boatman. The influence of Gil Vicente's *Barca de la gloria* may also be seen in Valdés' dialogue as the occupants of the boat are judged and taken to their final destination in the hereafter.

The advent of picaresque literature was not only a signal achievement for prose fiction in general but an important step in the development of satire as well. Roman novels like Petronius' *Satyricon* and Apuleius' *Golden Ass* contributed significantly to the formulation of this genre, and works such as the *Danza de la muerte*, *Libro de buen amor*, *El corbacho*, and *La Celestina* foreshadowed its emergence in Spain. At a time when idealism dominated Spanish literature, especially in the form of books of chivalry, the picaresque offered a refreshing alternative, and its realism reflected the economic decline brought about at first by the absence of the Moors and Jews after their expulsion from the Peninsula and later by the influx of precious metals from the New World that passed through Spain on their way to European creditors. Although numerous picaresque works were written, three in particular—the anonymous *Lazarillo de Tormes*, Mateo Alemán's *Guzmán de Alfarache*, and Francisco de Quevedo's *Buscón*, which appeared in the seventeenth century—represent the best of the genre and mark specific phases of its development.

In contrast to the heroic knight of the tales of chivalry, the protagonist of this form of narrative, the *pícaro*, is an anti-hero who, instead of performing great deeds, finds his way from one misadventure to the next. The *pícaro*, usually a young delinquent of humble origins, recounts his own experiences to someone in authority, and the structure of his narration is episodic. Serving a continuous line of masters, he struggles to overcome his poverty, especially his hunger, and comments critically on the various levels of society that his employers represent. The tableau he describes captures the essence and vitality of the period and provides an excellent opportunity for the exposure of discrepancies between appearances and reality.[45]

The extreme pessimism and utter disillusionment of seventeenth-century Spain are best expressed by Francisco de Quevedo, whose brilliant satire in both prose and poetry distinguish him as a literary genius and the Peninsula's most outstanding satirist. His profound perception of his nation and his disturbing view of the empire made him a symbol of a critical age, and his biting criticism is the most influential voice in the development of satire on both sides of the Atlantic. Grotesque caricature and the sharpness of his attack are characteristic features of his satire, but his contributions to the art extend into many aspects of its form and content. His *Sueños*, written and published throughout the early 1600's, was his crowning achievement and won him the greatest fame. In this prose work Quevedo uses a dreamlike sequence to review a lengthy procession of character types and to uncover abuses and corruption everywhere. Victims chosen from the ranks of professionals to the level of ordinary citizens suffer his scathing attacks for their impropriety, but he reserves his severest criticism for women. *El buscón*, which follows his *Sueños* in importance, is also an exceptional piece of writing and marks the culmination of the picaresque novel. Quevedo continued to expose the imperfections in human nature and all human endeavors in other notable prose works, such as *Premáticas y aranceles generales, Orígenes y definiciones de la necedad,* and *El caballero de la Tenaza.*

Quevedo's poetry, although secondary to his prose, demonstrates similar variety and skill. As an advocate of *conceptismo,* he often derided the *cultismo* espoused by Góngora and his supporters, and his *Aguja de navegar cultos* is an excellent example of this. He did not, however, limit himself to literary matters in his poetry, and his politically oriented remarks about Philip IV's favorite, the count-duke of Olivares, resulted in an imprisonment that had ruinous effects on his health.

Major contributions to seventeenth-century satire were also made by Miguel de Cervantes and Baltasar Gracián. *El ingenioso hidalgo don Quijote de la Mancha,* published in two parts in 1605 and 1615, was destined to be the greatest masterpiece of Spanish literature. Cervantes' parodic treatment of chivalric works resulted in the creation of the first modern novel, and its overwhelming success as a new artistic form of expression is a clear demonstration of the enormous reconstructive potential of parody. He also wrote *Rinconete y*

Cortadillo and *El coloquio de los perros* in the picaresque vein, and in the latter he uses animal characters who engage in conversation about human imperfection. Creatures of lower orders appeared as well in *La mosquea* and *La gatomaquia*, parodic epics by José de Villaviciosa and Lope de Vega, respectively.

Baltasar Gracián, a contemporary of Quevedo, who shared with him a highly pessimistic view of society, is noted for his moralistic approach to human beings' shortcomings. In his final prose work, *El criticón*, he reviews the European way of life and gives instruction on the importance of being virtuous in the search for immortality. Within the framework of an extended journey, two characters, the sophisticated Critilo and the naïve Andrenio, travel about the countryside commenting freely on what they see, and their dialogue is meant to encourage the reader to rise above the disharmony and malevolence that appear to pervade earthly existence.

The eighteenth century did not contribute as much as the preceding one to the development of satire in Spain, although the period did demonstrate continued interest in this critical mode through the reiteration of previously explored aspects of it. Diego de Torres Villarroel, a disciple of Quevedo, wrote his picaresque autobiography, and in his *Visiones y visitas* he emulated Spain's most famous satirist by taking him on an imaginary tour of Madrid and pointing out the changes that had taken place since his last visit to the capital. The Jesuit father José Francisco de la Isla also satirized elements of eighteenth-century society in his novel *Historia del famoso predicador, Fray Gerundio de Campazas, alias Zotes* in which he attacks the pompousness and obscurity of pulpit oratory. Although his other work, *Aventuras de Gil Blas de Santillana*, is a translation of the French novel by Lesage, it is recognized for the exceptional clarity of its picaresque theme, a characteristic not found in Lesage's original.

Instructed, therefore, by this Peninsular literary heritage, which ran the gamut of satiric expression, colonial satirists found the means to reshape the most prevalent vision of New World reality and so became a dissenting voice within Spanish American society. One by one, they reflected upon their personal circumstances, and perceiving the problems afflicting them, they conveyed their own view of life in accordance with their individual literary skills. Their works, always written with courage and daring and frequently with creativity and wit, offer a startling portrait of the colonial period based on an unofficial version of Spain in the Indies. Its varied expression and general development over three hundred years are the subject of the following chapters.

2. The Sixteenth Century: The Conquest and the Years That Followed

The conquest of the powerful Aztec civilization gave the Spaniards a sense of accomplishment and their Crown a source of pride, but it was also an immediate cause of dissension among them. Frequently at the center of controversy was the conqueror himself whose grandiose promises brought little tangible reward to the common soldiers who had supported him loyally throughout the Indian campaigns. Bernal Díaz del Castillo dutifully presents this issue in his *Historia verdadera de la conquista de la Nueva España* with the hope of arriving at an equitable solution,[1] but other early writers were not as conciliatory in their treatment of this alleged injustice. Francisco de Terrazas, for example, in his epic poem *Nuevo Mundo y conquistas* takes umbrage at Hernán Cortés' false assurances to his troops in Cuba when the captain pledges "por premio a cada cual un reino entero" ("to each man an entire kingdom for a prize") if they will follow him to the Mexican mainland.[2]

Even Bernal Díaz was cognizant of the satiric tone used by some of his comrades in referring to their leader, and his mention of an incident in Coyoacan, Mexico, provides documentation of one of the first examples of satiric verse to be written down in the New World. *Pasquines*, or lampoons, were a customary expression of discontent in Spain, and a member of Cortés' force, suspicious of his division of spoils after a series of victorious battles, decided to chide him publicly by painting abrasive phrases on the town walls. At the outset of these pranks, Cortés responded cleverly and in a good-natured tone, but as criticism persisted, he took measures to discourage such dissent. After Cortés had written "Pared blanca, papel de necios" ("White walls, the paper of fools"), however, one of his men, demonstrating the relentless scrutiny to which prominent figures would be subjected, replied, "Aun de sabios y verdades, y Su Majestad lo sabrá muy presto" ("Even of wise men and truths, and His Majesty will know it soon").[3]

The controversy over inequities created by the conquest continued long after the subjugation of the New World's indigenous populations and appeared to intensify as Spain's colonial administration extended its control over much of two continents. The distribution of royal grants and privileges was a particular point of contention and proved to be a divisive force within early Spanish American society that would have eventual political ramifications as well. Creoles, whose forefathers had actually fought for the land, were often denied access to these benefits while new arrivals from the Peninsula, who enjoyed preferential treatment from the Crown, became their customary recipients. The resultant rivalry between these two groups is evident in some of the earlier satiric works written by *criollos*, as they boldly attacked the figure of the *peninsular* and symbols of his supremacy in the New World.

An anonymous sonnet, probably written during the late 1500's but published just after the turn of the seventeenth century, provides a portrait of the vilified Spaniard, or *gachupín*, as he was called. Beginning his poem "Viene de España . . ." ("He comes from Spain . . ."), the sonneteer alludes to the advantages acquired in the Indies by this ordinary emigrant with no visible means of support and chides him for his arrogant and ungrateful attitude toward the generosity of his new country.[4] Similar resentment is expressed, again by the poet Terrazas who was a Creole, in a versified complaint directed toward his birthplace, the "Ingrata Patria" ("unappreciative country," i.e., New Spain).

> Madrastra nos has sido rigurosa,
> Y dulce madre pía á los extraños;
> Con ellos de tus bienes generosa,
> Con nosotros repartes de tus daños.[5]

> (Stepmother, you have been rigorous with us
> and a sweet, pious mother to the foreigners;
> with them, generous with your benefits
> and with us you share your risks.)

The rift among Hispanics, however, was not the only obstacle to the fulfillment of Spain's utopian dream in the New World. Other problems, which were not merely social but extended into the political, economic, and moral aspects of life in the colonies, began to surface, and the general disintegration of colonial society became a frequent theme of satiric criticism. One of the first works of satire to portray this breakdown in Spanish America is a poetic description of New Spain's illustrious capital. This anonymous poem, which begins disillusioningly "Minas sin plata . . ." ("Mines without silver . . ."), is a probable parody of Juan de la Cueva's "Epístola al licenciado Sánchez de Obregón, primer corregidor de México" ("Letter to Licentiate Sánchez de Obregón, the First Indian Agent of Mexico") in which the Spanish poet finds six particularly beautiful things about the city and enumerates them. The first three items, houses, streets, and horses, pay tribute to the imposition of Spanish culture on the former Aztec capital of Tenochtitlan, and the last three extol its feminine pulchritude. The satiric sonneteer, on the other hand, after mentioning the initial triad ironically, proceeds to deride the city's female residents, who, according to him, are continually engaged in gambling and prostitution. Apart from Mexico's moral decay, the poet goes on to allude to other areas of decline which include failing mines, disobedient servants, and opportunistic courtiers.[6] Despite the brevity of this attack, it is indicative of the leveling procedures engaged by colonial satirists to create a topsy-turvy vision of the New World, and it anticipates the lengthier works in which the cities of North and South America as well as the Caribbean area are exposed.

Cristóbal de Llerena

Because the theater proved to be a successful vehicle of communication in the conversion of the Indians and a popular form of entertainment among colonists as well, it was viewed initially by several sixteenth-century writers of satire as being an expeditious way of making their views known to large groups of people. The presentation of dramatic pieces containing criticism of the government, however, quickly met with serious opposition, and as a result, several playwrights suffered the immediate consequences of their boldness. Just as Fernán González de Eslava had faced imprisonment in 1574 for including a reading in his theatrical program that mocked New Spain's viceroy, so, too, a Creole churchman on the island of Hispaniola was punished by civil authorities after he staged an interlude critical of Santo Domingo's municipal management. Plays were customarily presented throughout the Indies during the celebration of Corpus Christi, and in accordance with this tradition, Cristóbal de Llerena, an instructor at the University of Gorjón, directed his students in the 1588 performance of a sketch that he himself had written for the festivities. Although the *entremés* was performed in Santo Domingo's cathedral, it was a secular piece inspired, perhaps, by the lighter, or carnivalesque, side of this religious observance. Because it created such an uproar among city officials, however, its author was promptly banished to South America.[7]

Since the theatrical production resulted in the deportation of a clergyman without a trial, the Church immediately became embroiled in the controversy, and this prompted the Dominican archbishop, Don Alonso de Avila, to write Philip II on the accused playwright's behalf.[8] This letter provides what little is known about Llerena, and the attachment of the *entremés* to it assured the preservation of his only extant work for posterity. According to the correspondence, Llerena, who was probably born around 1550 of Spanish parents, occupied numerous positions at the University of Gorjón. Apart from his duties as professor, chaplain, organist, and accountant, he often found time to engage in creative writing. Although the archbishop refers specifically to his religious poetry, it is evident that his theme varied and that such a deviation may have brought him into conflict with civil authorities prior to 1588. After a year-long exile in New Granada, however, he returned to Santo Domingo and resumed his post at Gorjón. Without further interference from government officials, he concluded his career in the rectorship and lived at least ten years into the next century.[9]

The controversial interlude penned by Llerena depicts the extraordinary decline of Santo Domingo, the principal settlement of the island Columbus described on his first voyage as "la más hermosa cosa del mundo" ("the loveliest thing in the world").[10] Hispaniola had been under Spanish domination for nearly a century when this dramatic piece was written, but with gold supplies exhausted and Indian labor decimated, it had ceased to be a vital part of the empire. The island drifted into neglect with the conquests of Mexico and Peru, and this resulted in serious economic reversals and left the coastline unprotected from the growing number of buccaneers in the Caribbean area. Implying that Santo Domingo's colonial administration was responsible for the colony's deteriorating condition, Llerena describes the island community gripped by poverty and fear and riddled with moral decay.

Llerena's exposure of a colonial city's ills, like the anonymous sonnet critical of Mexico City, is yet another precursory piece, which anticipates the more elaborate satiric descriptions of other American metropolises, and it is evidence of the early transfer of this theme of classical and Christian origin to the New World. Juvenal's depiction of Roman decadence in his *Satires* is the most famous example of this literary motif and counters precisely the time-honored concept of *laudes civitatum*. Placing humankind in a more general context of a world community, Saint Augustine also uncovers human weaknesses by contrasting the City of God with the City of Man, or *caritas* versus *avaritia*.[11] Llerena's attack on a major municipality of the New World, however, is not merely the continuance of literary tradition. It was designed to deal a severe blow to one of the basic principles of the Spaniards' colonization as well. Spain's intention to establish permanent settlements based upon order and governed by reason were at the heart of its plan to realize legally visionary goals for America. These urban areas, therefore, were the conscious reflection of Spanish ideals, and their destiny as the center of colonial life was preordained.

In order to focus on the gravity of current problems besetting the Europeans' first city in the New World, Llerena juxtaposes Columbus' vision of the Caribbean islands as the location of an earthly paradise with a satiric profile of a declining Santo Domingo almost a century later. This juxtaposition also calls into question the Admiral's validation of his discovery in biblical tradition and levels the eschatological importance of his mission by contemporizing events in the Garden of Eden. Llerena also reflects critically on the process of making myths, especially myths of origin, by haphazardly substituting classical elements for some of the biblical ones, changes that contribute additionally to the confusion and incongruity he wished to convey. As suggested by Llerena's *entremés*, therefore, the Spaniards moved into the idyllic habitat after the expulsion of Adam and Eve only to witness a reenactment of the loss of its perfection, again as a result of human failings. Instead of the ominous appearance of a serpent, however, the birth of a far more hideous creature disrupts the lives of Santo Domingo's citizens. It is a consequence of humanity's fallen condition rather than its cause, and it serves as a possible prelude to another banishment, this time of Spanish colonial administrators in the Indies. If biblical parallels are enforced, then, the destined recovery of paradise by Columbus would also ironically signal its destruction and the exile of those who desecrated it for a second time. While this might be a welcome prospect for those who suffered under the yoke of colonialism and awaited the restoration of their land to its natural state, the ramifications of a second Fall on an imperial scale could have even graver repercussions for New World residents than those of the first.

Structuring his entire interlude around the birth of a monster by the *bobo* Cordellate, an event taken from Horace's *Epistola Ad Pisones*, Llerena uses the most fundamental form of the grotesque as an emblem of colonial Santo Domingo.[12] With a woman's head, a horse's neck, a bird's body, and a fish's tail, the creature resembles the fantastic Roman ornamentation for which the term *grotesque* was first coined.[13] Four classical figures are called upon to interpret the monstrosity's appearance, and their reaction predictably dramatizes the effects of this radical distortion as a technique. Edipo and Delio are amused by the freak and express comic and even absurd interpretations, the former blaming everything on Santo Domingo's female population and the latter citing Ovid and Terence in search of a philosophical explanation. Proteo and Calcas, however, find the monster's appearance shocking, and it is through their augury that Llerena delivers his most destructive criticism.

A strong defense and favorable trade concessions from Spain were tantamount to the island's survival, and these issues lie at the very center of Llerena's satiric *entremés*. The 1586 sacking of Santo Domingo by Sir Francis Drake had been devastating to the city, and Calcas predicts another raid with similar consequences. Foreigners, however, are not the only ones who took advantage of Hispaniola's isolation. As Proteo points out, greedy ship captains were often the beneficiaries of the strict economic rules imposed by the Spaniards on the island's trade and commerce. After dutifully sending raw materials to Spain, colonists were still forced to pay exorbitant prices for manufactured goods that were either imported or smuggled into the Indies.

The insensitivity of colonial administration to Santo Domingo's plight and its constant preoccupation with its own well-being are reinforced through Llerena's caricature of royal officials. They are described generally as a corrupt group in one of the prognostications, and the author relies on the actions of two councilmen to add to this negative portrayal. As overbearing lackeys, these individuals stand out beside the pathetic figure of the *bobo*, who represents Santo Domingo's population at large. Once happy and prosperous, Cordellate is now distraught by the area's impoverishment and stunned and mystified at what his oversized belly has produced. Neither official accepts any blame for this misfortune, and they both chide the poor simpleton for what they claim is his irresponsibility. Unwilling to believe that Santo Domingo has fallen victim to Spain's exploitive imperialism, the two reject the interpretations and predictions of Calcas and his companions and hurry off to the town hall at the conclusion of the skit to inquire what the official view of this phenomenon will be.

Although Llerena strikes primarily at government mismanagement, he broadens the scope of his attack slightly to demonstrate how maladministration has created a general climate of relaxed standards in which other undesirable elements of society are permitted to thrive. These types are named only and do not appear in the play, but reference to them suggests the profile of Santo Domingo's society. Notaries, lawyers, and theologians are mentioned for their deviousness, but women, condemned by Proteo as disorderly beings "cuyas galas, apetitos y licencias van fuera de todo orden natural" ("whose trappings, appetites, and licenses are outside all that is natural") (127), are attacked unmercifully. While all of the major characters agree that women are accountable to some extent for the city's deplorable state, Edipo attributes the monster's entire repulsive composition to aspects of a woman's character.

> Es la mejor mujer instable bola.
> La más discreta es bestia torpe insana;
> aquella que más grave, es más liviana,
> y al fin toda mujer nace con cola. (126)

> (The best woman is an unstable ball,
> the most discreet is a dumb, insane beast;
> she, who is more serious, is more frivolous,
> and finally all women are born with tails.)

Women are often singled out as symbols of both physical and moral decay in satiric works, and their denigration provides the most common theme in colonial Spanish American satire.[14] While misogyny has a long and varied tradition, Llerena's scathing portrayal of women probably originated with the interpretation of the Fall as the result of Eve's weakness. This perspective is clearly demonstrated in Motolinía's description of a dramatic representation of that Bible story performed throughout Mexico after the arrival of the first friars,[15] and this view was no doubt reinforced by the general body of patristic literature with which Llerena was acquainted.

In addition to contributing to the universal undercurrent of antifeminism apparent in literature, Llerena may have taken advantage of its popularity and relative safety as an amusing diversion away from the more sensitive issues to which he alludes. Sexual promiscuity is often used by satirists as an expedient leveler of idealistic aspirations and an abundant source of scabrous humor, and in the case of this play, complaints about women may have served as a unifying factor among the male members of the audience as well. Llerena's depiction of women staving off poverty through prostitution may also have been included to counter the excessive descriptions of conquerors' brave female companions that appear in some accounts written by early New World chroniclers.

Llerena's use of the grotesque adds theatricality to his interlude with the hilarious appearance of the makeshift monster on stage, but the boldness of its entrance and the shocking nature of its composition provide the cutting edge of the churchman's satire. The ridiculous figure is a succinct statement, which captures the essence of Llerena's criticism and presents a challenge to traditional symbols of authority, and its disquieting aura conveys the uncertainty and difficulty of the times with a sense of urgency. The real effectiveness of the grotesque, however, can only be understood by placing the island's deteriorating circumstances within the context of its early history. Only then do the hideousness and abnormality of this strange creature reach their greatest expression and reveal the process of decay that Santo Domingo had undergone.

In 1492 Columbus thought that he had discovered the gateway to enchantment in the Caribbean area. El Dorado, the Amazon women, and the Fountain of Youth were among the many myths and legends pursued by the early Spaniards, but not quite a century later, a frightful chimera, a harbinger of doom, stood perplexingly at the entrance to the New World. Utopia and the terrestrial paradise had vanished, if they ever existed, and all that remained was horrifying, according to Llerena. Carefully mapped out by the Admiral's brother Bartholomew, the city of Santo Domingo was the first permanent Spanish settlement in the Indies. It was the symbol of the Isabeline utopian dream to be duplicated throughout Spain's overseas possessions.[16] Instead, the colonies had become an administrative nightmare, and Llerena portrays the chaos and the irrationality of the society that subsequently sprang up there by using the monster's incongruous composition as the embodiment of urban disintegration that would mark the decline of a culture and the eventual fall of an empire. Royal administrators blindly served the Crown and lined their own pockets, and such irresponsible conduct, Llerena contends, brought nothing but destruction to the community. Viewed in this light, there is little to separate these Spanish officials from the pirates who ransacked the American seaports at will.

The grotesque figure's dominance over the action of the *entremés* is also indicative of an environment lacking in spirituality, an aspect of the work that undermines a principal justification of the conquest and ultimately reveals the hypocrisy of the Spaniards' alleged religious convictions. Even Columbus' role as the savior of the so-called heathen races through their evangelization was a failure on Hispaniola, although it succeeded in other parts of the Americas. The island's Indians suffered under Spanish rule and quickly fell victim to its harsh regimentation and lack of humanitarian principles.

According to Llerena's view, therefore, virtually nothing remained of the idyllic garden spot Columbus reportedly discovered on his first voyage. The Spaniards had been tempted by the island's rich resources, and their consumption of them had transformed the serpent of Genesis into a monster of the apocalypse, the apparent offspring of the epitome of grotesque figures, the devil himself.

Whether Llerena envisioned the cataclysmic end of the world, as predicted by Columbus, or whether he actually detected the precise fissures in the union that bound Hispaniola to the rest of the empire, it is clear that he perceived potentially destructive forces to be at work in Santo Domingo. The separation of the city's people from their government is blatantly depicted in the play, and Llerena indicts the colonial administration for creating this breach. This point of view, though sensed by some observant *peninsulares*, was primarily espoused by irate *criollos*, and Cristóbal de Llerena is one of the first writers, whose identity is known, to take this particularly Spanish American position in a literary work. Llerena's perspective and outspokenness represent a glimmer of a national consciousness that would eventually spread throughout Spain's possessions and would ultimately result in the dismemberment of the Spanish American empire. Ironically, however, Santo Domingo would not participate in this movement because of the infiltration of French corsairs, who took over the entire island in the seventeenth century. While much of Spanish America was gathering forces to challenge Spain, some Spanish speakers were resisting the influence of France and the continued domination of its colony, present-day Haiti.

In addition to expressing a controversial minority opinion in early colonial discourse, Llerena is also a pioneer in the employment of the grotesque as a principal vehicle of satire. His interlude is a good example of the pre-Quevedan concept of this technique, which appropriately conveys the historical reality of Santo Domingo as a grotesque spectacle. Llerena is one of the earlier writers to broach the topic of the apparently fraudulent ideological foundations of New World historiography, and his radical rewriting of both history and myth turns tragedy into absurdity, a transformation designed to alienate the audience from its own historical heritage.

In terms of the development of New World satire, this brief play represents an intermediate step between the early *pasquines* and the lengthy satires written by the poet Mateo Rosas de Oquendo before the end of the century. Satiric themes and techniques, however, did not reach their fullest expression in theatrical works of the colonial period because of the vulnerability of the performing arts to government censorship. This official vigilance did not deter such playwrights as González de Eslava from taking an occasional jab at

Crown policy but made women and lovers appear to be more attractive objects for sustained satiric attack. Interludes written by Juan del Valle y Caviedes in the seventeenth century and Pedro Peralta Barnuevo and Jerónimo Monforte y Vera in the eighteenth illustrate this persistent tendency in viceregal theater.[17]

Mateo Rosas de Oquendo

The Peninsular-born poet Mateo Rosas de Oquendo is presently recognized as being Spanish America's first known writer of genuine satires. Although fragments of his poetry initially appeared in Baltazar Dorantes de Carranza's 1604 publication of *Sumaria relación de las cosas de la Nueva España*,[18] the popularity that he achieved during his lifetime was due primarily to the circulation of copies of his work in manuscript form. Very little is known about Rosas de Oquendo, who was also known as Juan Sánchez, except what he himself tells us in his poems, especially his *Sátira a las cosas que pasan en el Pirú, año de 1598* ("Satire about the Things That Happen in Peru in 1598").[19] In this work he leads his readers to believe that he was thirty-nine years old in 1598, placing his birth around 1559, and that he served in the army in Italy before traveling to America. His decision to leave Europe, he confesses, resulted from a number of unfortunate amorous relationships; however, this did not dissuade him from pursuing women in the Indies, it would appear, as his narration of numerous romantic encounters indicates.[20] Rosas de Oquendo probably arrived in the colonies between 1585 and 1588, and from Lima he made his way to Tucumán.[21] Historical documents attest to his activities in the Río de la Plata region, where he accompanied Juan Ramírez de Velasco in the founding of the city of La Rioja in 1591 and became its first public treasurer. As recompense for his service to the Crown, he was awarded tracts of land in the province of Santiago del Estero. A serious account of the subjugation and settlement of northern Argentina is said to be contained in his twenty-two canto history of the area entitled *La famatina*. The manuscript was lost, however, after the death of Governor Ramírez de Velasco, who intended to publish it for the author.[22]

Either in 1593 or shortly thereafter, Rosas de Oquendo apparently left Argentina and returned to Peru, where he supposedly became a member of the staff of the viceroy, Don García Hurtado de Mendoza, the Marquis of Cañete.[23] His lengthy stay in Lima gave him much insight into the daily life and customs of the city and essentially provided him with the material for his two principal works, *Sátira* and *La victoria naval peruntina* ("The Little Peruvian Naval Victory"). At some time after 1598, Rosas de Oquendo moved to New Spain, though perhaps not directly. There he made the Mexicans bear the brunt of his satiric attacks in several short poetic compositions. Although it is believed that he spent some years in Spain's northernmost viceroyalty, his exact whereabouts after arriving there and the date of his death still remain a mystery.

Sátira a las cosas que pasan en el Pirú, año de 1598, Rosas de Oquendo's best-known poem, holds yet another major colonial city up to scrutiny, and its considerable length (more than two thousand lines) permits a more extensive development of the theme than that contained in the anonymous poetic description of Mexico City or Llerena's interlude. Moreover, Rosas de Oquendo's encoding of multiple parodies in the manner theorized by Bakhtin distinguishes his poem as one of the more complete examples of Menippean satire written in sixteenth-century Spanish America.

Founded by Francisco Pizarro in 1535 and designated by him as the City of Kings, Lima was a spectacular showplace of the Spanish Empire in the New World rivaled only by New Spain's capital. Astounding profits from Incan gold and Potosí silver had provided for its opulence and grandeur, and this splendor was reflected in its prestigious viceregal court. Beneath the city's lavish facade, however, lay tremendous deprivation, and it is the vast discrepancy created by these extremes, rather than a gradual historical decline as described by Llerena, that led Rosas de Oquendo to expose Lima's social ills. Declaring that Peru is "tan rrico como ynorante" ("as rich as [it is] ignorant") (2), Rosas de Oquendo quickly penetrates the capital's deceptive exterior, and decentering the focal point of traditional discourse, he concentrates on the marginalized sectors of society by immersing himself in the teeming subculture of its street people. Matters of discovery, conquest, and acculturation are then recontextualized to fit the unconventional focus of the poem, and when perceived by the ordinary person faced with daily survival in an urban setting, they take on mundane and even seamy proportions.

Rosas de Oquendo engages carnivalesque inversion in the rendering of every aspect of his *Sátira* from its individual tropes to its parodic framework, and this technique is particularly evident in his initial scanning of Lima's rabble. Anaphoric enumerations create a sense of confusion and crowding in his introduction of a city turned upside down, and oxymoronic comparisons contribute to the poem's incongruity and antithesis. Depicting the capital as a "mar de miserias" ("sea of misery") into which he will now hurl himself, he appears to inventory the multitudes randomly:

> . . . quántos pobres bisten seda,
> quántos rricos cordellate
>
> . . .
>
> quántos padres ai sin hijos,
> quántos güérfanos, con padres;
>
> . . .
>
> quántos habladores, mudos,
> y quántos mudos, hablantes;
> quántos cobardes, balientes,
> quántos balientes, cobardes!
>
> . . .
>
> quántos ynfames, ylustres,
> quántos ylustres, ynfames. (3–5)
>
> (. . . how many poor people dress in silk,
> how many rich people in corduroy
>
> . . .
>
> how many parents, oh! without children
> how many orphans with parents;
>
> . . .
>
> how many silent speakers,
> how many talking mutes;
> how many valiant cowards,
> how many cowardly brave men!
>
> . . .
>
> how many notable scoundrels,
> how many infamous notables.)

On this occasion Rosas de Oquendo transcribes social contradiction into a conflict of words through the antagonistic pairing of terms and places in contention the very meaning and function of language. This focus on basic lexicology, however, serves as important preparation for the understanding of similar procedures of reversal at work on a larger scale as entire rhetorical models are later called into question.

Rosas de Oquendo's view of Lima assumes the structure of a confessional letter of farewell written as he leaves the city for Mexico or Spain. This is the first of several parodies that he undertakes and the one that provides a unified framework for the intercalation of the others. Letters became an excellent source of information about the New World encounter, and they provide documentary evidence of Spain's imperial progress. In the name of God and king, both Christopher Columbus and Amerigo Vespucci, for example, announced their historic discoveries to the European world in correspondence, and Hernán Cortés likewise wrote a series of *cartas de relación* to the Spanish monarch describing his founding of the city of Veracruz and the conquest of the Aztec Empire.[24] Rosas de Oquendo questions the use of letters in the establishment of authority and legal status in the New World and reappropriates Lima for those who were absent from its founding. In keeping with the epistolary format, but with the intention of lowering the correspondent's lofty purpose, the poet facetiously speaks of his many humorous escapades with a sense of achievement and acknowledges that sex and money were his primary goals. Time and experience prevented him from writing the favorable reports of his predecessors, and he openly admits that he is glad to be leaving the viceregal capital.

While immediately leveling the political aspirations expressed by early Europeans, Rosas de Oquendo also seeks to deflate their spiritual values as well, and so to dispel indirectly the seriousness of their commitment to religious conversion. As if passing from a life of complete freedom and independence into a penitential period, the poet recounts his South American adventures ostensibly to unburden himself of guilt. Although these admissions bear some resemblance to a homily, the poem ultimately becomes more of a *sermon joyeux* with its emphasis on comedy and its tendency toward mockery. In this respect, the point of view of Rosas de Oquendo as the narrator and his attitude toward his account in the *Sátira* may be compared to those of Juan Ruiz in his *Libro de buen amor.*[25] Both men purport to be writing from experience, and they appear to express sheer delight at being alive. Although at times they espouse high moral standards and intermittently condemn the relaxation of such norms, they generally speak of sin from the point of view of a participant and demonstrate their complete surrender to the carnival spirit unleashed prior to the observance of abstinence and penitence. Contradiction also permeates the attempts of these two authors at self-parody, as the ridiculous portraits they paint of themselves not only place their attractiveness in serious doubt but jeopardize their record of seductions as well. Describing himself as a skinny fellow with red hair and big, black eyes, Rosas de Oquendo pretends to personify the incongruity he sets out to create in his poem.

In addition to casting doubt upon explorers and conquerors in their own writings, Rosas de Oquendo contests as well their portrayal as epic heroes, a measure that questions the relationship of early Spanish culture in the New World to classical literary tradition. Heroic narrative poetry enjoyed a revival with the discovery and conquest of America, and the genre is distinguished by such poets as Francisco de Terrazas, Pedro de Trejo, Juan de Castellanos, Alonso de Ercilla, and Pedro de Oña. Rosas de Oquendo, however, debunks both the explorer and the conqueror as literary figures by assuming the roles himself, as a streetwise *limeño*, and then, in picaresque fashion, by behaving like an irresponsible, fun-loving individual out for a lark.[26] Enmeshed in the inner-city environs, therefore, he became motivated by basic instincts rather than high ideals and embarked upon his own personal conquest of the New World. The one he undertakes, however, is not of a martial nature but that born of physical desire. Viewing the massive miscegenation that took place in the Americas ironically, Rosas de Oquendo changes it from the outcome to the purpose of the conquest, implying that the main reason the Spaniards came to the New World was to have sexual relations with its inhabitants.

Transforming himself into a New World Ulysses, Rosas de Oquendo demonstrates the explorer's relentless desire to wander and his thirst for adventure by making his way from one woman to the next and by showing a particular preference for wives. His version of Homer's legendary character is completely humanized and contemporized, and instead of resisting temptation, he proceeds to succumb merrily to every form of it. Lima's streets become the Mediterranean and Aegean seas inhabited by fantastic creatures, who seek to test the hero's strength and endurance and ultimately to bring about his ruin. Scylla, Charybdis, and Circe all lurk in the dark, dangerous caverns of the downtown area, but on close inspection they are the notorious members of Lima's female population. Rosas de Oquendo's recollections, like those of Juan Ruiz, then become a guide to the art of lovemaking in the viceregal capital.

Unlike his epic counterpart, Rosas de Oquendo does not leave a wife behind, but he makes a special point of visiting the spouses of the adventurers who did. Departing from the character of the patient and faithful Penelope, these women were ready and willing to engage in adulterous affairs and often parlayed their services into a life of comfort if not one of extravagance. The rascality of the Lima housewife, moreover, made her the worthy companion of the *pícaro*, and in at least one respect she is able to outwit her adventurous lover. Within the context of Rosas de Oquendo's topsy-turvy version of the conquest, it is the conquered female rather than the supposed conqueror who, after surrendering delightfully to his advances, ironically receives the spoils from the victory.

Although Rosas de Oquendo portrays many women as being alluring enchantresses, he describes others as being grotesque, the obvious counterparts of the monsters of the deep encountered by Ulysses, and he singles them out as the real dregs of society and emblematic of the capital's deception and decay. Even before Christian antifeminism, misogyny was a frequent topic among satiric writers of antiquity, and it is an essential part of the legacy inherited by colonial satirists. Hesiod's story of Pandora, who unwittingly brought evil into the world, is considered to be a prominent source of women's negative portrayal, and Varro's criticism of marriage in his Menippean satires and Juvenal's attack on wives in his *Sixth Satire* are only two of the important works that perpetuated this theme. In keeping with misogynistic tradition, therefore, Rosas de Oquendo gives only passing attention to other societal types, such as impoverished noblemen, homosexuals, gamblers, ruffians, and so forth, and centers his inverted vision of Lima on spirited girls, prostitutes, ailing women, hags, and a particularly enterprising group that he calls *donsidueñas* (20). In order to identify contradictory elements within society as well as to divulge the disparity between their appearance and reality, Rosas de Oquendo creates a word in a manner similar to the formulation of mythological creatures in which two or more distinct life-forms are merged. Combining *doncella*, or maiden, with *dueña*, usually a matron, to refer to young "ladies" with the sexual experience of older, married women, the poet assails their virtuous posture and so discloses their lack of morality. Although neologisms fulfill the desire of some Americans for linguistic creativity in the face of the present lexicon's inadequacy to describe something new and unusual, they are not the only recourse that Rosas de Oquendo employs to characterize and lower these feminine wonders of the New World. Animal imagery and oxymoron contribute to the denigration of females as well and figure prominently in his depiction of Lima as an extraordinary place where the women are "corderos de día / y de noche gauilanes" ("sheep by day / and hawks by night") (4) and where virgins are capable of giving birth.

Having ridiculed the image of the dutiful woman in the epic in his portrayal of wives, Rosas de Oquendo takes aim at the presentation of femininity in lyric poetry as well. Deliberately countering the golden-haired beauties with pearly smiles extolled in the poetic portraiture of Petrarch and Garcilaso, he caricatures them quite simply as being bald and toothless. Throughout his entire poem, Rosas de Oquendo also rejects the spiritual affection expressed by the courtly lover and exhibits only carnal lust in his obsession with painted whores flaunting themselves in public for profit.

Although Rosas de Oquendo encounters other perils such as gambling and dancing during his journey down Lima's streets, he persists in according them sexual significance as well in order to stress the dominance of the lower body over the totality of human physical functions. Card playing, he insists, is like dealing with a pimp because in both cases you lose your self-respect, honor, and above all, your money. Debasement is also suffered by those who dance, for while executing the latest steps, they make highly suggestive gestures. Eroticism is a constant feature of Rosas de Oquendo's *Sátira*, and its explicitness in some instances has led several editors to abridge its publication. The poet's continual reference to acts of carnality acquire the monotonous pattern of daily routine and therefore lend credence to the impression that Lima is the scene of endless debauchery.[27]

In an effort to close the final gap in his circular narrative, Rosas de Oquendo renews his attack on Spanish conquerors in their own rhetoric, but this time he parodies their military discourse. Confessing that he, too, wished to portray himself in the best possible light in order to secure the maximum compensation from the Crown not only for himself but also for his descendants, he admits that he falsified some reports of the Argentine expedition that he sent back to the Peruvian viceroy. Revealing that he was not the victorious warrior that he made himself out to be, he concedes:

[Los pobres naturales] . . . nos dieron la tierra
con muy buenas boluntades
y partieron con nosotros
de sus asiendas y ajuares;
y no me dé Dios salut
si se sacó onza de sangre. (43)

([The poor indigenous inhabitants] . . . gave us the land
of their own volition
and shared with us
all their possessions;
and may God strike me dead
if an ounce of blood was spilled.)

Here Rosas de Oquendo trivializes the encounter and questions the ethical and moral conduct of its alleged champions. In the first place, the poet levels the formal legal procedures used by the Spaniards in taking possession of the land and making the inhabitants the subjects of the king of Spain, an intention announced in the reading of the *requerimiento* (requirement). As a result of this lowering, he removes totally any need to document or legitimize their subsequent appropriation of the New World. In the second place, Rosas de Oquendo portrays these unfortunate natives not as the ferocious and formidable adversaries of conquest histories but as the unwitting victims of pretentious Spaniards with a flare for the dramatic. The mention of their peaceful and generous nature, therefore, makes accounts of raging battles and Spanish heroism appear to be not only unnecessary but ridiculous as well. Even the New World's women were more of a threat than the Indian warriors, the poet insists, as the real battles that he was involved in took place between him and his girl friends.

In keeping with his role as conqueror, Rosas de Oquendo quickly became dissatisfied with his level of achievement and soon sought a new challenge, more recognition, and of course, greater rewards. Drawn toward Spain's wealthiest viceroyalty, he found that his previous dishonesty had ironically won him a government position in the service of the viceroy and that he would be right at home amid other opportunists like himself, who had similarly made their way to the viceregal court. His observations regarding Lima's privileged class are not contained in his *Sátira* but are the focus of his earlier *La victoria naval peruntina*.

Although Rosas de Oquendo's *La victoria naval peruntina* is a separate poetic composition from his *Sátira*, the two poems complement each other by providing a complete satiric profile of early Lima. Instead of centralizing the marginal, however, as noted in the previous discussion of his work, Rosas de Oquendo marginalizes the nucleus of viceregal society in *La victoria naval peruntina*. Scrutinizing members of the ruling aristocracy who were sent to the New World by Spain, he uncovers the same basic attributes of ugliness, corruption, and hypocrisy and concludes that only their manifestations differ from those of the lower classes. Anarchy and fraud prevail at court just as they do on the street, and money again controls lives, this time by buying power and influence. In lieu of the poverty and disease that afflict the common people, incompetence and ineffectiveness plague the nobility and similarly erode its dignity and integrity.

In his poem *La victoria naval peruntina*, Rosas de Oquendo satirically examines the character of Don García Hurtado de Mendoza, who governed Peru from 1589 to 1596, and his handling of the defense of the viceroyalty during an attack by English pirates. Don García, the eighth viceroy to occupy the post in Lima, was an immensely popular figure during his lifetime, and his exploits were celebrated in notable works of prose, poetry, and drama.[28] Fame had come to him early in his career, for in 1556 he was named governor of Chile and charged with the responsibility of pacifying the Araucanian Indians and extending Spanish territory southward after Pedro de Valdivia's death.[29] Although the viceroy was well past his prime by the time he employed Rosas de Oquendo, his image as the epitome of Spanish colonialism in America still remained intact. This fallacy consequently provided the poet with an excellent opportunity to expose a prominent royal official and to bring up pressing political issues that were directly related to the stability of the empire.

In order to compel his readers both to reevaluate the place of this symbolic figure and to consider the ramifications of his viceroyship on colonists, Rosas de Oquendo chose to juxtapose a satiric view of his employer with the portrait of Don García in Pedro de Oña's *Arauco domado.* The Chilean poet's epic was considered to be the most outstanding of the works commissioned by the Hurtado de Mendoza family after Alonso de Ercilla failed to accord Don García the importance he allegedly deserved in his masterpiece *La Araucana.*[30] Even Lope de Vega had praised Oña's artistry in his description of the sea battle between royal forces and English corsairs, the precise incident involving Don García that Rosas de Oquendo selected to level.[31]

Following the traditional portrayal of the Renaissance epic hero who personified both classical and Christian virtues, Oña characterizes Don García Hurtado de Mendoza as a symbol of perfection and the ideal embodiment of Spain's political solidarity, chivalric honor and pride, and religious zeal. In order to counter Oña's lengthy description of Don García as the legendary young captain of the Araucan campaigns, Rosas de Oquendo assumes the role of a picaresque poet in the viceregal court, ostensibly charged with praising heads of state and celebrating occasions of imperial importance, and caricatures Don García by glimpsing him after he has aged considerably and is in poor health.[32] His leadership now lacks the authority and decisiveness of the past, and he functions primarily as a figurehead encumbered by protocol and hindered by his own insecurity. Rosas de Oquendo narrates the events of his mock epic from a position of omniscience, a distance that may be indicative of his social isolation from his eminent employer and the distinguished entourage of the court.

The threat of attack by foreign agents was not a new one for residents of coastal Spanish American cities, as they had been the victims of a number of devastating raids since the middle of the sixteenth century. Sir Francis Drake was among the more successful pirates in American waters, and he was indeed responsible for major military defeats dealt Spain during the reign of Philip II. In 1593 this famous privateer appointed Richard Hawkins (who became known to his Spanish adversaries by the name of Ricardo Achines) commander of a squadron assigned to continue harassing Spanish settlements and disrupting trade along the Pacific coast of South America.[33] When the news of Hawkins' arrival on the western seaboard and his attack on Valparaiso reached Lima, the viceroy was understandably alarmed and took a personal interest in the preparation for his viceroyalty's defense. Don Beltrán de Castro y de la Cueva, his wife's brother, was placed in command of all royal ships and charged with finding Hawkins and destroying his fleet. Stormy weather, however, hindered Peruvian search efforts and forced royal vessels to return to the port of Callao for shelter and repair. When Don Beltrán and his men finally located Hawkins near a Chilean seaport, they discovered that his command had dwindled to a single ship after suffering losses in the Strait of Magellan.[34] On July 2, 1594, a bloody battle took place, and the gravely wounded English captain was taken back to Callao as Beltrán's prisoner.[35] At the time, winning this combat was viewed as an extremely important victory for the Spanish in their war against foreign intervention and a fine addition to Don García's distinguished career as a military officer and an administrative head of state.

In order to place this single event of Peruvian history within a satirical context in *La victoria naval peruntina*, Rosas de Oquendo parodically reverses numerous aspects of Oña's *Arauco domado*. After introducing himself as a person with all the restlessness, curiosity, and impertinence of a Spanish rascal, the poet then proceeds to assail his employer with the same zeal as that with which he was extolled by his reputed admirers. Not only does he strike out at the resultant image created by these colonial poets and historians, but he also attacks the fundamental validity of New World history.

Replacing the Chilean's numerous cantos of elegant and well-ordered royal octaves with what he himself describes as "verso burlando, / llano, suelto, corriente y trompicante / y a veces, con la priesa, salpicante" ("mocking verse / [which is] unadorned, light, common and faltering / and, at times, in haste, out of control") (74), Rosas de Oquendo shatters in only a few pages the foundations on which his predecessor's poem is based.[36] Determined to present a vision of a world inhabited by inept, ineffectual beings and fraught with chaos, he alternates randomly, it would appear, between the narration of indecisive and ambiguous occurrences and the description of grossly exaggerated characters whose relevance is uncertain. Triumph is removed as a possibility for Don García, and drama is immediately eliminated from the sequence of events when Rosas de Oquendo recounts the outcome of the sea battle and characterizes the victory celebration in colloquial metaphor as "para sólo un huevo / mucho cacarear de las gallinas" ("a lot of cackling / over only one egg") (73). Returning to what led up to this allegedly hollow triumph over the English, the poet accordingly selects and condenses several of the most inconsequential incidents and focuses much of his attention on a dock in the port city of Callao as somnambular figures wander aimlessly about in the dark. Even the poet's muse must be roused from slumber ostensibly for inspiration and guidance, but he readily admits that his efforts are futile as she is barren and her windpipe is mildewed (74–75). Rather than describe the actual battle,[37] he dwells only on the unfairness of the confrontation and the lack of valor demonstrated by its victors. Rosas de Oquendo concludes his poem by saying that this sea battle ushers in a new era of waging war and a different standard for measuring the success of armed conflict, which would astound prominent figures of the past, and is, in the final analysis, all a joke.

In addition to using the structure of the poem to convey his perception of Don García's tenure as viceroy and its ramifications for the empire, Rosas de Oquendo expresses his point of view on another level through the irregularity, incongruity, and abruptness of his language. On many occasions he twists Oña's own stylistic devices and imagery to achieve his satiric purpose and so creates new and shocking linguistic elements and metaphorical speech. Latinisms, for example, are a characteristic of *Arauco domado*, and Rosas de Oquendo often combines them with the items of his more mundane lexicon and places them amid trite expressions. Most notably, however, he delights in creating neologisms. Referring to the viceroy's sailors as argonauts, he describes them facetiously, and in imitation of Oña's frequent use of repetitive syllables, as the "terrífico terror terrificante / del aurífero mundo antarticado," ("terrible terrifying terror / of the auriferous, antarctic-like world") (73). Rosas de Oquendo emulates the variety of Oña's vocabulary by including the same antiquated words and maritime terms that are found in *Arauco domado* as well. He also intersperses Italian and Quechua within his Spanish verse and even creates an occasional hybrid. After renaming the City of Kings Limapacha, a deliberately clumsy effort at transcultural expression and one designed to mock the Spaniards most common means of New World appropriation, he even appears to make fun of the silliness of his own invention.[38]

The abundance of mythological references in Oña's epic is also reflected in Rosas de Oquendo's satiric piece, but in the latter work, the poet frequently robs the deities of their previous image. After invoking his poetic muse, Rosas de Oquendo playfully addresses Venus to ask for help by saying, "Y tú, fulgúrea madre de Cupido, / tus pechos musicales ordeñando, / infunde cacoquimia de conceptos /

en este mi evacuado entendimiento" ("And you, resplendent mother of Cupid / milking your musical breasts / infuse a concoction of concepts / in this my empty understanding") (74).[39] Neptune, as well, appears as the principal ruler of the seas, but according to Rosas de Oquendo, he is crippled by the first volleys fired by Don Beltrán's squadron on its departure from the harbor, and he is forced to cling to his trident to remain upright in the water. The tendency of poets to rely on such allusions, Rosas de Oquendo insists, results in the creation of "jerigonza de gitanos" ("gypsy gibberish").[40]

Sensorial imagery, which appears frequently in Oña's poem, is utilized by Rosas de Oquendo as well in the creation of complete scenes and single figures of speech alike. Mocking the Chilean's description of Don García's departure from Lima for Arauco, a ceremonious occasion with a military band, colorful decorations, and marching men in full uniform, he compresses it by repeating one representative element of each aspect of Oña's elaborate tableau.[41] By suppressing all superfluous detail, he drastically reduces the significance of the action as well as the man. After formulating plans for the defense of the coast in *La victoria naval peruntina*, the viceroy is depicted as a pathetic figure who attempts to recapture his former greatness by donning his old robes of office and parading around in them.

In a final effort to oppose Oña's elegance and erudition and to create comedy, Rosas de Oquendo introduces elements of vulgarity. Such allusions range from simple crudeness, as in his description of the muse, to scatological references. Venus, he hopes, will endow him with a form of flowing speech, which he likens to acute dysentery (74).

The focal point of Rosas de Oquendo's *La victoria naval peruntina* is his characterization of each of three principal figures who are presented as onlookers incidentally caught up in a series of unexpected circumstances. All of these portraits are short and superficial and portray their subjects in a uniformly unfavorable light. In *Arauco domado*, Don García was the undisputed center of attention in the scenes in which he was present, and secondary characters became involved in the action only to enhance his stature in the work. Rosas de Oquendo, on the other hand, reduces Don García's importance by making him share his prominence with an ugly, overbearing wife and an insipid brother-in-law and by depicting him as being dependent upon the conduct of others for his own success.

Light imagery is generally employed by poets when describing a man of Don García's position, and Oña follows this tradition by comparing him to the sun.[42] Rosas de Oquendo, on the other hand, downgrades his image to that of a pitiful form in shadow attempting to dispel evil, and perhaps comfort himself, by the light of a fire. Despite his heroism at the battle of Penco and in combat against the bravest Araucanian chieftains, as narrated in *Arauco domado*,[43] Don García's role in *La victoria naval peruntina* has been diminished to that of an observer who risks the lives of Creoles for his own aggrandizement and who sanctions an unfair fight against the enemy, a flagrant breach of the chivalric code. Rosas de Oquendo continually refers to the fact that Hawkins only had one ship to oppose the three Peruvian vessels and refers to him as "un inglesillo malaventurado" ("an unfortunate little Englishman") (73).[44] Pedro de Oña, however, concluded that the viceroy's defeat of both the Araucanians and the Protestants was more than just a military achievement but had religious significance as well. To convey this, he alludes to him in his exordium as Saint García,[45] a gross exaggeration according to Rosas de Oquendo's way of thinking. The latter facetiously dubs him "el cristiano Marqués" ("the Christian Marquis") and depicts him reciting the creed "como mejor puede" ("as best he can") (79).

Rosas de Oquendo deliberately ridicules a number of the more extravagant compliments Oña pays Don García, but this amusing tenor does not diminish the seriousness of his statement. In keeping with Don García's symbolic representation of Spain in America, the poet uses his waning career to mark a lackluster period in the empire's history and the faults of his administration to reveal grave weaknesses in the Spanish colonial system. Although Rosas de Oquendo gives no specific details of his mismanagement and malfeasance other than the Hawkins incident, Don García's provocation of a rebellion in Quito, his role in forcing Andean miners into the overproduction of mercury, his misappropriation of household expenses, and his favoritism in the assignment of prestigious positions and lucrative property were no doubt well known to Peru's residents at the time, as they have carefully been recorded by historians since then.[46]

The menacing presence of pirates during Don García's viceroyship proved to be his greatest challenge and one that was certainly met with immediate success. When placing the defeat of Richard Hawkins in a larger context, however, as Rosas de Oquendo appears to do, he treats it as only one encounter in an ongoing war with relentless enemies, and renewed piracy by France, England, and Holland during the next century would bear this view out.

Because female relatives of renowned men in the New World were often mentioned in both historical prose and poetry, Rosas de

Oquendo includes a portrait of Don García's wife. His purpose in portraying her, however, was probably to add levity to his work and to blame her, at least in part, for the incapacity of the male characters in his poem. Doña Teresa Castro y de la Cueva was the first viceroy's wife to accompany her husband to Lima,[47] and Pedro de Oña names her in the dedication of his *Arauco domado*.[48] Although he fails to provide a description of the vicereine, Oña is noted for his idealized descriptions of feminine beauty, especially in the case of chieftains' wives such as Caupolicán's Fresia.[49] Rosas de Oquendo appears to attack this tendency to praise prominent women excessively through his misogynic caricature of Doña Teresa, the only female target to be identified by name throughout his satiric works.

Doña Teresa's description, which matches those of her husband and brother in length, undoubtedly reflects her high visibility at court and her continual demand for attention from those around her. The many titles that she enjoyed as a member of the nobility both by birth and by marriage were obviously a point of great pride and prestige for her, and Rosas de Oquendo often improvises upon actual family names to lower her status. Imitating the ornate style of Oña's epic, he mockingly calls her the "Ninfa de Lemos, joya de Cañete" ("Nymph of Lemos, the jewel of Cañete") and the "Sultana occidental de todo Argete" ("Western sultana of all of Argete") (77), and in order to deride her for her unattractive appearance, he refers to her as the "Inclita mamacona de Galicia" ("Illustrious *mamacuna* of Galicia"). The last example is another attempt to counter satirically the Spaniards' tendency to claim aspects of indigenous America for their own by giving them Spanish names. Here, however, Rosas de Oquendo reclassifies, or dispossesses, a Peninsular woman by according her a native Peruvian designation. Originally *mamacuna* was a title granted to elderly matrons in charge of the Incan ruler's Virgins of the Sun; however, when it was incorporated into colloquial Spanish, it became a term used to describe a woman who was old and fat.[50] This impression is further emphasized by the poet's creation of the word "anchicara" ("broadface") to continue his caricature.

In addition to Doña Teresa's unsightliness, Rosas de Oquendo may have felt that she was a threat to the patriarchal system. Calling her "la gran Tamorlana de Cañete" ("the great Tamerlane of Cañete") and "Preste Juana de Lemos" ("Prester Jane of Lemos") (81), he criticizes her efforts to extend her influence into both political and religious spheres. His use of masculine allusions in this case is not to praise her for her strength and courage as Oña does in his creation of Tucapel's wife, Gualeva,[51] but to deride her for overstepping the bounds of a woman's traditional role and infringing upon that of the man.

Just as Rosas de Oquendo unmasked the viceroy and vicereine, so, too, he strips Don Beltrán of his dignity. Portrayed as a strong, brave, and skilled warrior in *Arauco domado*,[52] the "Príncipe anfibológico de Lemos" ("two-faced Prince of Lemos") (83) is conversely ridiculed for his weakness, cowardice, and incompetence in *La victoria naval peruntina*. Rosas de Oquendo's technique in illuminating Don Beltrán's traits is different from that displayed in his other two portraits in that he has him confess his shortcomings, crimes, and ambitions in a prayer. Here, the poet appears to chide the overconfident Spaniards for believing that God was always on their side and would even be of help to them against Protestants. Beseeching the Almighty for protection in this venture, Don Beltrán begins, "Soy un tonto y mísero gallego / pecante cotidie empanderado, / descortés, malcriado y arrogante" ("I am a foolish and miserable Galician / a continually sinning wretch, / [who is] discourteous, spoiled, and arrogant"), and his subsequent admission of greed in accepting this mission implicates the viceroy as well.[53] Wealthy on account of his family alliances, according to the poet, Don Beltrán intends to continue in his brother-in-law's footsteps to amass a fortune. In response to his plea, and reminiscent of the visions of famous warriors prior to engaging in battle, his appropriately named guardian angel, Miguel Angel Filipón, speaks to him; however, instead of reassuring Don Beltrán of his strength of character and ability as a seaman, he confirms his worthlessness but tells him not to worry, as he will be victorious. After all, he continues, even toads, insects, and women have on occasion been capable of vanquishing their foes (88).

By juxtaposing classical and Renaissance views of heroism with scenes of contemporary Peru in his *Sátira* and *La victoria naval peruntina*, Rosas de Oquendo demythologizes historical military and political leaders as epic heroes, either by taking them out of the heroic context traditionally accorded them in colonial writings or by contemporizing legendary figures of antiquity. This demythologizing, therefore, ultimately results in the reduced status of the epic in legitimizing Spanish imperial authority. More important, however, Rosas de Oquendo places both the past and future of the viceroyalty in doubt by presenting the capital as a hollow monument to previous accomplishments and the ineptitude and selfishness of colonial leadership as an imminent threat to the empire's security.

As a result of Rosas de Oquendo's satiric leveling, therefore, an innovative profile of postconquest Peruvian society emerges that not only recognizes economic, social, political, racial, and linguistic differences in Lima but focuses on its thriving popular subculture as well. This view of culture may lack the documentation of the official one, but by virtue of its nonexclusivity, Rosas de Oquendo suggests, it rivals the predominant vision in its extensiveness and exceeds it in its ability to depict the real essence of living in the New World. His descriptions of daily routine and perpetual tension, articulated in colloquial and street language, capture the readers' attention and even endeavor to supercede works of official colonial discourse in their power to instruct. Conversely, a behind-the-scenes look at the palace strips away the aura surrounding Don García and reveals a dullard who is detached from the people he serves and ultimately from the mainstream of colonial life. While such lackluster circumstances traditionally compelled New World writers to rely on previous utopian models to transform personages prominent in name only into individuals of distinction and even national heroes, Rosas de Oquendo implies that a satiric profile, fashioned from the point of view of the common person, would at least make the viceroy and his career more engaging as a literary topic and certainly more plausible to his subjects. Don García looks just as absurd in one context as he does in the other, however, a function of the dialogic created by the poet. Epic poetry and other works written in a heroic vein, Rosas de Oquendo contends, do not lead to an understanding of New World reality but contribute to the perpetuation of its myths and legends. His ultimate goal, therefore, is to prod his readers into a realization of their own environment and especially what individuals write about it, which can never be taken at face value. Because of this, heroic literature is for him a particular source of deception, and it cannot inspire greatness, only parody.

The place of Rosas de Oquendo in the history of Spanish American satire is a crucial one because he clearly pursues both the revisionary and revolutionary possibilities of parody in the fulfillment of a satiric design. By introducing the *pícaro* by name into the New World and utilizing both singular and multiple parodic reversal as important structural devices in the composition of lengthy literary works, he demonstrates the vitality of the two principal intertextual strategies employed by colonial satirists as well as the ability of these strategies to function interdependently.

Picaresque characters were especially appealing to colonial satirists because they proved to be an excellent model for someone who is not only alienated from society but who is also the antithetical embodiment of such heroic authority figures as the explorer, conqueror, or viceroy or of the chronicler, historian, or epic poet who

ostensibly documented their accomplishments. The *pícaro's* adventures were those of the ordinary man facing adversity and the
unexpected, and the results were predictably not momentous but
ridiculous and even absurd. Interest in these errant ne'er-do-wells
contributes significantly to the development of narrative, especially
fictional autobiography, throughout the colonial period, and it culminates in 1816 with the publication of Joaquín Fernández de Lizardi's *Periquillo Sarniento*, the first completely picaresque work
written in Spanish America and one considered for many years to be
its earliest novel.

Rosas de Oquendo's picaresque projection of himself as a plain-
spoken individual, whose antics undermine the foundations of the
prevailing culture and draw attention to the serious issues confronting others like himself, lends credence to the theory that the evolution of the picaresque subgenre in the New World paralleled rather
than mirrored that of the Peninsula.[54] Because copies of Spanish
picaresque writings did not enter the colonies in considerable numbers until the beginning of the seventeenth century,[55] it probably
was the actual relationship of these misfits to the rest of colonial
society and their ubiquity in the population at large that made them
compulsory literary characters in satirically oriented works. Youthful wanderers such as the one portrayed in *Lazarillo de Tormes* did
comprise a part of New World society, it appears, and Rosas de
Oquendo may, indeed, have actually been one of them. While the
dominant Spaniard was insistent upon carrying out a mythical conquest of the New World, the *pícaro*, as a representative of the opposite end of the social spectrum, was just as determined to discover
what he considered to be the real America and subsequently to con-
quer and colonize it. Rosas de Oquendo shatters the hopes of those
Spaniards who expected to do anything but struggle for survival in
the New World, and he contends, ironically, it is only the *pícaras*
who are able to achieve the economic independence and social mobility so sought after by the men.

Although Rosas de Oquendo uses many lowering procedures from
grotesque caricature to bilingual hybrids in order to fulfill the overall satiric design of his work, it is their ability to function in parodic
concert that distinguishes his satire. By means of parody, therefore,
the poet not only contests the hegemonic vision of the New World
but creates one of his own that is more relevant for the viceroyalty
of Peru because it reveals the chaos and contradiction that surrounded him. While he clearly demonstrates the effectiveness of
combining satire with parody, he failed to explore the full extent of
parody's constructive potential by devising a new form of expression

that was autonomous from the backgrounded text. This capability, however, was pursued with considerable success by Rodríguez Freile in the seventeenth century and Carrió de la Vandera in the eighteenth. Their utilization of parodic technique contributes significantly to the originality of their prose works and is consequently more directly involved in the development of fictional narrative during the colonial period. Rosas de Oquendo's varied use of parody, however, is the most enduring feature of his satire, and his pioneering efforts in its employment open the way for the complete renovation of Spanish American discourse.

3. The Seventeenth Century: The Growth of Colonial Society

Juan Rodríguez Freile

The life of Juan Rodríguez Freile, like that of many of colonial Spanish America's other satirists, must be pieced together from the information he gives his readers in his only work, *El Carnero*. Just as in the case of Rosas de Oquendo, however, some caution must be exercised in accepting it at face value, as the presentation of autobiographical elements, which are sketchy and often confusing, are clearly part of the critical framework of his account. Whether Rodríguez Freile's family had a close relationship with Archbishop Juan de los Barrios, the conqueror Pedro de Ursúa, or the founder of Bogotá, Gonzalo Jiménez de Quesada, is still a matter of conjecture; however, it is certain that the author's parents were among the first Spaniards to settle in Santa Fe de Bogotá and raise a family. In his account Rodríguez Freile was particularly intent upon establishing his father as a loyal supporter of the king and a lifelong Christian, and thus he hoped to regain at least a portion of the inheritance denied him by the Crown.[1] Rodríguez Freile's social status is a crucial factor in his presentation of life in New Granada, as he expresses the Creole resentment and frustration of being considered a second-class Spaniard, the result of his American birth, and of being treated more like the colonized than the colonizers. Reflecting this colonial milieu in which he played a peripheral part, Peninsular Spaniards dominate the world of *El Carnero*, and Indians, mestizos, blacks, and Creoles are relegated to marginal roles in the narrative's development.

Rodríguez Freile was born in Santa Fe de Bogotá in 1566 (53), and the days of his youth as a schoolboy and later a seminary student there provide a link between him and a number of events in New Granada that are the subject of his narration. When he was about fifteen years of age, he participated in the campaigns against the

Indians in Timaná and Pijao, a venture that must have lasted several years. At some time prior to 1585, the year in which he traveled to Spain, he became well acquainted with the judge Alonso Pérez de Salazar and joined his staff as a page. He accompanied his employer to the Peninsula after charges were made against the official for making a particularly harsh judgment in a case. Although Pérez de Salazar was cleared of any wrongdoing and reappointed to a government post, he died soon after his acquittal leaving Rodríguez Freile to fend for himself. Rodríguez Freile portrays him in *El Carnero* as one of the few honest and just officials to hold office during the first one hundred years of New Granada's history, and he describes his loneliness at Pérez de Salazar's death as that of an orphan in a strange land (242–243). Before his departure from Spain, the young colonist witnessed the 1587 burning of ships by Sir Francis Drake in Cadiz harbor, a prelude to the English defeat of the Armada the following year.[2]

Returning to New Granada by 1591, Rodríguez Freile married at the age of thirty-five and tried to eke out a living managing and farming the remaining estates in Guasca and Muenquevita that had been left to him by his father. Crop failures, however, led to his impoverishment and the subsequent loss of this property. With a sense of isolation, rejection, and utter defeat, the seventy-year-old Creole began writing his only work, a manuscript that would be completed two years later in 1638. It is known that by the early 1640s, Rodríguez Freile had died, but his work was not destined to be published for more than a century.[3]

The lack of a history dealing solely with New Granada provided Rodríguez Freile with an acceptable pretense for writing an account of its first century of Spanish colonization. Because the Chibchas had failed to reach the level of development attained by the Mayas and the Incas or to acquire the gold and silver of other Amerindian civilizations, the region was unable to offer the adventure and wealth the Spaniards so desired or to draw significant attention from the Crown. Purporting to remedy this oversight, Rodríguez Freile set out to inform his readers, especially the king, of New Granada's situation and to place it within the more general framework of universal history.[4]

Behind the mask of a New World chronicler and historian, however, Rodríguez Freile presents a satirical rewriting of New World and Christian history. By establishing ironic parallels between the history of Mexico and Peru, according to official accounts, and that of his own region, he mocks New Granada's uneventful past as well as its questionable present and points out the inadequate and outmoded means of conveying these circumstances through traditional forms of historiography.[5] The history of the Indies was an officially sanctioned form of colonial discourse that predominated during the sixteenth century, and it dramatically captured the most spectacular dimension of Spain's presence in America. Using parodic reversal as the principal vehicle of his satire, therefore, Rodríguez Freile systematically defamiliarizes his readers with this form of expression and subsequently questions the very nature of writing itself. Incongruities dispel the preconceived notions of what New Granada's history should be like, and they find Rodríguez Freile's distillation of events amusing yet averting. The tension created between the author's satirical projection and traditional ideology and rhetoric also opens up new interpretive strategies to colonial readers, a revelation designed to raise their competency at penetrating the artifice of the written page and discerning its true meaning. In addition to enhancing the cognitive ability of his readers, he introduces as well a discursive alternative to the original rhetorical model, a demonstration of the reconstructive powers of parody.

The first indication of unconventionality and the initial step in Rodríguez Freile's parodic process appears in *El Carnero*'s original title *Conquista y descubrimiento del Nuevo Reino de Granada* ("The Conquest and Discovery of New Granada").[6] Although it is composed from a common lexicon employed by chroniclers and historians of the time, the inversion of "conquest" and "discovery" signifies that a particular realization or disclosure followed rather than preceded the subjugation of the territory, and this immediate transgression anticipates the contradiction and disorder that seem to characterize Rodríguez Freile's account.

Further light is cast upon the nature of the awakening that is under way in New Granada in the work's dedication to Philip IV, a customary gesture to one's patron, Rodríguez Freile admits, but one that may have been a protective measure against official censorship. Reflecting upon this dedicatory preface after having read the prologue, it becomes apparent, however, that the elements of the monarch's encomium outline the precise reasons for the author's criticism (35). Although Rodríguez Freile recognizes the king's ability to reward loyal subjects for service and his responsibility to maintain peace and justice in the empire, he makes it plain that New Granada was not the recipient of these benefits when he describes the kingdom metaphorically as a "huerfana" ("orphan girl"). In view of the region's poverty and neglect, therefore, he undertakes a reimaging of this unfortunate waif by dressing her up literarily in "ropas y joyas prestadas" ("borrowed clothing and gems"), which he considers to be of great value (74). Through this textual adaptation, the author intends to make her more attractive as well as to conceal her original state. In a concluding wish for the Spanish ruler, which can only be a reminder of the false justification for the conquest, Rodríguez Freile expresses the hope that the king encounter more lands to subdue for Spain in the name of Christianity (35).

Continuing in a historical vein, but with an ironic tone, Rodríguez Freile applies the phrase "Golden Age" to certain parts of the colonial period, but its connotations are more economic than social or cultural. In reality it was an age of gold for Spain and Spaniards, as wealth from the New World flowed into royal coffers and the pockets of corrupt officials. It was a heyday for the unscrupulous and the incompetent and a triumph for materialism that resulted in the depletion of the region's critical resources. Not only does Rodríguez Freile uncover specific details of mismanagement in this manner, but he also demonstrates how a single term can refer to opposite historical phenomena.

Wishing to question the significance of the discovery of America, the justification for the conquest, the effectiveness of colonization, and even the character of the conquering Spaniard, Rodríguez Freile reduces the utopian dream of Spanish monarchs to a long succession of sexual encounters. Replacing eyewitness testimony and documentary evidence with scandalous rumors and gossip, as principal sources of information, he recounts these escapades with a feigned air of high adventure and martial achievement. The Spaniard, in keeping with the hegemonic vision of the conquerors as well as the exclusivity of New Granada's contemporary society, is still the focus of the action, but his unflagging participation in this alternate field of endeavor, as a dedicated, reliable, skillful, and enthusiastic warrior, is clearly presented as an anachronism.

Conquest remains the theme in *El Carnero*, but it most often takes place in the boudoir rather than on the battlefield, and the resulting alliances lead to a wide variety of crimes. Women, who were customarily ignored in many New World histories,[7] are principal figures in the work's action, and, Rodríguez Freile contends, they have contributed more than their share to the mayhem engulfing New Granada. They, in fact, are portrayed as prime motivators of history and responsible for inspiring lust, vengeance, and greed in the male population. Mocking the chivalric code, Rodríguez Freile frequently portrays men going into armed conflict at the behest of a woman, ultimately willing to die for love if need be. In most cases, however, these incursions are carried out against the woman's husband or her other concerned relatives.

By portraying women in this manner, Rodríguez Freile criticizes the official role of Spanish women in the colonization of the New World. They were thought to be crucial in the creation of a stable society, as they were central to the preservation and perpetuation of the family unit and consequently the key factor in maintaining Spain's economic, political, social, and racial supremacy. Marriage served as the foundation for this hegemonic system, as well as a means to control female sexuality, and as an institution and a sacrament, it was strongly supported by both Church and state. It is not coincidental, therefore, that in most instances in which women provoke crime in *El Carnero* they are the wives of prominent Spaniards. An excellent example of this takes place during the disastrous governorship of Doctor Lope de Armendáriz. In this episode of Rodríguez Freile's work, the wife of the public prosecutor, out of jealousy and a desire to get even, reports her husband's affair with an army captain's wife to a commissioner sent from Spain to investigate charges against various government officials.[8]

While New Granada cannot boast of a bloody subjugation of the territory, gory violence abounds in *El Carnero*, and injury, loss of life, and property damage occur daily, it would appear. So rapid, in fact, is the succession of shootings, stabbings, hangings, beheadings, and so forth that the savagery takes on the stylized comicality of a farce. Indians are featured at the beginning of the work to set the stage, but the acts of barbarity are so prevalent among the Spaniards themselves that they overshadow any uncivilized behavior by the aborigines. An indigenous population is hardly a prerequisite for committing atrocities, Rodríguez Freile's reader should conclude, when dealing with Spaniards in the New World. Even blood-drenched priests waiting to rip out the beating heart of their next victim, as recorded in Mexican chronicles, look pale in comparison to the episode of Juan de los Ríos, who was stabbed twice and had his tongue torn out as he struggled against two assailants. After subduing their victim, they cut out his heart and severed his nose, ears, and genitals and delivered them to the wife of his former employer (184–185). Given Rodríguez Freile's satirical perspective, therefore, history becomes a tragic log of crime and a shocking document of humanity's fallen condition.

In addition to recording events in New Granada, Rodríguez Freile places them within the greater framework of universal history and so provides for a moralistic interpretation for the particular course they are taking. Just as in the *Primera crónica general* of Alfonso X, for example, the beginning of history was viewed as human beings' creation, and events of the Testaments were often perceived as prophetic of their progress thereafter. Columbus himself felt that the discovery of America had eschatological significance, and he saw it as an opportunity to rejuvenate Christendom with his arrival at an earthly paradise and with the evangelization of its inhabitants.[9]

Rodríguez Freile's use of the Bible, ostensibly to legitimize his presentation of events in New Granada, may be a mockery not only of the Spaniards' attempts to validate Spanish American culture in myth and legend but of biblical writers as well, who spiritualized the realm of physical experience, especially when dealing with sexuality. Allegory has long been perceived by satirists as a rhetorical device that fostered self-deception and was employed by authors to conceal any trace of discrepancy or indelicacy. Rodríguez Freile endeavors to reverse the process of allegorization in *El Carnero* by presenting the spiritual and high-minded in terms of their physicality. Such satiric leveling tends to neutralize the allegorical aspect of the text and often limits its interpretation to a literal one.[10] By questioning the veracity of the Scriptures in this way, he may have intended to strike down the very tradition underlying all forms of the written word and to call for its immediate interrogation. The Bible was sacred to Christians, as it contained the word of God, and it represented absolute authority that was not to be doubted. Because the earliest books were generally religious in nature, the aura of their sacredness continued, and even as secular works were produced, they, too, it was assumed, reliably contained the truth. Rodríguez Freile may have hoped to conceal what could have been interpreted as an attack on the Church or Christianity by designating laic New World history as his prime target, and this may have provided him with a modicum of protection from ecclesiastical censure.

Humanity's Fall provides the central metaphor of *El Carnero*, which unites biblical tradition with New World history. Rodríguez Freile demythologizes foundational accounts by populating New Granada with Peninsular Adams and Eves who fall continually in Bogotá and the surrounding area.[11] The devil is depicted as an active force in the New World, and ironically he encounters much less resistance from the Spaniards than from the Indians, who, in order to be baptized, are portrayed fighting hand to hand with him in accounts by Motolinía, Las Casas, and Cieza de León. This is predictable, according to Rodríguez Freile, as he bitterly remarks that emigrants to the New World no longer have to be Christians of long-standing who were of neither Jewish nor Arabic descent. By portraying the Spaniards as giving in to every form of temptation, he casts a shadow over the sincerity of their conversion of the Indians and illustrates that they contributed more to their own perdition than to the salvation of any of the Indies' inhabitants. Just as Llerena conjectured some years earlier in his dramatic interlude, the Spaniards could be the ones expelled from the New World paradise this time, and Rodríguez Freile, as creator of the text, would like to evict them verbally from New Granada. His prediction of a tragic outcome for such a hedonistic life-style is ominous as he sees the end of the world with its condemnation of innocents as well as those responsible. In this case, Rodríguez Freile's fatalism could ironically anticipate yet another concurrence of Christian and New World history.

As Rodríguez Freile journeys through the first century of Spain's domination of New Granada, the metaphor of the Fall is applied not only to the loss of innocence and goodness but to the forfeiture of greatness and power as well. His history is divided, therefore, into the political terms of presidents of the Audiencia, a judiciary and legislative body that was an early symbol of royal authority in the New World, and he points out the ineffectiveness and corruptibility of these appointees, along with the entire administration that served them. Here, Rodríguez Freile even carries the Fall to absurdity within the context of *El Carnero*, as government officials literally tripped one another up in the fulfillment of their duties. When they were not enforcing meaningless rules and regulations, they were taking a spill off a torture rack, tumbling down stairs, or collapsing when bumped on the head. The Creole satirist also reveals the bureaucratic nightmare created by *visitadores* and the periodic *residencia* whose purpose it was to investigate all forms of indiscretion and to provide a judicial review of royal appointees.

A profusion of names accompanies the announcement of each newly arrived administration from the Peninsula, but the lack of an individual description for most of the officials contributes to the initial chaos and confusion of Rodríguez Freile's account rather than its clarity. Although such enumerations traditionally provided historical grounding for the events that unfold, the seemingly interminable procession of nondescript officeholders in *El Carnero* quickly emerges as a predominant characteristic of New Granada's government.

Focusing on sexual exploits that provoke crime, Rodríguez Freile presents a sequence of actions in a predictable pattern, designed to fulfill his didactic and moralistic purpose. Although he follows the formula of temptation, sin, consequences, and haphazard assignment of blame and punishment, he is able to bring in a variety of themes not commonly found in the histories of the period. A dozen or more ways to dispose of your lover's spouse heads the list of topics, and witchcraft, abortion, counterfeiting, jailbreaking, infanticide, kidnapping, and robbery follow somewhat behind. Episodes are based upon the relationship of cause and effect, and finality is often neatly provided by the triumph of justice, which may be meted out in poetic form or, for those who escape worldly judgment, death itself. The Crown's judicial system may be imperfect but God's is not, and only after dying can a just sentence be determined. Rodríguez Freile does, however, mention the involvement and injury of innocent people caught up in the schemes of unscrupulous individuals. They are the real victims, and he considers himself to be one of them.

The presence of Rodríguez Freile as the narrator of events provides a unifying factor for *El Carnero*. He, like the many participants in New World history who authored accounts, was an eyewitness to important happenings in the region, and he serves as a link between reality and the realm of fiction revealed in his numerous intercalations. Sometimes he views and presents events from his own perspective, and at others, he is an omniscient narrator who, with an air of mischief and humor, peers behind the closed doors of authoritative figures and passes down moral judgments on their behavior. Although at one point he laughs at himself caught up in the Spanish vision of New World prosperity, and even admits to having pursued the Golden Alligator like the conquerors who sought the illusive El Dorado (75), he structurally isolates himself from the mainstream of activity controlled by Peninsular Spaniards. After assuming the role of the *pícaro* and firmly establishing the picaresque as a form of Creole discourse, therefore, he repeatedly avoids first-person narration in the numerous episodes of his work, a clear transgression of the genre's norms, in order to reflect a facet of New Granada's sociopolitical reality.

The individual characters of *El Carnero* appear in such rapid succession that the reader is left with only the memory of social types. Women compose the most notable group, particularly the young, beautiful, and wealthy aristocrats. While ugly females are just a nuisance, according to Rodríguez Freile, he predicts that the attractive ones will bring an end to civilization as it was known. Spanish women were the purveyors of evil to the New World, he contends, and he historically traces the trail of destruction by members of their sex back to the Garden of Eden. Following the tradition of *El corbacho* and *La Celestina* in the expression of his misogyny, Rodríguez Freile even repeats the famous line spoken by Rojas' character Sempronio: "Por ellas es dicho: arma del diablo, cabeza de pecado, destrucción de paraíso" ("Women are called limbs of Satan, the fountainhead of sin, and the destroyers of paradise") (296).[12]

Rodríguez Freile's personal reasons for including misogynistic elements throughout his work are unsubstantiated by the text; however, antifeminism is an important aspect in the debasement of the chivalric code and often a characteristic of patristic or moralistic literature. His use of the theme may also serve another purpose, as his attack on women is so frequent and forceful that it may have been a diversion. A woman's moral character was often thought to represent a man's honor, and when she fell, it was consequently at his expense. Satirists who criticized women feared no retribution, since few in the colonies could read, and those who could spent time perusing works considered to be more appropriate for ladies.[13]

Rodríguez Freile's negative portrayal of Spanish men is just as common, but the moralistic conclusions about their behavior are minimized. Officials of both Church and state in *El Carnero* appear to be basically weak, and many demonstrate how easily they were guided by their passions and how quickly they defended their honor at all costs. To have subjected male characters to the scrutiny accorded the women, however, would have resulted in the direct condemnation of Spain's colonial administration.

After having made clear both his own critical position and the inquisitive approach his reader should take, Rodríguez Freile then embarks upon a series of negative, historically based episodes that fulfill his satiric design. One of the first he narrates, which is often considered to be the most imaginative and entertaining of *El Carnero*, is the case of Juana García, a freed slave who was accused of being a witch by the husband of a young, socially prominent resident of Bogotá (132–139). The wife, whose name is not revealed, solicited the services of a black *curandera* (medicine woman) to rid herself of an unwanted pregnancy. This indiscretion had come about during her husband's lengthy stay abroad, and news of his arrival in Cartagena with the flotilla drove her to take desperate measures and seek an abortion. After some deliberation, Juana García decided to discover the whereabouts of the husband and so determine the amount of time before his appearance in the capital. Preparing a washbasin, she conjured up the image of the lady's husband as well as that of his current female companion. Peering into the water, the *señora* remarked:

—"Comadre, aquí veo una tierra que no conozco, y aquí está *fulano*, mi marido, sentado en una silla, y una mujer está junto a una mesa, y un sastre con las tijeras en las manos, que quiere cortar un vestido de grana."

Díjole la comadre:

—"Pues esperad, que quiero yo también ver eso."

Llegóse junto al lebrillo y vido todo lo que la había dicho. Preguntóle la señora comadre:

—"¿Qué tierra es esta?"

Y respondióle:

—"Es la isla Española de Santo Domingo."

En esto metió el sastre las tijeras y cortó una manga, y echósela en el hombro. Dijo la comadre a la preñada:

—"¿Queréis que le quite aquella manga a aquel sastre?"

Respondióle:

—"¿Pues cómo se la habéis de quitar?"

Respondióle:

—"Como vos queráis, yo se la quitaré."

Dijo la señora:

—"Pues quitádsela, comadre mía, por vida vuestra."

Apenas acabó la razón cuando le dijo:

—"Pues vedla ahí," y le dio la manga.

Estuviéronse un rato hasta ver cortar el vestido, lo cual hizo el sastre en un punto, y con el mesmo desapareció todo, que no quedó más que el lebrillo y el agua. Dijo la comadre a la señora:

—"Ya habéis visto cuán despacio está vuestro marido, pues podéis despedir esa barriga, y aun hacer otra." (134–135)

("I see a country I don't recognize, and there is my husband, sitting on a chair. There is a woman standing by a table, and a tailor with scissors in his hand cutting out a scarlet dress." Said the gossip [Juana García], "Let me see." And when she looked she saw just as the other had said. "What country is that?" the wife asked. "Hispaniola, Santo Domingo."

Just then the tailor snipped out with his scissors a piece of cloth for a sleeve and threw it across his shoulder. Said the gossip, "Would you like to see me take that piece of cloth away from him?" "You can't do that?" "If you want it," she said, "I can take it." "Take it, my friend; take it by all means." Scarcely were the words out of her mouth when the other said, "Here it is," and gave her the sleeve. They continued to watch until the tailor had finished cutting out the dress. Then, in a second, the whole scene vanished, leaving nothing but the tub and the water. "Now," said the gossip, "you can see what a hurry your husband is in to get back to you. You needn't worry about being with child. You have time for another one for that matter.")[14]

Although novelistic elements are not uncommon in New World histories, the fact that Rodríguez Freile has elevated aspects of parody to create them is significant and illustrative of its constructive potential. Just as the modern novel emerged from Cervantes' parody of the chivalric novel in *Don Quijote*, so too the short story and novel advance with Rodríguez Freile's parodic inversion of New World historiography. Literary critics have focused especially on the character of Juana García, a socially marginalized figure that Rodríguez Freile has drawn openly from folkloric tradition. She, like the old go-between Celestina, is both real and fantastic, as she represents black culture, transferred to the Caribbean through the slave trade, and she is capable of magically transforming reality through her knowledge of the occult. More specifically, however, she threatens to reverse the patriarchal system imposed by both Church and state by asserting women's power over men through bewitchment.[15]

The events surrounding Juana García's witchcraft are crucial to Rodríguez Freile's satirical framework in that they establish a pattern of behavior in a society lacking in moral restraints. As a colonial Eve awaiting the Fall in her idyllic New World kingdom, the *señora* is portrayed as a pawn in the ongoing conflict between good and evil, and the devil makes his presence known through the person of the devious Juana García. While these happenings are not directly linked to governmental mismanagement, their occurrence just prior to the arrival of the first president of the Audiencia is not a good omen for the recently acquired territory of New Granada.

More important, however, is the method of Juana García's witchcraft, which gives insight into the creative process of Rodríguez Freile's satire. The scene that appears in the washbasin quite clearly links events in New Granada with those on the island of Hispaniola. While this may be an indication of the widespread immorality throughout Spain's overseas empire, the reference to the location of the Spaniards' first permanent settlement in the New World takes the reader back in time to the beginning of an era of discovery and conquest. The fact that a tailor is making a dress for a young woman is also vital to the significance of this episode in that the function of a tailor is not unlike that of the early chroniclers who allegorized the New World in their writings. A tailor, after all, is charged with making or altering clothing to suit an individual's taste and to meet a particular need. It is also important to note that he cuts his garments from previously made cloth and does not weave the fabric himself. Allegory is often characterized by its ability to cloak stark reality,[16] and it is generally formulated from existing literary tradition. When Juana García retrieves the sleeve of the woman's dress, ultimately leaving a portion of her body exposed, it is like taking a metaphor, or one aspect of an allegory, and revealing the truth behind it.

Rodríguez Freile's figurative representation of New Granada as an orphan girl in need of wearing apparel, which was mentioned earlier in the discussion of *El Carnero*, indicates that he was cognizant of what adding and subtracting from an image could do and the general impression that these changes created. Here again he uses a woman to allude to the land and her condition to refer to its status. Instead of removing something from his subject, however, as Juana García had done, Rodríguez Freile wishes to enhance his unwanted region's position in a manner similar to that of the chroniclers and early historians. In this case, however, he exercises satiric leveling by embellishing her with works of low style, such as *La Celestina* and the picaresque of popular origin, which are themselves accounts of social outcasts and contrast sharply with his biblical allusions.[17] His admission that he proposed to attire his orphaned land with borrowed accessories, like his literary predecessors, is also significant, as he acknowledges that there was no new linguistic system capable of capturing the uniqueness of New Granada's history. Borrowing from his Spanish literary heritage, therefore, was his only recourse.

In addition to modeling the character of Juana García on Fernando de Rojas' famous bawd, Rodríguez Freile also reveals the influence of the picaresque in this episode. Both Juana García and the Creole satirist invoke images with the purpose of exposing an adversary or destroying an enemy. Unlike the freed slave, who is exiled from New Granada by royal authorities for her practice of sorcery, however, Rodríguez Freile intended to get away with his mischief by transforming witchcraft into a literary mode,[18] a spirit that contributes to his stature as a devilish rascal and a persistent *pícaro*. *El Carnero*'s author also levels the grounding of early Spanish American history in classical and Christian myth by associating it with tales of superstition and the occult in his account, and he acknowledges the participation of members of a non-Western culture in the colonization of America and the continuation of subaltern cultural practices long after the Spaniards' arrival.

The case of Juana García was only one of many heard by Inquisitors and magistrates and recast satirically by Rodríguez Freile to expose the obsessive legalism of the Spaniards that slowed the process of colonial administration and at times impaired its ability to function altogether. However, when the archbishop wished to punish all those involved in this serious crime, he was dissuaded from doing so by Jiménez de Quesada, who thought that the incident might prove detrimental to the new territory as it was just getting started. For this reason, Bogotá's founding fathers suppressed the entire affair. The archbishop, nonetheless, must have issued some documentation on the subject of witchcraft, as it was mentioned by Rodríguez Freile in connection with other useless papers lost in the shuffle of bureaucracy.

> Pero este auto y el que hizo el señor arzobispo don fray Juan de los Barrios contra las hechiceras o brujas, nunca más parecieron vivos ni muertos; lo cierto debió de ser que los echaron en el archivo del fuego. (147)

> (The offending decree, like the one Bishop Barrios launched against witches, was never more heard of, alive or dead. It may be assumed somebody threw it into the fire for safe keeping.) (79–80)

The power of the archive was well known in official circles, and the only way to deal with a potential problem of this sort was to deny it permanent written representation. In this respect, then, this fiery repository may have been similar to the so-called *carnero*, from which Rodríguez Freile allegedly retrieved discarded documents.

El Carnero is a pivotal text in the development of discourse in the New World, as it clearly demonstrates the constructive potential of parody in the fulfillment of a satirical design. The exposure of Spain's utopian dream with its related challenge to the authority and reliability of the written word, therefore, serves only as a point of departure for Rodríguez Freile's defamiliarization of works generally classified as histories of the Indies. His primary goal is to reeducate colonial readers by heightening their awareness, enhancing their sensibilities, and providing them with alternative interpretive possibilities to their traditional expectations.

The first priority in this proceeding, and a measure that ensures the desired response from Rodríguez Freile's audience, is to instruct the reader on how to read judiciously and how to go about interpreting the meaning of a text. Once aware of the manner in which a work is encoded by the author, the reader may then proceed to decode his or her message accurately. In the case of *El Carnero*, Rodríguez Freile begins the lesson with the title of his satire, and he continually reminds the reader of his point of view as he reduces the term of each Audiencia to its most absurd aspect.

After establishing a need for a viable alternative to the history of the Indies, Rodríguez Freile's next step is to create it as well in the process of formulating his parody. This he achieves by sifting through the predominant form of discourse written during the sixteenth century, and elements of epic poetry and the chivalric novel as they contributed to its inception and composition, and by experimenting with his narration. Ambiguity blocks the facile interpretation previously accepted by many readers, and departing from the rigid factual framework based upon chronology and copious detail,

Rodríguez Freile moves toward a more unstructured arrangement of events in which he plainly places aesthetic concerns above historical ones. By doing this, however, he does not sever the bonds between the intratextual world he projects and the extratextual reality in which he exists. Although his role more closely resembles a storyteller than a chronicler or a historian, the Creole author does not compromise his commitment to the truth but simply indicates that it is presented within a more flexible framework.

By distancing himself from the dominant Spanish conceptualization of history espoused by numerous early colonial writers, Rodríguez Freile calls for its demythologizing, and he opposes their tendency of looking solely to the past, especially for the restoration of a golden age, in the presentation of events of recent memory. Such evasion only postpones the consideration and resolution of current problems and deludes the citizenry into having a false sense of security and well-being. Through a heightened consciousness of one's own situation as well as an inquiring posture toward tradition, Rodríguez Freile proposes to deal more effectively with the present and to initiate change for the future.

While rejecting certain aspects of his Spanish literary heritage, Rodríguez Freile adapts others to his portrayal of the American scene, and he favors the use of nontraditional works, such as *La Celestina* and the picaresque, as principal instigators of discursive change. His recasting of the powerful Celestinesque figure as a member of a marginal race in the New World, however, not only enhances *El Carnero* from a creative standpoint but also opens up a new dimension for her interpretation, which has alternative cultural implications. The same is true of Rodríguez Freile's adaptation of the picaresque when he himself acquires anti-heroic characteristics to fulfill his role as mock chronicler and mock historian in his account. His structural displacement of the *pícaro* from the center of the action to the periphery of the events is vital to his message, as it demonstrates the alienation and isolation of Creoles in a Peninsular-dominated society.

By refocusing previous historiographical priorities with the intention of raising the social and political awareness of both readers and writers in the New World, Rodríguez Freile transforms the presentation of the history of New Granada into a fictional account with historical grounding. Because of this artistic experimentation, *El Carnero* emerges as one of the earlier manifestations of the desire to renew viceregal prose, and its precursory status in the development of Spanish American narrative reveals the role of both satire and parody in this renovative process.

Sor Juana Inés de la Cruz

The satire of Sor Juana Inés de la Cruz, though a lesser-known aspect of the distinguished Mexican nun's literary production, is yet another dimension of the creative genius that confirms her position as the most renowned writer of colonial Spanish American letters. Markedly aggressive and strikingly provocative, this small portion of her complete work attests to her protest against the rigid language of patriarchal discourse that denied her expression of herself and her femininity and against the hierarchy of gender it imposed. Dispersed among her prose, poetry, and drama, her satiric composite of colonial life focuses on the inequality between the sexes and the subsequent disharmony it creates. Believing that each individual should be judged on his or her own merits and not be granted privileges or refused them on the basis of gender, Sor Juana challenges the conventional masculine views of women as members of society, as representatives of the Church, and as literary characters as well. Either by reversing these images of womanhood or by adapting them to her own purposes, she emphatically and convincingly disputes the masculine prerogative to define femininity, in both literary and real terms, and then preside over its fulfillment. In works ranging in tone from the burlesque to the vitriolic, therefore, Sor Juana subverts the patriarchal system of signs and codes and appeals to men to look beyond tradition and to consider seriously the role of women in contemporary society.

Born with an insatiable intellectual curiosity, Sor Juana began a quest for knowledge following her infancy that initiated her lifelong defiance of established conventions.[19] Driven by her own self-perception, she tricked her sister's teacher into giving her reading lessons before her third birthday, and from that day forward her determination to circumvent rules and regulations in pursuit of study only increased. Denying herself childish pleasures and later disregarding the cosmetic concerns of a young girl, she disciplined herself severely to learn as much as she could in the shortest period of time. She even considered dressing like a man to be able to attend lectures at Mexico City's all-male university but had to resign herself to poring over the numerous volumes contained in her grandfather's library. With this preparation, however, she later withstood the thorough examination of noted professors, who had assembled at court at the viceroy's request, and her performance proved to be a milestone in her career as well as in the intellectual history of New Spain.

Sor Juana's disinclination toward marriage left her no other choice but to enter a convent, the only acceptable alternative in seventeenth-century Spanish America for a single woman who wished to live away from home, and this she did in an effort to continue her education in seclusion. Although she wrote numerous works with religious themes, her interests went far beyond the theological concerns of her vocation. Within the context of conventual life, therefore, she continued the secular writing begun when she was the vicereine's lady-in-waiting, and in her leisure she even pondered mathematical and scientific problems at the insistence of her good friend Don Carlos de Sigüenza y Góngora. Because she devoted much of her time to these endeavors, whose goals were unrelated to the Church, she incensed her superiors and thus became the center of controversy. Reduced physically and psychologically by repeated interruptions and queries, she eventually ceased writing and may have withdrawn from life itself. Even her final poems and the renewal of her vows hint at her desire for death in advance of the epidemic that struck the capital and invaded the Hieronymite convent. There, aiding her stricken sisters, she herself fell ill with the plague, and on April 17, 1695, she died.[20]

The idealized vision of femininity set forth in courtly lyric poetry is the target of several of Sor Juana's more comical satiric poems.[21] In these compositions she questions the codified metaphorical language used to describe female subjects and the subsequent mythology about women it has engendered. Although the Renaissance concept of womanhood, derived from a combination of chivalric and Neoplatonic views of love, was certainly not the only factor to shape men's attitudes toward and expectations about women, it undoubtedly had some bearing on the relationship between the sexes in colonial Spanish America. Young girls were encouraged to follow this vision of both physical and moral perfection, and they were often judged by men, and even some women, on their ability to approximate this ideal.[22] In accordance with courtly tradition, poets extolled the immaculacy of the lady, who was the embodiment of perfect beauty and the source of divine inspiration for men. Her flawlessness was defined in encomiastic terms, and her loveliness was likened to the splendorous phenomena found in nature. A woman's youth and attractiveness were often compared to the exquisiteness of a flower, especially the rose, and celestial light conveyed her radiance or prominence. Her facial features were generally the focus of her poetic portrait, and her eyes, metaphorically described as stars, planets, or suns, were a reflection of her divinity.

This time-honored poetic vision of a woman became conventionalized in colonial lyric poetry, and the components of its formula were employed in the characterization of both imaginary and real women. For this reason, the portrayal of leading Spanish American women in the Church, state, intellectual community, and a poet's own circle of friends almost always resembles that of Petrarch's Laura, Garcilaso de la Vega's Isabel Freyre, or Quevedo's Lisi. Even Sor Juana had followed this tradition in her series of poems dedicated to "Laura" and "Lysi," the vicereines Doña Leonor María de Carreto and Doña María Luisa Gonzaga y Manrique de Lara, respectively.[23] Although the poet did attempt to direct attention away from features of their outward appearance and more toward aspects of their inner character,[24] for her to have departed significantly from this tradition might have cast a shadow over these honorable women. While being the ultimate compliment of the time that praised a woman in the most mellifluous and hyperbolic terms, it nonetheless set her apart from the functional activities of society, established her presence as ornamental, and measured her accomplishments by her ability to influence men to excel. Not surprisingly, the women who had attained the greatest success in imitating this image resided at the viceregal court, the most visible locus of hegemony and patriarchy in New Spain, and they no doubt contributed to the artificial atmosphere there that Sor Juana sought to avoid. In both her *comedia, Los empeños de una casa,* and her *Sainete de palacio,* a short intercalated piece within the same program, Sor Juana criticizes court life, a real stroke of irony considering that these works were written precisely for the nobility and performed in the viceroy's palace.[25]

The idea of exploring feminine beauty to create levity in "El pintar de Lisarda la belleza" ("The Painting of Lisarda's Beauty") is probably a derivative of the burlesque mythological fables written during the baroque period.[26] Góngora's "Fábula de Píramo y Tisbe," considered to be the most outstanding representative of this literary category, may have served as enticement for the poet to compose her own comical portraits, and Jacinto Polo de Medina's "Fábula burlesca de Apolo y Dafne" directly shaped her representation of Lisarda, a debt she mischievously denies. Her inspiration, she avers, was the devil, who placed the temptation of being an artist in front of her. Now, instead of portraying Lisarda's beauty with elegance and grace, she will present it in a colorful and colloquial manner. This jocular intention is reinforced by the incongruity and dissonance of the *ovillejo,* an awkward verse form that consists of the unlikely blend of highly regularized rhyme and lines of randomly varying length.[27]

Although the stated purpose of this lengthy poem is to delineate elements of Lisarda's attractiveness, this objective quickly becomes a pretext in Sor Juana's efforts to examine and relay, with a semblance of spontaneity, aspects of the creative process facing the poets of her time as well as the nature of womanhood. She, therefore, is the work's principal character, and she internally deliberates the matters involved in artistic expression, a procedure that also occasionally includes dialogue with an imaginary audience. As the artist, then, it is her task to paint the portrait of a lovely woman with her pen, and the result of her work is both amusing and thought provoking.

Vacillation, doubt, and frustration engulf the creative process that Sor Juana experiences as she attempts to choose from the scant materials with which she can work. Artists before her had metaphorically used up the natural resources to such an extent that she jokingly complains that the stars have dimmed, the flowers have faded, and precious stones have lost their value. Reluctantly, therefore, Sor Juana begins her portrait by piecing together the paltry remains, and thus she questions the basic concepts of metaphorical assignation in female portraiture. The delays are not over, however, as she pauses and tries to resume her description by inarticulately interjecting the word "pues" ("well") into her poem. It is here that Sor Juana declares Lisarda's existence as a real person and separates her subject from the mere visual impression that reveals nothing about the content of her character.

> Es, pues, Lisarda; es, pues . . . ¡Ay Dios, qué aprieto!
> No sé quién es Lisarda, les prometo;
> que mi atención sencilla,
> pintarla prometió, no definilla.
> Digo, pues . . . ¡Oh qué *pueses* tan soeces!
> Todo el papel he de llenar de *pueses*.
> ¡Jesús, qué mal empiezo! (I, 323)

> (She is, well, Lisarda; she is, well . . . Oh Lord, what difficulty!
> I don't know who Lisarda is, I promise you;
> my simple work
> promised to paint her, not to define her.
> I say, well . . . Oh what vulgar "wells"!
> I am compelled to fill the entire page with "wells."
> Jesus, what a bad start!)

Even consultation with her muse proves fruitless as Sor Juana claims that her particular inspirational goddess, who is now experiencing the trials and tribulations of a mortal existence, is being crowded out by those of other poets, thus making creativity and originality impossible.

Resigning herself to coping with these problems, Sor Juana finally starts her portrait of Lisarda and is immediately faced with describing her hair. Gold and sun rays were the more common figures of speech chosen by previous lyric poets, but when she interprets them literally rather than figuratively, she confirms that they have, indeed, been depleted for poetic purposes. As a consequence of the lack of a metaphor to cover her subject's bare head, therefore, she is forced to declare that the beloved is bald, an indignity Sor Juana conceals with a wig. Although false hair appears to be quite a departure from the golden strands and sunshine, these components are now actually very similar, according to the poet, in that they have all become ordinary, superficial, and incompatible with human form.[28]

Pretending to forget her burlesque intention for a moment, Sor Juana compares Lisarda's broad forehead to the sky. This deliberate slip produces a combination of high and low styles in the poem and moves her hurriedly to Lisarda's next feature where the poet whimsically considers the importance of maintaining rhyme in women's portraiture, no matter how detached from reality the description may become. At one point, she even thinks jokingly that it would be easier to describe Lisarda more poetically if she had been named something else. After deciding that Lisarda's eyebrows are like *arcos*, since they resemble Cupid's bow, the first thing that comes to Sor Juana's mind to rhyme with *arcos* is *zarcos*. Blue eyebrows would not only be inappropriate from her standpoint, but she thinks that Lisarda would be upset about them too. Convinced that *arcos* is still the right word, she decides to make it refer to the arches of aqueducts, since water in the form of tears flowed from Lisarda's eyes from time to time. Feigning a sense of satisfaction with the originality of her choice, Sor Juana remarks poetically: "¿Esto quién lo ha pensado?" ("Who else would have thought of this?") (I, 325). While satirists generally tend to reduce metaphorical language to its literal interpretation, it is necessary to retain it as a possibility, as in this case, when it contributes in some way to the contradiction and absurdity they intend to create.

While ostensibly continuing her portrait of Lisarda's femininity, Sor Juana gradually introduces adjectives that are simple, obvious, and derived from colloquial usage. Above all, they lack the connotative reference to her subject's gender and allude to general characteristics held in common by both sexes. Lisarda's eyes are declared to be "buenos" ("good"), and mention of her nose, too, is reduced to a mere formality and a pun on the verb *seguir,* meaning "to follow" as an infinitive and "straight" in its participial form. The poet herself is hardly the traditional paragon of colonial womanhood either, as she portrays herself patting her head and chewing her nails, clearly perplexed by issues extending far beyond the parameters of her poetics.

Lisarda's cheeks present a particular challenge for Sor Juana's artistic talents, and finally in frustration she concedes that if her subject wants a colorful countenance, she can buy her own paint, referring to her makeup. Cosmetics, in a sense, like the clothing in Rodríguez Freile's *El Carnero,* are similar to the allegorical and metaphorical trappings devised by writers to enhance their subject matter. In this case, however, cosmetics are generally applied by the women themselves in an effort to hide flaws in their natural condition. The poet does finally acknowledge Petrarchan tradition when she says that Lisarda's cheeks look like roses, but she immediately revises this illusion; they are, after all, human cheeks and are therefore made of flesh. To conclude the portrait of the maiden's face, Sor Juana compares her subject's mouth to a piece of dried beef rather than coral, since it is both red and salty, and she further justifies her selection by insisting that the former is actually a more appropriate description of this aperture because it is something edible. The substitution of one metaphor for another here, although Sor Juana's is more closely related to the function of Lisarda's mouth, only illustrates that she can be just as absurd as the courtly poet in selecting the descriptive imagery of her portrait.

Noting that her creative energy is cooling down, Sor Juana again merges the literal with the figurative when she endeavors to put this frost to use and depicts Lisarda's throat as snowy. Her decision to do this, however, has now created an additional problem because Lisarda's hands are the same color, and traditionally poetic comparisons cannot be repeated. After ruling out the imagery associated with marble and silver statuary, Sor Juana states quite plainly that they are functional and made of flesh and bone. Continuing the cursory treatment of Lisarda's remaining features, Sor Juana explains that one line is all she needs to describe the girl's waist, since she is extremely thin. If rhyme is to be such an important determinant in a woman's portrait, Sor Juana jokingly suggests that the size of the subject's features should dictate the length of their description.

In her rush to finish, Sor Juana quickly uses a pun to contrast Lisarda's delicate foot to the long and heavy poetic meter of *arte mayor,* and she signs her portrait just as an artist would. Having completed her description without succumbing completely to traditional poetic language, she announces the conclusion of her poem. Not only has she exhausted her theme, albeit hastily, but she is tired and not getting paid, a commentary, no doubt, on the excuses given by poets for their lack of ingenuity.

Sor Juana's portrait of Lisarda is not a satire of baroque style but an amusing critique of the elaborate imagery that had become stale and tedious after years of usage and that resulted in the defeminizing of female portraiture. Poets who consistently employed it, therefore, engaged in a form of unintentional self-parody, as they did not offer a demonstration of their creativity but proof of their own artistic inadequacies. By disassembling in a dilatory manner the component parts of the Petrarchan code, Sor Juana illustrates how barren it had become, and the resultant decomposition exposes the traditional tropes as being a garish conglomeration of inanimate objects that are alien to female form. As a woman, Sor Juana is acutely aware of the need to renovate feminine portraiture, and her concern is not only poetic but humanitarian as well. For this reason, she redirects the attention of the poets of her time as well as her reader to a more plausible perception of woman's presence, which is not dependent entirely upon her outward appearance, but portrays her as a capable and concerned individual.

Sor Juana not only advocates this reorientation toward truth and reality in her presentation of Lisarda but also boldly embraces it in the portrait she offers of herself. No physical profile is given of the poet; however, she is meticulously portrayed in the process of performing an activity. In this respect, she demythologizes the static image of womanhood at the height of its perfection and dispels as well the aura surrounding literary creativity by describing it as being the result of exploration and experimentation. Although her own description is presented within an imaginative context, she demonstrates through her actions that she is a real woman who wonders, doubts, commits errors, and corrects them. A woman, Sor Juana would have her readers believe, is not merely an inspiration for artistic creation, but a potential creator of art as well.

Courtly conventions are also held up to scrutiny by Sor Juana in a series of five burlesque sonnets written in forced consonantal rhyme. Parody, however, characterizes her criticism in these poems, and the chaotic scenes she creates are reminiscent of episodes of the picaresque. As a form of literary diversion, this type of poetry was technically constructed around sequences of fourteen final words in each line, supplied to the poet by another person. Their diversity and dissonance are essential to the farcical comicality she evokes, and they effectively oppose the mellifluousness and erudite intricacies of baroque verse.

The women portrayed in these sonnets are obviously not the aristocratic ladies of lyric poetry nor are they graced with the dignity and patience of Lisarda. They are instead plain, ordinary women, who are readily available and overly responsive, and in this respect, they are not dissimilar to the subjects of misogynistic portraits penned by numerous male satirists. The complaints Sor Juana expresses about them are not entirely critical, however, as they make a mockery of the wistful protests of a spurned courtly lover. Placing more importance on their actions than on their physical description, an approach that reiterates her belief that looks are deceiving, Sor Juana presents an often bawdy account of the tumultuous relationships they have with their male companions. Characterizing them in the order of their presentation: Inés is a loudmouth, Teresilla is an adultress, another woman named Inés is mean, Beatriz is derisive, and Nise is deceitful.[29]

In her third sonnet, Sor Juana comically undermines the very premise of courtly love by debasing its principal objective and by interpreting the effects of the lover's attachment to the beloved literally rather than figuratively. Inés is still perceived as the object of the suitor's affections, but it is the sheer physical pleasure of her company that attracts him to her instead of her uplifting spiritual qualities. Bound to her by this intense carnal desire, therefore, he recounts several of the consequences of his passion, traditionally compared to symptoms of a disease or the results of a wound. Trembling and restlessness are certainly among the outward manifestations of love; however, his unsteadiness is due to a very real fear of her, and his insecurity is a reaction to her lack of morality. The suffering he experiences, then, is the result of blows from the beloved's fist during her fits of temper, and his longing over her inaccessibility is caused by her frequent meetings with other partners outside the house. Despite all this, however, he dedicates himself to her and states that he will follow her anywhere whether to bed or out into the street.

Sor Juana further weakens the irreproachable positions of the admirer and his ladylove in her fifth sonnet, in which she assails other canons of courtly bent. Nise's boyfriend, for example, is not distracted by his feelings for her to the extent that he·fails to see her for what she really is. Love, therefore, has not blinded him, and he refuses to assume any semblance of humility in their relationship. Conventional contrasts of light and dark and heat and cold play a role in the description of their association, but their original figurative significance has obviously been changed. The man's traditional dark disposition, therefore, is now quite literally taken to be the actual color of his skin, as Nise's intended is a mestizo or mulatto. Although the reassignment of this adjective from his nature to his physical appearance works out cleverly within the design of her sonnet, it may also be interpreted as a racial slur. He is not deceived by any aura Nise allegedly possesses, and he harbors no illusions about her. Her brilliance, it seems, is due to her ability to cook up schemes and can hardly be described as a fatally attractive light. Repelled by her continual trickery rather than consumed by his own passion for her, he is justified in his chilly reaction toward her.

Apart from countering various aspects of the courtly concept of womanhood within each of the sonnets examined, Sor Juana composed another designed solely to expose the strictly limited perspective of traditional feminine portraiture. In her first sonnet, therefore, she presents a description of Inés in which auditory imagery takes precedence over the visual. The characterization is encased in a reprimand delivered by the woman's mate for her excessive chattering, a characteristic that Sor Juana imitates with the strident cacophony of a forced rhyme. "Caca" is one of the words included in these verses, and it captures not only the harsh-sounding tone of Nise's speech but the common vulgarity of her language as well. Poetic dissonance is also reinforced through the use of onomatopoeia, which further emulates the intensity and irritation of her utterances.

Men's failure to consider feminine qualities other than the most outwardly visible is also given burlesque treatment in Sor Juana's *Los empeños de una casa.* In one of the more uproarious scenes of this comedy, the buffoon, who has coincidentally come over to Spain from the Indies, dresses up in female attire to escape from the house where he is being held. Don Pedro, who is the play's patriarchal figure, becomes the object of ridicule when he recognizes the clothing of his ladylove and approaches the silly servant. Failing to discern that the person in Leonor's gown is a man, the head of the household begins making amorous overtures (IV, 149).

Sor Juana's sonnets, which are undoubtedly her most eccentric satiric works, demonstrate her ability to create humor and poetry through the suggestion of only a few words and to comment critically as well on the literary conventions and contemporary decorum. Her use of parody of courtly love poetry not only exposes the tremendous exaggeration inherent in this form of encomiastic verse but also demonstrates that efforts to correct its excesses may result in an equally distorted view of womanhood. In this respect, one overreaction is to a certain extent responsible for the other. The higher the expectations men have for women, the greater their disillusionment when the goals are not met. Sor Juana deals with men's forcefulness and constancy in their criticism of women in her poem "Hombres necios," but there she takes advantage of misogyny as a literary theme and explores its comic possibilities.

Although Sor Juana appears to direct her reproof toward the lower classes, this may have simply been an aspect of her parody in opposing ladies of the aristocracy and their gentlemanly admirers. Her tone, however, in bringing this behavior to light is not condemnatory but jovial and is readily conducive to a good, hearty laugh. In addition to this, the placement of these sonnets within the context of Sor Juana's life makes them even funnier, as they appear to be so clearly inconsistent with her religious calling and her reputation as the period's most outstanding baroque poet.

Sor Juana's best-known satire is found among her *redondillas* and is often referred to by its first lines: "Hombres necios que acusáis / a la mujer sin razón" ("Stupid men who accuse / woman without any grounds" (I, 228–229).[30] Ridiculing the male population in general for its inconsistency and presumptuousness regarding female morality, the poet presents a convincing defense of women as well as a sharp protest against men's customary superiority. Because of the forcefulness with which she expresses the woman's viewpoint, this poem is frequently cited as an early example of feminism in the Americas. If, however, her verses are viewed as a parody of feminine satire in which the man is now held up to the scrutiny to which he subjects women, that, then, adds humor to her composition. By choosing this particular strategy in order to present her criticism of men, she also demonstrates that feminine satire can become just as conventionalized and formulaic as the idealized vision of womanhood. Sor Juana was well acquainted with the misogynistic perspective and its presentation in literature, as she used it in the creation of male characters in *Los empeños de una casa*. The father of the beautiful Doña Leonor vilifies women, for example, when he thinks his daughter has run away with Don Carlos, thus bringing dishonor on the family name (IV, 48–49). Don Juan, the suitor of Doña Ana, is also outraged to find another man hidden in her bedroom when he himself has slipped into the house without her knowledge (IV, 76–77).

"Hombres necios" is a carefully constructed piece of argumentation based on the premise that complaints about women have resulted from the antithetical demands men place on them. Mockingly, therefore, Sor Juana assumes the authoritarian role customarily occupied by a male, and she mercilessly examines the conduct of men by pointing out, not coincidentally, flaws generally attributed to women. Satiric leveling is carried out by forcing men to occupy the same position that they have traditionally accorded women. Ostensibly permitting the opposite sex to judge its own behavior, Sor Juana patronizingly leads male addressees through a series of rhetorical questions. In this way she grants men the same consideration they have given women, as they are not allowed to reply to the charges she makes, and her queries are designed to elicit only negative responses.

Sor Juana's assault on the male character is systematic and complete, but its ingeniousness lies in her ability to criticize men through their own literary creation of women. She was a master at following the rules set by men, and her reoriented application of them for satiric purposes is devastating. Although she begins the questioning quite simply, her interrogation intensifies as the verses continue, and each query reveals another unfavorable aspect of manhood. To expose the general irrationality of men in their relationship with women, she asks: "¿Por qué queréis que obren bien / si las incitáis al mal?" ("Why do you want them to be good / when you incite them to be bad?"). Continuing to shed light on the type of individual who would do such a thing, she condescendingly reduces the situation to a visual example and inquires: "¿Qué humor puede ser más raro / que le que, falto de consejo, / él mismo empaña el espejo, / y siente que no esté claro?" ("What damp whim can be more odd / than that which, lacking in counsel, / smudges the mirror itself, / and then regrets that it isn't clear?").

With a negative vision of the male projected, her questions become more abrasive but still deal with superficial flaws when she calls attention to his indecisiveness and the fact that he is never satisfied.

> ¿Pues cómo ha de estar templada
> la que vuestro amor pretende,
> si la que es ingrata, ofende,
> y la que es fácil, enfada?

> (Well, how do you want her to be tempered
> who seeks your love,
> if she who is ungrateful offends you
> and she who is too easy angers you?)

Coming to the heart of the matter, Sor Juana reduces the issue to a moral one, and her tone becomes accusatory. Cleverly she uses chiasmus to delineate the obvious options.

> ¿Cuál mayor culpa ha tenido
> en una pasión errada:
> la que cae de rogada,
> o el que ruega de caído?
>   ¿O cuál es más de culpar,
> aunque cualquiera mal haga:
> la que peca por la paga,
> o el que paga por pecar?

> (Who is more to blame
> in a sinful passion:
> she who falls because she's begged,
> or he who begs because he's so fallen?
>   Or who is more to blame,
> whatever the evil done:
> she who sins for pay,
> or he who pays for sin?)

Her ultimatum, therefore, is emphatic: "Queredlas cual las hacéis / o hacedlas cual las buscáis" ("Either take them as you make them, / or make them as you like them"). Maintaining her criticism of men as well as her intention of parodically paralleling the principles of feminine satire, she concludes by equating men with the symbols of evil, which she announces in unmodified succession. That men are the embodiment of "diablo, carne y mundo" ("the devil, the flesh, and the world") echoes the charges brought against Eve and reiterated by Llerena, Rosas de Oquendo, Rodríguez Freile, and Caviedes that women are diabolical, physical, and materialistic beings.

While men have been criticizing women for centuries, it is not unreasonable to think that women as well might have just as many complaints about men. Cleverly using a literary device that would be easily recognized by her contemporaries, she counters men's criticism and then exceeds their artistry. Her most serious point, however, is that men have wrongly determined the standards of womanhood, and their unrealistic expectations have generated unwarranted criticism. "Hombres necios," however, is not the only work in which Sor Juana exposes the very real injustices facing colonial women. Intellectual rather than social inequality is the concern of her famous correspondence with the bishop of Puebla. Although the dilemma presented in her letter is far more isolated and intricate than the issue she addresses in this poem, "Hombres necios" may have served in some respects as a poetic predecessor of the criticism that she levels at her superior.

Although Sor Juana's letter to Bishop Manuel Fernández de Santa Cruz, *Respuesta a Sor Filotea de la Cruz* (*Reply to Sister Philothea of the Cross*) (IV, 440–475),[31] cannot in itself be considered a satire, its elaborate composition reveals an impressive command of satiric techniques, such as sarcasm, irony, understatement, and masking, which permit her to devise her own system of signification. Even her ostensibly sincere recounting of the development of her inclination toward letters contains picaresque elements, which divulge the rascality of a precocious child and define the relationship of the talented woman in colonial society as one of alienation. Her defense of women, as well, while being a brief history of their accomplishments, becomes a humiliating lesson when recited to her superior. Using these devices in concert, therefore, Sor Juana endeavors to criticize the Church for its backwardness and to ridicule one of its leaders for his arrogance and ignorance. While Erasmism, a very obvious source of anticlerical sentiment, may have influenced her response to some extent, an intriguing possibility lies in the inspiration she may have gathered from the satiric writing of her order's founder, Saint Jerome.

Although he is most noted for his translations of the Vulgate, which serve as a cornerstone of modern Catholicism, Jerome was an outstanding Christian satirist of antiquity. Critical of certain clergy members for their failure as models of the faith, he frequently used satire as an instrument for reform, and it penetrates his numerous historical, polemical, and exegetical works as well as his letters. He, too, was the object of much criticism among his colleagues because of the importance he attached to pagan literature and his approach to religious texts, regarded as revolutionary at the time. These differences led to numerous controversies between Jerome and his fellow churchmen, and the resulting confrontations antagonized several ecclesiastical leaders. One of these disputes, which arose when Augustine of Hippo questioned his intellectual authority to speak out on a particular matter, provoked a famous exchange of correspondence between the two. Jerome wrote to his distinguished rival, who was incidentally a bishop at the time, from a monastery in Bethlehem where he had taken refuge from the corruption of the world.[32]

As a member of the Hieronymite religious community, Sor Juana was no doubt well acquainted with the writings of its founder, and she quotes his works as an authoritative source in her *Respuesta*. Whether she was fully aware of the extent to which he used satire as a mode of expression or of the circumstances that precipitated its utilization is unknown; however, she could not have failed to perceive his unmistakable association with the art form. Jerome actually referred to himself as a satirist and acknowledged it as a force that ultimately brings about positive results. The tone of his criticism, therefore, must have exerted some influence on Sor Juana although it is clear that his satiric writings in their entirety would not have appealed to her. While attacking members of the clergy for their arrogance and false erudition, for example, he also ridiculed women and poets.

On November 25, 1690, the bishop of Puebla wrote to Sor Juana to praise her for her explication of a sermon, written some years earlier, by the Portuguese Jesuit Antonio Vieyra. The letter accompanied a published copy of Sor Juana's work, whose printing he had commissioned. This tribute to her was inspired, he writes, because of the author's exceptional display of knowledge and her extraordinary ability to expound upon it, and for those reasons, he also entitled it the *Carta atenagórica*, or "Letter Worthy of Minerva." Apart from this recognition, however, the bishop included some harsh criticism for the illustrious nun in his letter and sent it to her under the pseudonym Sor Filotea de la Cruz, ostensibly a concerned churchwoman offering sisterly advice. While his motives for concealing his name in this way are not precisely known, since Sor Juana knew he had published her work and had written her the letter, they could be construed as a demonstration of attitudes ranging from collegiality to condescension. Sor Juana may have been additionally incensed, however, by the fact that the bishop assumed a female identity and then proceeded to defeminize it. Although he was sincerely convinced that it was his duty to chide Sor Juana on this occasion, the poet resented his outspokenness, and she cleverly uses satire as a means of chastizing him for it.

The elements of satire in Sor Juana's *Respuesta* are incorporated within the rhetorical structure of polite correspondence, which, in this case, is additionally influenced by the apologetic tone often taken by women and the tendency toward confession frequently employed by nuns.[33] Imitating the bishop, she uses the epistolary format and redirects aspects of his letter devised to stress his critical purpose to suit her own satiric design. This adaptation enables her to defuse his argument and to dismantle his image, while reaffirming her own position as an eminent writer and intellectual. The assertiveness with which Sor Juana exercises her role as a satirist is particularly notable at the beginning and at the end of her lengthy reply because rhetorical amenities, which provide at least some de-

gree of concealment, are more prescribed at the extremities of a letter than in its main body. By extravagantly reciting customary expressions of courtesy, therefore, she creates a vital atmosphere of
ambiguity that entices her reader to interpret her remarks ironically.
Her opening statements are, of course, the more crucial as they immediately set the sarcastic, mocking tone that extends throughout
much of the letter. Instead of being an initial declaration of humility
or cordiality, therefore, her greeting to her superior is a thinly veiled
announcement of the outpouring of resentment and outrage to
follow.

Sor Juana's first matter of concern regards the very nature of her
response to the bishop, and the deliberations she shares with him
clearly demonstrate her use of irony. Instead of revealing how deeply
angered she is by his invasion of her highly valued privacy, she
wisely chooses terms that convey precisely the opposite impression.
She refers, for example, to the unauthorized publication of the *Carta
atenagórica* as a kindness and pretends to muse over how to repay
him fully and in a manner worthy of his position. Silence was even
an alternative to her difficult situation, but, she contends, employ-
ing baroque antithesis, "explica mucho con el énfasis de no expli-
car" (IV, 441) ("it explains a great deal through the very stress of not
explaining") (25). Disregarding the traditional canon of reticence for
women and breaking a strategic silence after the receipt of the bishop's letter, then, she begins the delicate task of voicing a protest yet
still remaining within the confines of acceptable communication
according to ecclesiastical standards.

Just as the bishop employed masking in presenting himself as Sor
Filotea de la Cruz, so, too, Sor Juana uses it in her communication
with him. The principal identity she assumes is also the one assigned to her by the bishop, and it is precisely this literary image
of a conservative cloistress through which she channels her most
damaging criticism and ultimately her liberal views. Her purpose
in doing this, however, is not to place herself on an even par with
her addressee but to distance herself as much as possible from him.
Using distortion, Sor Juana inflates the already egotistical figure
looming behind Sor Filotea by making ingratiating remarks, and she
diminishes even more the meager stature given to her through expressions of false modesty. When placed in close proximity, these
hyperbolic images stand in sharp contrast to one another as Sor
Juana describes the bishop's correspondence as a "doctísima, discre-
tísima, santísima y amorosísima carta" ("most learned, most prudent, most holy, and most loving letter") and alludes to her own

work as "borrones" ("scribblings"), the product of a "torpe pluma" (IV, 440) ("clumsy pen") (17, 19).

After expanding the bishop's image to the extent that she desired or dared, she then deflates it as quickly as possible to create the greatest shock. This technique had been used by the bishop to some extent in his letter, as he presents his dissatisfaction with Sor Juana's intentions after overwhelming expressions of praise for her work. Taking her cue from him, therefore, she employs this strategy, and because his augmented image has a greater distance to fall, her criticism acquires an even sharper sting.

Embedded within Sor Juana's letter to the bishop is a brief autobiographical sketch of her early life that appears to resemble the numerous accounts written by religious women in compliance with the requests of their confessors or other church advisors. These *vidas* often contained the narration of mystical experiences and even miracles, and as one of the few forms of discourse specifically authorized for women, they are an important source of information regarding colonial womanhood. Sor Juana, however, in describing the emergence of her particular God-given talent, juxtaposes a satiric view of her youth with the angelic and martyrlike behavior expected of prominent religious women in times of adversity. In the first place, she is protesting the prejudicial treatment that she has received from the bishop because her so-called divine gift is not limited strictly to religion but may be applied to other disciplines as well. This intention is followed by her rejection of his entreaty, so typical of male ecclesiastics, to provide him with her self-justification.[34]

Parodically reversing the model of the hagiographic autobiography inspired by Teresa of Avila, Sor Juana rewrites the *vida*, and the results of her efforts are not unpredictable. Just as the conqueror, as the ideal man, became a *pícaro* through satiric leveling, so, too, the perfect woman acquires picaresque characteristics in this same demythologizing process. Her rewriting, therefore, not only serves as a prelude to the exposure of Puebla's chief religious leader but also contests the limitations imposed on women by forms of autobiography and its frequently intercalated mystical discourse. Although recent studies have shown that the language and imagery of mysticism provided female religious with an opportunity to liberate themselves from patriarchal suppression, the discursive strategy of the mystic is reliant upon the creation of interior space for self-expression.[35] Sor Juana, on the other hand, advocates the expansion of women's horizons in an exterior dimension, and in a manner comparable to the freedom offered to men.

Under the guise of obeying the bishop, Sor Juana replaces examples of piety with trickery in her picaresque profile. Prevarication, misrepresentation, and circumvention were all considered by the young Juana, if not carried out by her, and she provides evidence that these ruses were used not only to gain access to and acquire knowledge but also to put this knowledge to work even after her adolescence. In addition to living by her wits and taking risks to serve her own interests, she may even have physically resembled the *pícaros* of New Spain who found themselves isolated from the mainstream of colonial society. By cropping her hair and expressing a desire to wear pants, she was the antithesis of the image of femininity so customarily espoused by notable religious women. Even her continual craving for knowledge fulfills the requisite use of hunger as a motivating force in a picaresque narrative, and her escape from the court to the convent corresponds to the Spanish rascal's flight from one place to another only to encounter a more difficult situation.

> Pensé yo que huía de mí misma; pero ¡miserable de mí! trájeme a mí conmigo y traje mi mayor enemigo en esta inclinación, que no sé determinar si por prenda o castigo me dió el Cielo, pues de apagarse o embarazarse con tanto ejercicio que la religión tiene, reventaba como pólvora, y se verificaba en mí el *privatio est causa appetitus.* (IV, 447)

> (I believed that I was fleeing from myself, but—wretch that I am!—I brought with me my worst enemy, my inclination, which I do not know whether to consider a gift or a punishment from Heaven, for once dimmed and encumbered by the many activities common to Religion, that inclination exploded in me like gunpowder, proving how *privation is the source of appetite.* (51)

Her assumption of the role of a *pícaro*—that is, the identity of an individual of low station of the opposite sex—also provides an additional counter to the bishop, as it parodically parallels his usurpation of an ordinary nun's persona in his letter to Sor Juana.

Although the picaresque characteristics of the *Respuesta* are concentrated mainly in Sor Juana's brief recounting of her youth, there is some evidence to indicate that the *pícaro*'s defiant and critical posture influenced her attitude, and perhaps her actions, in later years. The bishop's stance toward her, for example, could be considered another in the series of obstacles to the development of her inclination to study, and her customary response to such opposition may therefore have led to his ultimate discrowning in the poet's letter. While the thought of a picaresque nun in the colonial period appears to be farfetched at first glance, a young woman did actually escape from a Spanish convent during the sixteenth century to disguise herself as a man and to fight in the campaigns against the Indians in Peru and Chile. After she was seriously wounded and her true identity revealed, she returned to the cloister in Spain, but only after receiving a special dispensation from Pope Urban VIII to wear pants in the daily performance of her conventual duties.[36] In a poetic letter written by one of Sor Juana's admirers, Juan del Valle y Caviedes compares her to the nun ensign, as Catalina de Erauso was called, because both women made important contributions to early Spanish American history that were deemed extraordinary for their gender at that time.[37]

The discrowning of the bishop, then, which may be taken as an extension of the picaresque elements found in her alleged *vida*, is accomplished when Sor Juana ably disarms his case against her while further building upon her argument for the acceptance of women as capable and responsible individuals. It is in this counterattack that the real ingeniousness of the *Respuesta* and the satiric magnitude of its composition begin to be unveiled. The revelation of numerous inconsistencies in the bishop's communication, is not only damaging to his authoritarian stance but also enables Sor Juana to deflect his criticism of her and to make his complaints self-incriminating as well. Because contradiction abounds in the bishop's letter, he appears to be a confused person who accuses people hastily and without just cause. Sor Juana holds his behavior up to scrutiny through a series of interrogatives in her *Respuesta* and thus invites either the bishop himself or the public at large to arrive at this foregone conclusion.

> ¿De dónde, venerable Señora, de dónde a mí tanto favor? ¿Por ventura soy más que una pobre monja, la más mínima criatura del mundo y la más indigna de ocupar vuestra atención? . . . ¿Qué entendimiento tengo yo, qué estudio, qué materiales, ni qué noticias para eso, sino cuatro bachillerías superficiales? (IV, 440–441, 444)

> (Why do I receive such favor? By chance, am I other than a humble nun, the lowliest creature in the world, the most unworthy to occupy your attention? . . . What capacity of reason have I? What application? What resources? What rudimentary knowledge of such matters beyond that of the most superficial scholarly degrees?) (21, 37).

Following these tongue-in-cheek queries, which reflect upon the accuracy and rationality of his description of her, Sor Juana shifts the blame for her present predicament away from herself and portrays the bishop as its instigator. If writing and the promotion of an author's works are not desirable, why has he written her a letter that necessitates a reply, and why has he published her work? Again utilizing traditional concepts of womanhood to her advantage, she deliberately plays up her obedience, an alleged virtue expected of women, by contending that she only wrote at the insistence of others and certainly never with the intention of publishing anything. The author of the *Respuesta,* Sor Juana invites the bishop to believe, is a nonthreatening person who definitely does not want any trouble from the Church. To have written on religious matters, therefore, would have been too presumptuous of her because it might have brought her into conflict with the Inquisition. Given these circumstances, then, the bishop, like the men in her poem "Hombres necios," appears to be responsible for the very thing for which he criticizes her.

With regard to the charge that she had neglected her religious obligations, Sor Juana presents her rebuttal from several angles in order to prove that the bishop knows little about her and even less about women and their role in the Church. Apart from the *Carta atenagórica,* which provides conclusive evidence of Sor Juana's prolonged study and profound contemplation of ecclesiastical matters, she further documents her participation in religious writing by offering to send the bishop copies of several of her devotional compositions. These short works, which, as a testament to her selflessness, do not bear her name, were originally written for her sisters but later printed for public use. Even her writing of poetry may be vital to the Church, she points out disdainfully, as the words to hymns are an integral part of the sacred ceremony.

When discussing the vital role of women in history in the *Respuesta,* Sor Juana carefully focuses on those mentioned in the Bible as an obvious lesson for the bishop. Of particular importance to Sor Juana are the famous female members of religious communities who have been recognized for their contributions to Catholicism. Sister María de la Antigua, Teresa of Avila , Saint Birgitta, and the Nun of Agreda, for example, were all permitted to study and write under the auspices of the Church, and their writings account to some degree for their recognition.

After establishing the fact that women can contribute to the Church and that they have played a role in its growth for years, Sor Juana goes on to advocate the extension of their responsibilities to include teaching, a view that supports her contention that women must be educated. Here, she faces her greatest intellectual challenge because the opposition to this idea is considerable and of long duration, and some of its opponents are quite well known. Sor Juana's display of knowledge about religious history and doctrine in this part of the letter is brilliant, and her presentation conforms masterfully yet ironically to the traditional Scholastic methodology adhered to so closely by the Church. Scholasticism, as the foundation of colonial thought during the sixteenth and seventeenth centuries, helped to sustain hegemonic ideology because it relied completely on the past to provide solutions to present problems and accepted without question the Bible, religious writings, and certain classical texts. By examining the statements of such prominent Church figures as Paul and Jerome, Sor Juana carefully uncovers ambiguities and contradictions in their statements about the comportment of women in church and the participation of females in religious ritual. By reinterpreting their words or placing them in another context, she demonstrates how a method of inquiry, like language itself, may be easily manipulated, and she successfully refutes their declarations to solidify her own position. Even the world's greatest authorities could learn from women, Sor Juana contends in one of the most humorous statements of the *Respuesta,* and she sarcastically solicits the confirmation of "Sor Filotea."

Pero, señora, ¿qué podemos saber las mujeres sino filosofías de cocina? Bien dijo Lupercio Leonardo, que bien se puede filosofar y aderezar la cena. Y yo suelo decir viendo estas cosillas: Si Aristóteles hubiera guisado, mucho más hubiera escrito. (IV, 459–460)

(But, lady, as women, what wisdom may be ours if not the philosophies of the kitchen? Lupercio Leonardo spoke well when he said: how well one may philosophize when preparing dinner. And I often say, when observing these trivial details: had Aristotle prepared victuals, he would have written more.) (113)[38]

After pointing out the numerous discrepancies between the bishop's thinking and his actions, Sor Juana deals yet another blow to his image by defining a fool and making it sound curiously like the description of an ecclesiastic.

Dijo un discreto que no es necio entero el que no sabe latín, pero el que lo sabe está calificado. Y añado yo que le perfecciona (si es perfección la necedad) el haber estudiado su poco de filosofía y teología y el tener alguna noticia de lenguas, que con eso es necio en muchas ciencias y lenguas: porque un necio grande no cabe en sólo la lengua materna. (IV, 463)

(A wise man has said: he who does not know Latin is not a complete fool; but he who knows it well is qualified to be. And I would add that a fool may reach perfection [if ignorance may tolerate perfection] by hav-

ing studied his tittle of philosophy and theology and by having some
learning of tongues, by which he may be a fool in many sciences and
languages: a great fool cannot be contained solely in his mother tongue.)
(127, 129)

Because of the deliberate vagueness of this definition, it may also be
applied to the Church at large as a repository for dull, narrow-
minded people. Her recounting of an incident in which the abbess
of her convent denied her the privilege of reading books corroborates
this, and she alludes as well to the intolerance of some of her sisters
toward her supposedly evil inclination. Referring to their failure to
understand and their persistence at interrupting her, Sor Juana ironically states "que no les ha costado afán el saber. ¡Dichosos ellos!"
(IV, 451) ("that they have not been plagued by the thirst for knowledge: blessed are they") (73). Just as she must have disapproved of
the ladies-in-waiting, therefore, for conforming to masculine images
suggested by courtly love poetry, so, too, she chides other women
who adopt the male view of the nun that bishops, confessors, and
priests endeavored to impose upon them.

In the final paragraphs of the *Respuesta,* Sor Juana is concerned
about how her letter will be received. Attempting to cushion her
previous remarks yet still wishing to make a point, she neutralizes
the concept of criticism by stating that it, like praise, is a subjective
judgment. She also declares ironically that censure is preferable to
approval because it is less likely to encourage the development of
inherent human weaknesses. This preference, then, provides justification for her response to the bishop's critical comments in kind
and permits her to deliver them under the guise of saving him from
his own condition.

Rhetorically begging her addressee's pardon for any possible mis-
interpretations, especially in the reply's familiar form of address, Sor
Juana facetiously invites him to change whatever is not suitable.
Several paragraphs earlier, she had noted the predictability of the
bishop's correction of any work of hers and the importance of accepting the inevitable.

Sor Juana's entire letter, therefore, is a testament to the ability and
accomplishment of a real woman, for in her efforts to assert herself,
she has proven herself to be far more intelligent and much more
talented than her male adversary, the bishop of Puebla. While hiding
behind the static image of an ordinary nun, she also forges an entirely new image for Spanish American women as active participants and achievers, and she distinguishes herself not just as an edu-

cated woman but as one of the more outstanding intellectuals of the entire colonial period.

Although Sor Juana obviously took numerous precautions in presenting her position and in answering the bishop's criticism, the letter's mocking tone is only thinly veiled. Such superficial concealment may have been deliberate and the manifestation of a real desire to release the suppressed frustration that had been mounting over the lengthy controversy surrounding her. At the very least her expressions of dissent were viewed as an act of insubordination by the Church, and at most, they were perceived as the advent of a rebellious spirit within the ranks that could ultimately challenge the institution's patriarchal authority.

The exact repercussions of Sor Juana's *Respuesta* can only be surmised, although it is obvious from several of her comments in the letter that she was not optimistic about the outcome of her reply or her own future. The archbishop, Francisco Aguiar y Seijas, reportedly withdrew his support from her as did her longtime confessor, Father Antonio Núñez de Miranda, and in this respect, she may have been an undocumented casualty of the Church's stringent censorship.[39] Soon after sending the letter to the bishop, she stopped writing altogether and became more reclusive than ever. Unwilling to accept the role that was assigned to her yet unable to continue her defiance, she probably hoped for a permanent end to her situation and one that would not be long in coming.

Because Sor Juana's success has been so overwhelming in the traditional genres of prose, poetry, and drama, her achievements in what has been considered a minor art form will remain as a little-mentioned aspect of her literary production. In general terms, however, her satire provides additional proof of her enormous versatility and uncovers recessed aspects of her personality as well. She obviously enjoyed humor and delighted in its creation, and she was also capable of using it aggressively in the interest of social justice. Sor Juana was the only satirist to utilize fully the complexity and ambiguity of the baroque style in pursuit of her targets, and amid the paradox, contradiction, hyperbole, multiple meanings, and other technical devices that normally accompanied it, she revealed a truly original profile of herself.[40]

In judging the quality of her satire, her contributions to its history are clear. Her exposure of the conflict between the sexes, although related to some extent to seventeenth-century social customs and literary styles, transcends time because of its continued relevance. The feminine perspective on this issue is highly unusual for the colonial period, as relatively few women could read and write, and even for those who could, satire was regarded as an unlady-like mode of expression. Sor Juana, however, effectively challenged time-honored ideas about women and invited men to find the real woman behind the various masculine images.

By means of this critical mode, therefore, Sor Juana contends that feminine satire, Petrarchan portraiture, and even formal correspondence in which women are addressed do not lead to an understanding of reality but only contribute to the perpetuation of myths about them. The vision she creates of colonial life, however, not only captures the contradiction and disharmony that surrounded a woman; it is also indicative of the disorder perceived by the Creole and the intellectual. Although Sor Juana uses literary models on numerous occasions in her own writings, they are employed, she would have us believe, merely as rhetorical devices. There is far more evidence to indicate that she failed to identify with the view of woman that these paradigms projected and certainly rejected the role they ostensibly had in the intellectual and cultural formation of colonial womanhood.

Although the precise changes Sor Juana would make in the literary presentation of women are only suggested, and although the impact new images of womanhood would have on men is only hoped for, her proposal for social reform is clear and constructive. Education for women is a sound solution to elevating the woman within colonial society and, when put into action, would in part achieve the goals that Sor Juana so desired. By writing satire, she also established an actual role model for other intelligent, talented women, who must openly question, test, and criticize conventions that are thrust upon them. Sor Juana was probably the only female satirist in the history of colonial Spanish American satire, and considering her contributions to this art form, she must be regarded as the most outstanding satirist of New Spain prior to the nineteenth century[41] and second only to Juan del Valle y Caviedes during the viceregal period.

Juan del Valle y Caviedes

Juan del Valle y Caviedes has long been considered the colonial period's best satirist, and his success rests solidly upon his poetic skills, his knowledge of Peninsular satire, especially that of Francisco de Quevedo, and his capacity for improvisation. As a poet, he was second only to Sor Juana Inés de la Cruz in seventeenth-century Spanish America, and he even counted the Tenth Muse, as she was called, among his many admirers. Unlike the famous nun, however, he resisted the intricacies and obscurity characteristic of the baroque age. Popular concerns dominate his satire, and his language and verse forms are distinguished by their clarity and their lack of complication. Caviedes' tendency to avoid the elaborate literary style of the times may be compared to Quevedo's opposition to Gongorism in Spain, and it is, indeed, the Peninsula's greatest satirist who serves as his most pervasively influential model. Despite the influence and inspiration he obtained from the master's works, however, the Peruvian setting is apparent in his satiric poetry, and he is regarded as a contributor to literary *criollismo*, the perspective espoused by colonial Creole writers.

The biography of Juan del Valle y Caviedes, although erroneously embellished in the nineteenth century by Ricardo Palma,[42] has been reconstructed more judiciously in recent years on the basis of the poet's marriage certificate and last will and testament, which were uncovered in Lima's archives by Guillermo Lohmann Villena. Born in Porcuna, Andalusia, at some time between 1645 and 1648, Caviedes left Spain for the New World at an early age. He was probably accompanied on the trip by his uncle, and their arrival in Peru, it is conjectured, took place about 1657. Because he grew up in the colonies without the benefit of family position or special privilege, he was quickly assimilated into the social milieu of the viceroyalty, an experience that accounts for the considerable extent of his Americanization. As a young man he worked in the mining industry of the Andean cordillera, but after his marriage to Beatriz de Godoy Ponce de León in 1671, he settled down in Lima, where the couple raised their five children. Caviedes made a very modest living during these years probably working as a merchant.[43]

In 1683 an ailing Caviedes made out his will thinking that death was imminent. While poetic references to several later events in Lima's history attest to his recovery from this illness, his unfortunate experience as a patient undoubtedly left an indelible impression on him, as his poetry is noted for the intensity and frequency of his attacks on members of the medical profession. There is no known record of his residence in Lima after 1696, and his name does not appear in the municipal census of 1700. A document written by the Peruvian playwright Jerónimo de Monforte y Vera states that his last years were sad ones, as he slowly drifted toward the brink of insanity. Although only three of Caviedes' poems were published during his lifetime, he became widely known in Peru with the circulation of his works in manuscript form. The publication of his poetry in the eighteenth-century periodical *Mercurio Peruano*, however, brought renewed interest in his literary production and ultimately led scholars to evaluate its merits.[44]

The satiric vision of Lima presented by Caviedes emerges from the collections of his poetry rather than from a single work. The absence of some form of narrative unity that would link one poem directly to another, however, does not deny the existence of organizational features in his satire but places each poetic composition in a more imaginative context. This dreamlike quality, which generally isolates characters and situations from the extended framework of Spanish American history, enables readers to delve into their own imagination for the relationship of his poetry to reality, which adds to the appeal and universality of Caviedes' work. In this respect, the loose construction of his collections resembles the general plan of Quevedo's *Sueños* or a rapid series of picaresque scenes.

When taken as a whole, however, Caviedes' character sketches provide a review of numerous contemporary social types living in the multiracial and bilingual viceregal capital, and as products of the environment, they are, in the poet's estimation, reflections of the state of the viceroyalty. Each character embodies a form of social breakdown, and this degeneration is generally symptomatic of a community whose members, out of self-interest, seek to advance themselves at the expense of or detriment to others. Although Lima's nobility, religious devotees, professionals, and general misfits are all targets of Caviedes' satire, his most determined efforts at exposure and ridicule are directed at doctors and women.

Because Caviedes perceives the world to be an illusion created by appearances, he, too, bases his revealing projection of it on the visual and the pictorial. The most striking image that catches his eye repeatedly is that of human form, and it is, consequently, the deformation of the portrait that becomes the focal point of his satire. Portraiture is a purveyor of the human image, and as such, it has been viewed since ancient times as a magical entity with extraordinary powers. The public conception of a person is one's most valuable possession and is closely associated with honor and reputation. Recognizing its vulnerability, Caviedes undertakes the satiric leveling of laudatory exposition in order to disrupt the customary relationship of identification and admiration that people developed toward traditionally revered social types, and his ability to devise creative caricatures through reimaging establishes him as a master of the grotesque and a creator of the fantastic.[45]

Caviedes' satire of members of the medical profession and their practices is contained in his collection of poetry entitled *Diente del Parnaso* ("The Tooth of Parnassus"). Although he claims that personal reasons, most notably his close encounter with death at the hands of Lima's quacks, prompted him to write this work, the choice of a doctor as representative of the city's social ills is an excellent one. While their ability to diagnose and treat patients was far from scientific in the seventeenth century, doctors allegedly possessed the potential to alleviate human pain and suffering and to eradicate disease, and because of their dedication to this ideal, they commanded a certain amount of authority and respect within the community. Caviedes deals a forceful blow to this collective image, however, by contending not that they had neglected their duty but that they had maliciously devoted themselves to precisely opposite goals. Fear rather than trust, Caviedes insists, should be the response of those who seek their services. While he appears to have a number of grievances against physicians, what probably inspires his harshest criticism is that the profession stands to profit from the dead. Caviedes was well acquainted with the tradition of medical satire and paraphrases the complaints and advice of authorities from antiquity to the seventeenth century in his "Romance jocoserio a saltos" ("Serio-comic Ballad by Leaps and Bounds"). Among the names he mentions are the great philosophers Aristotle and Augustine, the Roman satirists Juvenal and Martial, and Spanish writers from Cervantes to Calderón (111–123).

In numerous poems, predominantly written in ballad form, Caviedes acquaints his audience with the dangers of consulting one of Lima's medical practitioners. The tone of his attack, though it may conceal feelings of resentment and bitterness, is overtly humorous, and his comic allusions frequently give way to hilarity. Reducing both characters and situations to absurdity, Caviedes begins *Diente del Parnaso* by providing a list of outrageous errata, which serves as an introduction to his own system of signification and could be used to transform any serious seventeenth-century treatise on medicine into a parody. Here, the tragic irony of death constituting a medical cure is reduced to the trivial substitution of one word for another ostensibly to correct a minor copying or printing mistake. Where you find "doctor," he states, it should read "verdugo" ("executioner"). Replace "receta" ("prescription") with "estoque" ("sword"), "sangría" ("bloodletting") with "degüello" ("throat cutting"), "medicamento" ("medicine") with "cuchillo" ("knife"), "purga" ("purgative") with "dio fin el enfermo" ("death sentence"), and so forth (6–7). By prefacing his satire of doctors in this way, Caviedes also calls into question the authority and reliability of scientific discourse, a new and emerging form of hegemonic expression. Science became increasingly important during the poet's time, and some colonial intellectuals envisioned it as providing many of the answers to the problems facing humankind and society at large. While undoubtedly offering a number of possibilities for the betterment of daily living for the general population, its powers were also overestimated in some circles, and this inevitably led to its mystification. Caviedes counters this tendency by inferring that scientific exposition, like other discursive forms, contains errors and therefore warrants similar scrutiny.

After noting the failure of doctors to treat their patients effectively, Caviedes offers to the infirm personal advice in which his own philosophy of satire emerges. In a sense, he places himself in the physician's position, as a diagnostician, and prescribes the laughter derived from his poetry as a remedy for human malady. Caviedes, therefore, ascribes curative or sanative powers to his satire and offers it, in an extended context, as a panacea for what ails society. Although Caviedes, like the doctor, believes he has a cure, he cannot be compared to a member of Lima's medical profession in other respects.[46] In the first place, he quips, he does not get paid for his foolishness, and in the second, his errors are not life-threatening. Appearing to brag about the impact his poetry will have, he even suggests that the city's doctors should underwrite the publication of his manuscript, for his work ostensibly fulfills their responsibilities (18–21).

In order to dramatize the danger in which doctors place the public, Caviedes presents their incompetence not as an isolated threat but as a full-scale conspiracy perpetrated by members of the profession and Death, to whom he dedicates *Diente del Parnaso* (5, 8–11). His presentation of Death as the ruler of a dark empire, the militaristic relationship of the physicians to their leader and to their enemies, who are patients, and the characterization of doctors were inspired principally by Quevedo's *Sueño de la Muerte*. Caviedes may have been drawn to this work not only because the Peninsular satirist describes doctors but also because he places the figure of the warrior in a negative light.

By recontextualizing Quevedo's description, Caviedes recasts the sixteenth-century Spanish conqueror as a seventeenth-century Peruvian doctor and then equates him with the modern-day mercenary, the English pirate. This change in referentiality, while still satirically leveling both military and medical men as heroes, brings to the fore several current issues, such as the changing or changed view of the conquest, the growing threat of pirates, and above all, the security of the viceroyalties from both Spain and its foes. Caviedes transhistorically condemns militarism as an instrument of authority, be it foreign or domestic, and he places conquerors, doctors, and pirates on the same plane for their part in causing death and destruction in the Western Hemisphere. The poet's suggestion that the conquerors could have been invaders from hell, as they spread devastation among those they pretended to help, is particularly important because it calls attention to the widening breach between Spain and its American colonies.

Although the portrayal of doctors as agents of a foreign power and the practice of medicine as a declaration of war have apocalyptic implications in this instance, Caviedes jokingly finds some positive use for the diabolical and warlike nature of Lima's physicians. Proposing that they along with the pharmacists would be worthy adversaries for the English corsairs led by Bartholomew Sharpe, he expresses the hope that the next time that the port is under siege that the defense of the City of Kings will rid the place not only of pirates but also of two deadly local menaces (38–39).

While Caviedes condemns all doctors, he focuses on Lima's more prominent malpractitioners, who were introduced by Death during a roll call of troops. While the setting in which they are presented is imaginary, he grounds his vision in reality by actually naming doctors who, for one reason or another, have been noted in historical documentation. The descriptive features of any one of them are rarely concentrated in a single poem, although the poem may be specifically about that person, and the individual profile emerges little by little as the reader advances through the volume of poetry. Quick epithets identify the doctors with death, and rapid visual imagery reveals some aspect of their individuality, which is usually a negative feature of their appearance. The poet also delights in placing incriminating dialogue directly into the mouths of his targets and frequently devises occasions in which doctors converse with one another or with the figure of Death.

Francisco Bermejo y Roldán, for example, was one of the more distinguished physicians to become the subject of Caviedes' satire. As an outstanding professor of medicine at San Marcos for a number of years, he was elected to the rectorship in 1690.[47] Only two years after assuming this post, he was named chief physician of Peru and thus became the highest-ranking health official in the viceroyalty. In his "Los efectos del Protomedicato de Bermejo escripto por el alma de Quevedo" ("The Effects of the office of Royal Physician Bermejo Written by the Soul of Quevedo"), Caviedes mocks his target's title by referring to him as the "protoverdugo" ("chief executioner") and places him in situations that reflect not only on his lack of professionalism but also on his efforts to impose his unethical conduct on both colleagues and patients. As a member of the Royal Board of Physicians, Bermejo was responsible for examining all prospective doctors to determine their ability to uphold the standards of the profession. In this same poem, Caviedes parodies one of these tests by having the doctor interview an English intern for a hangman's apprenticeship (126–134).

Continuing to describe Dr. Bermejo's incapacity to carry out his professional responsibilities, Caviedes charges him with taking advantage of his female patients in "Respuesta de la Muerte al médico" ("Reply of Death to the Doctor"), a poem in which he also criticizes women. Common among the treatments he prescribed for them was "jeringas por delante" ("injections administered in the front"), an apparent remedy that the ladies sought out, according to Caviedes (27). On a more serious note, however, the poet accuses Bermejo of negligence in the deaths of the viceroy's son in "Habiendo escrito el excelentísimo Sr. Conde de la Monclova un romance" ("Ballad to the Count of Monclova") (224) and of the doctor's own father in "Carta que escribió el autor al doctor Herrera" ("Letter to Doctor Herrera") (74). Whether these accusations are true or not has never been confirmed.

Another of the *Diente del Parnaso*'s targets was Francisco Vargas Machuca, who had the honor of occupying the chair of medical methodology at San Marcos, or as Caviedes called it, that university's "Cátedra de Venenos" ("Distinguished Professorship of Poisons") (51). Apart from remarking on the deadly effects of his skills, the poet also refers to him as a "loro de Avicena" ("parrot of Avicenna") to denote his tendency to engage in the mindless recitation of various principles of medicine (62). As a prominent scholar, Machuca had authored a number of studies regarding matters of health, and among them was a treatise on the adverse effects of eating cucumbers (54–58). Caviedes attacks his conclusion—that their seeds are poisonous to Indians—and makes his stupidity on this occasion appear to be exceeded only by his ridiculous admission that he is a virgin (51–52). Although Caviedes finds this surprising statement hard to believe, since he is an associate of Bermejo's, the poet declares in his *décimas* that chastity at his age is un-Christian and inhuman and hardly relevant to the presentation of his credentials.

Pedro de Utrilla is also among the numerous doctors excoriated by Caviedes, but his literary portrayal focuses more on his race than his profession. Although the poet calls him a "condor de la cirugía" ("condor of surgery") (43) because death quite literally provides him with something to eat, his status as a zambo, or person of African-Indian descent, inspires most of Caviedes' imagery. "Licenciado Morcilla" ("Licentiate Blood Pudding"), "bachiller Chime-nea" ("Bachelor of the Chimney"), and "doctor de Cámara Oscura del rey Congo de Guinea" ("Doctor of the Dark Chamber of the king of the Congo") are but a few of the jabs that the poet takes at the doctor's blackness (42), and he ridicules him as well for the mixture of blood in his veins. When the so-called "el cachorro" ("mongrel pup") marries a middle-aged mulatto woman, Caviedes predicts a colorful brood and jokingly requests a "cachorrito barcino de la pri-mera camada" ("spotted one from the first litter") (141–142). Ra-cial prejudice is also a factor in his portrayal of the Indian doctor, Lorenzo, whose halting Spanish he imitates in several poems (47, 86–87).

By carefully choosing such doctors as these, Caviedes extends his criticism to other groups within Spanish America's social spectrum. This extension would include such sensitive sectors of the popula-tion as the government and the intellectual community as well as target members of the racially mixed lower classes. In this respect, Caviedes' concern for the health of Lima's residents subtly conveys his reservations about the stability of viceregal society and even of Spain's overseas possessions in general.

As the chief physician of Peru, for example, Bermejo was a mem-ber of the viceroyalty's colonial administration and an appointee of the king or the viceroy. Caviedes not only harps on his incompe-tence as a doctor but criticizes him as well, although indirectly, for his ineptitude as a royal official. Chosen more for his loyalty to the Crown than for his ability to heal, how, then, could he effectively examine and license prospective practitioners and adequately warn the populace of threats to public health? As a professor and rector of South America's most outstanding university, Bermejo should have been at the forefront in the development of medical technology. In-stead he relied on traditional methodology and even attributed a measles epidemic to an astrological phenomenon.[48] Caviedes' attack on some of Peru's more learned men becomes clearer in his derision of Machuca's treatise on cucumbers. If a layman like Caviedes fails to see any logic in the doctor's research and treatment, how could physicians conduct themselves seriously and meet their responsi-bilities effectively? Both of these men illustrate the need for educa-tional and pedagogical reform, and in the case of the latter, the poet points to learning by rote, or "parroting," as a major drawback to the present system of instruction.

In contrast to the indirect criticism that Caviedes levels at offi-cials and intellectuals through his medical satire, his attack on phy-sicians whose families were members of the lower classes is bold and shocking. Again casting a shadow over the selection of candidates permitted to practice medicine, Caviedes continually derides Pedro de Utrilla about his racial makeup, while any malfeasance on his part is secondary. In this respect, the poet reflects the general atmosphere of racial tension existing in Lima at the time and indicates that much of it stems from the resentment toward representatives of the masses who aspire and attain positions of social prominence and economic security.

In his *Diente del Parnaso*, Caviedes encourages the reader to laugh at adversity by finding humor in illness, deformity, and death, and he achieves this quite appropriately and effectively through his use of the grotesque.[49] His exploration of its potential is much more extensive than that of any of his Spanish American predecessors and more creative than any other satirist of the colonial period. Its most ingenious expression is found in his caricatural sketches of doctors, although Caviedes employs it to a considerable extent in his satire of women as well.

The principal type of the grotesque to be found in Caviedes' medical satire is the macabre, and it is indicative of the gradual replacement of the Fall, as the predominant metaphor used by colonial satirists to describe aspects of New World living, with death. By the middle of the seventeenth century, they had begun to perceive the situation to be more than just "paradise lost" but as an entire civilization on the brink of extinction. In addition to Death appearing as a character, portrayed typically as a skeleton with a scythe, every activity and accoutrement of the doctor reveals him as either a disciple of the Deity of Darkness or Ruler of Hell, a harbinger of doom, or an emissary of the grave.

Several of the lowering strategies used by Caviedes throughout *Diente del Parnaso* were probably derived from Quevedo's elaborate description of doctors in his *Sueño de la muerte*. Metonymy is frequently used by satirists in the demystification process, and it counters precisely the elaborate metaphorical language found in colonial portraiture.[50] Reducing the image of doctors in this way, therefore, Caviedes presents them in terms of their material possessions, and he makes these trademarks synonymous with extermination. All physicians are equipped with purges, syringes, and syrups, for example, and these are equated with lethal weapons or deadly substances. Gloves and rings are also associated with them as are collars, glasses, degrees, and mules, which they customarily rode to visit patients. The "pera de barba," the most commonly used metonymic reduction devised by Caviedes, was a particular pear-shaped style of fashioning one's whiskers in vogue during the poet's time, and it became a veritable sign or emblem of the doctor. In his poem "Remedios para ser lo que quisieres" ("Recommendations on How to Be What You Want"), Caviedes reverses the traditional significance of the beard found in Spanish literature and transforms it from a symbol of dignity, wisdom, and experience to one of fear and certain death. Depersonification is also employed by Caviedes when he compares the natural disasters that frequently befell Peru with the violent and often fatal effects of a medical consultation. Because tremors and earthquakes are like getting medical assistance, Caviedes remarks, doctors should be feared as much as those dreadful occurrences are (9).

The second type of the grotesque deals with monsters and the monstrous and may be expressed by the severe distortion of the human form or the composition of a being consisting of incompatible, nonhuman parts. Just as Llerena used it in portraying the imperfections in sixteenth-century Santo Domingo, so, too, Caviedes employs it, although on a larger scale, in describing the defects of an aspect of Lima's society a century later. Because the devil best represents this category, and because Caviedes, like Quevedo, links doctors to the underworld, this form of the grotesque may also be associated with the apocalypse. The first physician was the devil, according to the viceregal poet (119), and he portrays doctors as embodiments of evil who attack the health of the body rather than the soul.

Caviedes also describes a number of deformed people and cruelly presents them as monstrosities. According to superstition, a distorted physical appearance reflected a moral or ethical flaw in a person's character, and this may have been one of the reasons why Caviedes chose to attack some doctors who were physically impaired. Although it would be considered insensitive and appalling today, the manner in which Caviedes made fun of hunchbacks and people who were blind in one eye was typical for his time. The life of the colonial Mexican playwright Juan Ruiz de Alarcón, who went to Spain as a young man and became an outstanding writer of the Golden Age, is a shocking example of the treatment accorded persons with disabilities. Contemporaries of his, such as Góngora, Lope, and Quevedo, devised ingenious insults to hurl at him and competed with one another in the creation of the most offensive remark.[51]

The technique of comparing men to animals of a lower order is a common leveling procedure employed in Caviedes' medical satire, and the poet deems it especially appropriate in describing deformities because people who possessed them were thought to be less than human and the relationships they maintained devoid of civilized conduct. Animalization is evident in the description of the humpbacked Dr. Liseras whom he calls a "mono de la medicina" ("monkey of medicine") and a "gimio de los curanderos" ("chimpanzee of quacks") (32). Creatures of lower order are also used in comparisons to debase the individual further, and on another occasion a man with a hump is referred to as a turtle (318) and to be even more degrading, a spider (240). Fruits and vegetables are not excluded from the imagery, and in one instance a hunchback is referred to as a "cohombro retorcido" ("contorted cucumber") (56). Distortions such as these are not just used to depict physically handicapped persons but are considered the supreme insult to anyone by denying that person human form.

Apart from the doctors who possessed an obvious characteristic that immediately lent itself to the grotesque, Caviedes often created his own monsters through literary disfigurement, a process that becomes formulaic in many of his poems. Reducing a person's description to the most prominent feature of his physical appearance, usually related to his size, shape, or color, Caviedes uses it metonymically to represent the entire individual. He then finds something with which to compare it and combines that equivalent with a symbol of the trade in order to discredit not only the individual doctor but the medical profession as well. The greater the separation from the human race, the less chance there is for the reader's personal attachment, and the greater the opportunity there is for comedy and absurdity. However bizarre Caviedes' creations, they may indeed represent the doctor from the point of view of the patient because many of the images could be drug induced or the result of a high fever. Don Antonio García, because he is mature and rotund, is like a ripe fig falling off a tree as he descends from his mule, for example, and Francisco Ramírez is a squash with pants, glasses, gloves, and rings (57). When doctors are ridiculed as a group, their killer instinct is emphasized by redundant images of death, one of a general nature, the other specifically dealing with his calling. In Caviedes' dedicatory poem, a physician is variously defined as: an "exhalación a mula" ("bolt of lightning on a mule"), a "volcano graduado" ("volcano with a degree"), and a "veneno con guantes" ("poison with gloves") (9–10).

Despite dealing with medical satire, Caviedes does not use, to any extent, the third form of the grotesque, in which bodily functions or malfunctions are emphasized. To have focused on the serious aspects of the illnesses they dealt with would have only served as a distraction; the poet's primary objective, however, was to expose the doctors themselves who were incompetent protectors of the public, as a symptom of an ailing society. The relationship of actual disease to the social spectrum, though, does become an issue in his satire of women. In Caviedes' portraits of doctors, therefore, the lancing of a boil, the removal of a gigantic kidney stone, and the administering of purges become a part of the grotesque situation but remain secondary to the hyperbolic figures they encase. Perhaps his funniest scatological reference in this regard is interwoven into the portrait of the doctor known as Pico de Oro. He is such a handsome man, he himself believes, that he narcissistically looks for his own image in the urine specimens of his patients (107).

In order to illustrate that Lima's doctors were not only out of the mainstream of scientific developments but far behind the times because of their antiquated mode of thinking, Caviedes places his misshapen figures in situations that are often ingenious and range from the purely fantastic to the historically related. In "A un desafío que tenía el dicho corcovado con un cirujano tuerto sobre salir discordes de una junta" ("To a Duel That a Hunchback Had with a One-Eyed Surgeon, over Differences Arising from a Consultation") (34–37), for example, two of Death's "campeones galenos" ("Galenic champions") engage in hand-to-hand combat in caballeresque fashion to determine how to put a patient out of his misery. Although the surgeon is recognized only by his defect, the other physician is the deformed Dr. Liseras, who is mentioned a number of times in *Diente del Parnaso*. After using several adjectives, such as *corcovado* (humpbacked), *jorobado* (hunchbacked), and *gibado* (gibbous), to describe the latter's disfigurement, Caviedes then adds an Americanism, *corcuncho*, to the list. This defect is the most important element of his caricature and is the object of derision throughout the poem. Arming himself with the tools of his trade, which he ironically thinks will protect his life, Liseras dons two barber bowls used for bloodletting to cover his hump and domed chest and draws his syringe against his opponent's surgical probe. Caviedes states that they faced one another "hombre a hombre" ("man to man"), but corrects himself since Liseras is only "hombre medio" ("half a man") in his doubled-up condition.

With two loyal supporters about to kill themselves, a situation that Death concedes comes up often between doctors, the macabre figure steps in to arbitrate their dispute, and the rationale expressed for saving them is, of course, incriminating to the doctors. Thinking of the loss in numbers, the Grim Reaper would be sacrificing "diez mil muertos por dos muertos" ("ten thousand dead bodies in exchange for two"). Death then proposes that they become friends again and work toward a common goal. The two embrace, although not without difficulty because of Lisera's deformity, according to Caviedes, and they go hand in hand to make a house call on the patient waiting for a "cure."

One of Caviedes' poems dealing with actual events in the viceregal capital concerns a law prohibiting mountain people from eating cucumbers. This legislation issued by the viceroy, the duke of Palata, was based on a report submitted by Dr. Machuca, which concluded that cucumbers were poisonous to Indians. In his "Habiendo presentado el doctor Machuca un memorial para que se desterrase la semilla de los pepinos por nociva, se responde lo siguiente" ("Response to Dr. Machuca's Petition to Ban the Cultivation of Cucumbers Because of Their Harmful Effects") (54–58), Caviedes questions Machuca's officially documented findings, which he had allegedly based on medical science, and attacks the doctor for having arrived at his conclusions intuitively. Ironically following the scientific method more closely than Machuca, the poet offers satirical proof that the doctor is in error as he parodies this authoritative form of discourse.

The lack of scientific evidence or even common sense in Machuca's contention leads Caviedes to ridicule his warning unmercifully, and he labels the document "por simple, por majadero, / por tonto, por imperito, / por incapaz, (y) por idiota, / . . . como lo es quien lo escribió" ("as simple, stupid, / crazy, half-witted, / incompetent, (and) idiotic / . . . as its author is"). If cucumbers are outlawed today, Caviedes contends with feigned indignation, tomorrow it will be grapes, the next day, figs, the next, melons, and as all fruits are banned, other foods such as bread, meat, cheese, and wine will be added to the list. Then we will all surely die from hunger.

After tearing this particular prohibition down, Caviedes comes up with his own list of precautions to mimic the actions taken by Machuca. According to the poet, it is the pear that proves fatal when it is the infamous "pera de barba" worn by doctors. Continuing in this vein, he declares that people should, in fact, beware of this entire family of so-called "físicas frutas que matan" ("physical fruits that kill"). Dr. Avendaño is a sweet potato; Doctors Bermejo and Lorenzo are yuccas; Dr. Utrilla, the elder, "por ser calvo y denegrido" ("because he is bald and black"), is an eggplant; and his son is a pod. Closing his poem, Caviedes concludes that the seed to eradicate, therefore, is not that of the cucumber but the more deadly one that produces bad doctors.

Although Caviedes is probably better known for his caricatures of doctors, his scathing portraits of the dregs of womanhood, contained in his other collection of poetry entitled *Poesías varias y jocosas* ("Varied and Jocose Poems"), comprise a large portion of his satire. Among the females satirized by Caviedes, Lima's streetwalkers are the most frequent targets, and he particularly takes issue with their commercialization of love. In a relationship akin to the one in which he places doctors, women are, ideally, the creators of life, rather than its protectors, and the guardians of a man's heart instead of his health. As paid consorts, therefore, these women have betrayed a sacred trust, and their betrayal exemplifies the basic weaknesses of womanhood and of humanity in general. Unlike his predecessors, however, Caviedes is less concerned about the moral degeneration that prostitution causes within society than he is about the health threat that it poses to its participants. In this respect, however, the obvious presence of these women on Lima's street corners places the viceroyalty in double jeopardy, as they not only constitute a blot on its collective honor but literally risk the physical well-being of its citizens as well.

Since aristocratic women in the viceroyalties were often described in the Petrarchan code, Caviedes juxtaposes this ideal vision of womanhood with satirical portraits of those at the opposite end of the social spectrum. Although conventional feminine portraiture had been thoroughly challenged by Sor Juana Inés de la Cruz, Caviedes carries his parodic reversal of it to extremes by devising grotesque profiles of females that are scabrous and often pornographic. Like his mentor Quevedo, Caviedes had written traditional love poetry, and he was well acquainted with its excesses. Apart from its literary extravagances, however, it concealed a very real issue of promiscuous intimacy behind the facade of an ideally platonic relationship. Although the cause of disease in general remained a mystery in seventeenth-century Peru, venereal disease was known to be the result of indiscriminate sexual contact. After making fun of the various aspects of soliciting in numerous poems, therefore, Caviedes jolts his readers with explicit descriptions of the devastation of syphilis to warn them of the grave consequences of promiscuity.

Mocking the stance of the chivalric admirer, Caviedes assigns pastoral names to Lima's whores and simply calls them "damas" ("ladies") when referring to them collectively. A woman's appearance is still her most outstanding characteristic, but instead of choosing his female subjects for their attractiveness, he selects the more unsightly ones. Ugly women, old hags, and half-breeds are among those he considers to be the more visually displeasing, and he focuses on their instinctive behavior. In contrast to his love poems in which he emphasizes the beloved's facial features because they reflect a woman's beauty as well as her divinity, Caviedes concentrates on her sex organs to divulge her most common aspect and likewise her animal nature. This inverse portrait not only provides ample opportunity for the poet to allude to copulation but also permits him to incorporate other lower-body references, such as defecating, urinating, and breaking wind.

An excellent example of this third form of the grotesque to be found in Caviedes' poetry is contained in the poem "A una dama que rodó del cerro de San Cristóbal" ("To a Woman Who Rolled Down the Hill of Saint Christopher").

> Al caer mostró por donde
> suele el pepino amargar,
> que es por donde el melón huele
> y las damas hieden mal.
>   En tanto cielo mostró
> las causas de tempestad,
> por donde llueve y por donde
> a veces suele tronar.
>   · · ·
>   Paraíso en que se libran
> las sucesiones de Adán
> por donde heredamos todos
> el pecado original.
>   El sol le vino a dar donde
> dice que a nadie le da,
> aunque las cosas de Juana
> tienen poca soledad. (154–155)

> (As she fell she exposed
> what is known as the cucumber's bitter part,
> which is where the melon smells
> and women stink the most.
> Openly she revealed
> the causes of a storm,
> where it pours and
> often thunders.
>   · · ·
>   Paradise from which Adam's
> successors are set free,
> where all of us
> inherit original sin.
> The sun shone on her

where they say it never shines,
although Juana's parts
are never lonely.) [52]

Although Juana is clearly the target of the poet's satire here, the reader must also consider a larger context in which moral degradation is tied to the forfeiture of political power. Saint Christopher's hill is, indeed, an actual place near Lima, but Caviedes' linkage of a literal fall and the mention of a sacred figure named Christopher in the poem's title seems to echo the previous attempts of Llerena and Rodríguez Freile at demythologizing.

In addition to using the metaphorical language of courtly love to extol prominent women, colonial Spanish American writers also praised them by attributing masculine characteristics to their demeanor, another code challenged by Caviedes. This tradition, which may be traced back to such famous females of classical mythology as Athena (Minerva), Artemis (Diana), and the Amazons, was revived by some of the earlier Spanish chroniclers to describe women in the New World. For the native American women of nonsedentary cultures as well as the wives of Spaniards sent from the Peninsula to assist their husbands in colonization, life was a daily struggle and frequently a question of survival. As a result of this strenuous lifestyle, they were forced to develop a certain amount of physical strength, and many demonstrated skill and courage with arms. Since the Spaniards considered the warrior to be the ideal male, and since femininity was customarily associated with weakness and cowardice, women who were perceived as being unusual in any positive sense were accorded "manly" characteristics and often portrayed within a military context. Bernal Díaz del Castillo ascribed masculine traits to Doña Marina in his *Historia verdadera de la conquista de la Nueva España*, for example, and Father Bartolomé de Las Casas as well follows this tendency in describing the assertiveness and bravery of the wife of Panama's governor Pedro Arias de Avila in his *Historia de las Indias*. The most famous account of the New World's warring women, however, is found in Fray Gaspar de Carvajal's chronicle of the Orellana expedition that sailed South America's mightiest waterway.[53]

By the seventeenth century, military imagery was still being used by eminent authors wishing to pay tribute to female achievers in a male-dominated society. Caviedes was among them, and he used it in the previously mentioned letter addressed to Sor Juana Inés de la Cruz. Praising the illustrious Mexican nun's intellectual accomplishments, he refers to her as an Amazon and compares her to the nun ensign, Catalina de Erauso (454). Although Caviedes followed this persistent tradition in offering the ultimate compliment of his time to his extraordinary female contemporary, he was also clearly aware of the urgent need for changing this now tired depiction of feminine unconventionality. In his "Pintura de una fea buscona en metáfora de guerra" ("Portrait of an Ugly Camp Follower in War Metaphor"), he parodies aspects of the application of this masculine imagery to female subjects when he crudely compares parts of the camp follower's body to instruments of war and her sexual activities to recruiting procedures. To continue to mock the elegance of courtly love poetry, Caviedes begins his description, in lumbering *pie quebrado*,[54] with the lower part of her body and gradually works his way up to her head.

> En variedad de soldados
> tendrás de todas especies,
> pues siempre te harán infantes
>   los jinetes.
> Tendrás en tu compañía
> gente que levantes y eches,
> pues todo cabe en las muchas
>   levas que tienes.
> Artillería tendrás
> tan sólo con que te lleves,
> pues saben todos la buena
>   pieza que eres.
>   . . .
> Bombas tienes en los pechos
> porque revientan de leche,
> por pezones, infiernillos
>   de pebete.
>   . . .
> Adarga con mascarón
> es tu cara con afeite,
> y los carrillos de almagre
>   dos broqueles. (244–246)

(From a variety of soldiers
you will have every kind,
but you will always make infantrymen (infants)
    out of cavalrymen (riders).
You will have in your company
people that you pick up and draft,
for everyone fits into the many
    maneuvers that you have.

    Artillery you will have
simply to be loaded,
for everyone knows what a good
    piece you are.

     . . .

    Bombs you have in your breasts
because they burst with milk,
for nipples, you have little
    fuses.

     . . .

    Your face, with cosmetics,
is a leather shield with a hideous mask
and your rust-colored hair is arranged
    like two escutcheons on your head.)

After ridiculing every aspect of pandering from crafty go-betweens to lisping harlots, Caviedes extends his ironic perspective to include the serious consequences of indiscriminate sex, and it is here that he links social disease with intense suffering and death.

    El amor cobra en dolores
lo que le prestó en cosquillas,
conque a pagar viene en llanto
deuda que contrajo en risa. (187)

    (Love takes its payment in pains
what was lent in tickles,
for you pay with tears ·
what you acquired in laughter.)

Grim humor characterizes his more precise descriptions of female syphilitics in Lima's Charity Hospital, and he deals openly with the ravages of such a dangerous and controversial disease. In a reference to Belisa's general condition, the poet foreshadows a tragic end for many of the unfortunate victims:

    Un esqueleto es su cuerpo,
de tantas anatomías,
como las tientas le han hecho
en el mondongo y las tripas. (188)

    (Her body is a skeleton
from so many examinations
due to so much probing
in her intestines and entrails.)

Although annoying and embarrassing ailments have occasionally been the object of satiric commentary, Caviedes' bold treatment of serious illness is an unusual approach for a satirist to take, and his choice of addressing it in his satire of women rather than doctors is significant. Such shocking observations were intended to create a sense of alienation in the reader and thus serve as a stern warning, and it is perhaps through this frankness that the poet saw a solution to the actual spread of devastating social disease, truly a symptom of an ailing society.

The satire of Juan del Valle y Caviedes stands out among that of other colonial writers because of the extraordinary rapport that he establishes with his reader. Although he obviously draws upon elements of the Peruvian setting, the relevancy of his themes remains intact after three centuries, and their development, which may be detached for the most part from extended historical circumstances, contributes to his universal vision of humanity and society. Neither the advancements in medical technology nor the advent of the feminist movement has dissuaded critics from such age-old targets as physicians and women, and because both societal types continue to form an integral part of quotidian life, they are still held up to rigid scrutiny. Doctors are still chided for the wealth that they accumulate, and the rising number of malpractice suits filed against them continues to undermine complete confidence in their ability. Women, too, have not changed in the eyes of their detractors, and their characterization as loose, deceptive, aggressive, or crass is only modified slightly to accommodate a contemporary scene.

An intriguing facet of Caviedes' satire, however, which is related to both of his principal targets, is his attitude toward sickness and disease, a timeless preoccupation that has probably surpassed the fear of war in all eras. Because medicine has still not eradicated illness, which stands as an ever present threat to the life and happiness of every individual, his observations and advice are as pertinent today, for someone in an industrialized society, as they were for the colonial *limeño*. When placed within the larger context of seventeenth-century Spanish America, however, Caviedes' mention of the physical disorders of Lima's residents may also serve as a metaphor for the social and political instability in Peru resulting from internal causes.[55]

Sickness has been portrayed in literature since the time of Plato, and because its specific origin was not known then nor was it apparent in seventeenth-century Peru, it was regarded as a mysterious phenomenon. Caviedes demystifies it to a large extent by not taking it seriously, although he carries it to the other extreme by inferring that one's physical condition may be changed simply by altering one's mental attitude. Caviedes' inference, which has maintained its currency to the present, is a very positive one when coping with misfortune, and he appeals to his readers to take control of their own lives and to see the humor in any situation no matter how grave. Even the imagery of warfare provides a common link between Caviedes and his modern reader as today physicians speak of the "crusade" against cancer, the "invasion" of the body's healthy cells, and the ability of "victims" to "combat" the disease with their own "defenses." Caviedes, however, presents the reversal of this in that the enemy is not the disease but the doctors, who use their weapons against their patients rather than against harmful organisms.[56]

Venereal disease in Caviedes' feminine satire, on the other hand, is accorded very different treatment from that of the rarely identified infirmities of the patients of Lima's quacks. Because the source of this tragic scourge was known during Caviedes' time, he reasoned that not only could it be prevented but if contracted it could be treated and possibly cured. Although it is presented as a shockingly grotesque consequence of human weakness, Caviedes does not dwell on its punitive effects nor on its moralistic implications.[57] Instead, his explicitness in describing the ravages of the disease are intended to create public awareness of the painful and perhaps fatal results of this preventable affliction. Although some of society's worst problems are those that it inflicts upon itself, Caviedes still believes that average citizens are capable of dealing with the important issues that confront them, and he warns that unsubstantiated solutions proposed by any single sector, including the scientific community, should routinely be viewed with skepticism.

In addition to the transcendence of several of Caviedes' more important themes, his presentation of them in short, clear-cut segments enables him to strike at his targets quickly and accurately. Although his literary style is unmistakably that of his time, he does not use the intricacies of the baroque to conceal his intent. His communicative skills as well as his talent for writing poetry facilitate the transmission of his ideas simply and smoothly so that attention is drawn to his startling caricatures rather than unusual situations or settings. While Caviedes' challenges to poetic portraiture and other forms of encomiastic verse do not constitute a new direction for colonial satirists to follow, his parody of scientific discourse does provide an additional rhetorical target on which they could take aim.

It is through his use of the grotesque, however, that Caviedes creates his greatest humor and delivers his most serious message. Although Quevedo's works introduced him to this art of distortion, he brings his own interpretation to it and indeed advances its creative possibilities beyond the parameters established by the Spanish master. The grotesque influenced satire throughout the colonial period from the pre-Quevedan concept of it in Llerena's dramatic interlude to the elaborately perverse tableaux of Esteban Terralla y Landa's *Lima por dentro y fuera*, written during the latter part of the eighteenth century. Caviedes, however, proposes the most radical expression of it in his fantastic portraits of doctors, and the key to his creativity is not in the amount of detail he presents but in his ability to reduce an image to its more absurd components. This synthesis defies logical grounding to the extent that the readers can participate in the textualization, or writing, of the poem by filling in the gaps with their own specifics. Caviedes, therefore, creates a unique set of meanings based on traditional signs and symbols in *Diente del Parnaso*, and their importance and depth are determined by their interpreter.

Although Caviedes criticizes numerous members of Lima's social spectrum for a variety of reasons, he expresses as well a sincere faith in the ability of ordinary people like himself to control their own lives by benefiting from experience and by not fearing the unknown. An alert, sensible individual, therefore, can improve the quality of his or her own existence, and this, in turn, the poet hopes, will provide for the growth of a safer, saner society.

4. The Eighteenth Century: A Prerevolutionary Setting

Alonso Carrió de la Vandera

El lazarillo de ciegos caminantes, Alonso Carrió de la Vandera's account of his inspection tour of South America's postal system, has long been recognized as an outstanding work of the eighteenth-century colonial empire because of its versatility.[1] The contemporary setting offers a detailed profile of prerevolutionary society and invaluable information regarding the intricate network and management of commercial trade routes in the colonies.[2] In recent years the extent of its artistic creativity has been explored from various perspectives, and these studies have confirmed its importance in the early development of narrative in the New World.[3] Satire infiltrates the exposition of both historical and literary themes in *El lazarillo* and contributes in no small measure to the prominence it has attained in viceregal letters. Carrió's life is intimately intertwined with the events surrounding his character the Inspector, and thus it provides a guide to their interpretation. The depth of his knowledge of the New World, his reasons for incorporating satiric commentary, and his choice of literary devices to express it all become apparent as the facts of his residency in the Indies unfold.

Alonso Carrió de la Vandera enjoyed a professional career of some distinction in the New World, and his activities there are documented not only by his own written testimony but also by numerous public records. Although the exact date of his birth is unknown, he states in *El lazarillo* that he arrived in Lima in 1746 at age thirty. He also mentions that he had spent ten years in Mexico prior to his coming to Peru, which would establish 1736 as an approximate date for his arrival in the Indies from Spain (459).

During the first fifteen years Carrió spent in the New World, he traveled widely in the viceroyalties as a merchant. In 1750, however, he decided to settle down in Peru and married Petronila Matute y

Melgarejo, a socially prominent lady of Lima. Soon after, he began a series of government appointments that included Indian agent, supervisor of mines, and subdelegate of estates. His tenure in these posts was interrupted in 1762 when he joined the cavalry regiment of nobles formed by Viceroy Amat to defend the Peruvian coast against pirates. Five years later he was commissioned to accompany 181 Jesuits to Europe after their expulsion from Peru and Chile.[4]

The year 1768, the date of Carrió's arrival in Cádiz, was an important one for the history of the postal service in Spanish America. Since Ferdinand's reign, it had been under the direction of Lorenzo Galíndez de Carvajal and his descendants, but measures taken by Charles III to consolidate his power led to its incorporation into the Crown's administration. With the marquis of Grimaldi as the superintendent general of mails in Spain and the Indies, José Antonio de Pando was named administrator of the mail service in the viceroyalty of Peru in 1769, and on January 12, 1771, Carrió was appointed second commissioner in charge of inspecting the system of mails and posts from Buenos Aires to Lima. The successful completion of this mission, he was led to believe, would qualify him for a permanent, more prestigious position in the City of Kings.[5]

Convinced of the need to carry out his assignment and looking forward to returning to South America as a government employee, Carrió left Spain aboard the *Tucumán* on February 16, 1771, for an eighty-four-day voyage to Montevideo. Observations of his crossing were recorded in his *Diario náutico*, which today only survives in fragmentary form. By July he was in Buenos Aires, where he met Domingo Basavilbaso, who was in charge of that city's postal system. Out of their friendship a political alliance evolved that pitted them against their superior Pando and his policies concerning the management of the mails.[6]

On November 5, 1771, Carrió and his company began their nineteen-month tour of duty that would take them across much of South America's rugged terrain and over a distance of nearly three thousand miles. Juan Moreno Monroy, who guided the group on its departure from Buenos Aires, soon left it to establish additional posts on an alternate route. At Córdoba, however, Carrió was joined by Calixto Bustamante Carlos Inca, who accompanied him through the Andes to the city of Potosí. He is the amusing amanuensis Concolorcorvo of *El lazarillo* and the individual believed for some years to be the author of the work.[7]

When Carrió arrived in Lima on June 6, 1773, the reception he got was not what he had expected. Changes in the postal system recommended by Pando in his report, *Reglamento General de Correos del Virreinato*, had been ratified only the year before, and they took precedence over any reforms Carrió could propose. Angered by the hasty actions of his superior, he subsequently lodged a formal complaint against Pando. A committee appointed by Viceroy Amat was charged with mediating the situation, but its deliberations became protracted and its findings were inconclusive.[8]

By 1775 or 1776 Carrió had finished *El lazarillo*, and it went to press in Lima. This elaborate version of his journey, which was immediately sent to officials in Madrid, was designed to present his side of the dispute but in a manner that would not arouse ill feelings or cause punitive repercussions. Apart from generally hiding his hostility behind satiric technique, he provided false information on the work's title page in order to protect himself. Giving the impression that *El lazarillo* was a report routinely filed at the conclusion of his mission and not the result of growing frustration and bitterness, the publication date is given as 1773. The publishing house, listed as La Rovada (Something Stolen), was probably an invention of Carrió's devised either to shield it from having published an unlicensed work or to indicate indirectly that it represents a target of his satire. Gijón, Carrió's birthplace in Asturias, appears as the location of *El lazarillo*'s printing. Although these details have puzzled scholars since the appearance of the first edition, the naming of Concolorcorvo as the author has stirred up the most controversy. Carrió, however, claimed responsibility for the work in correspondence dated 1776 in which he states jokingly that he did this in order to spare himself the expense of having to give copies to all of his friends.[9]

Although Viceroy Amat[10] thought highly of Carrió and although his successor, Viceroy Guirior, belatedly named him to the post of accountant of the Lima mails, Carrió did not let the matter rest. After assuming office in 1777, he continued his attack on Pando in a *Manifiesto* for which he was taken to court. Carrió was imprisoned for a short time as a result of this litigation and urged to retire by his superiors in Spain. Little is known about him after his release from confinement, although a 1782 document presented to the viceroy indicates his persistent attempts to bring economic reforms to the colonies. On January 17, 1783, he died in Lima and was buried there in the convent of San Francisco.[11]

Although Spain had failed to fully realize its utopian dream, even after two centuries of New World rule, the monarchy refused to abandon its original idealism maintaining that, with prudent management, America still possessed the means to fulfill its projected goals. Pursuant to the orders of the enlightened despot Charles III, therefore, the Crown implemented plans for the modernization of Spain, which provided for the consolidation and strengthening of the entire empire. Carrió and other investigators like him were instrumental in this imperial reorganization, and it was they who would bear the responsibility of extending this philosophy to the colonies. For this reason, the administrative and technological advancement of Spanish America was supposed to be Carrió's principal concern during his journey, and he was commissioned to design a well-organized network of communications and transportation that would be safe, efficient, and self-supporting. Resultant prosperity, it was hoped, would filter down into other aspects of the economy and provide social and political stability for the region. This, in turn, would tighten or at least maintain Spain's grip on the colonies at a time when ideas of revolution circulated in Europe and in British North America.

When Carrió realized that his proposed changes in the commercial system of South America were not even considered by his superiors, since these measures did not benefit Spain directly but contributed more specifically to the prosperity of its protectorates, he became disillusioned over the Crown's lack of commitment to reform. This attitude consequently distanced him from the perspective of the dominant Spaniard and brought him closer to the way of thinking of restless Creoles. It also prompted him to view his inspection tour ironically and thus present it as a satire in *El lazarillo.*

In order to attack the status quo as well as to alert his readers to the dangers of society's present course, Carrió depicts viceregal roads and highways as being traveled for the most part by fools and those who take advantage of them. Negligence, thoughtlessness, ignorance, greed, and vanity characterize these types, and they represent unproductive or underproductive sectors of society. Women, Indians, blacks, nobles, officials, and clergymen, for example, are particular obstacles to progress, and Carrió encourages a reevaluation of their utility, not in the interest of social justice but with the intention of developing their economic potential.

The basic literary framework used by Carrió to convey his vision of life in the viceroyalties is that of a traveler's account.[12] Not only does it easily accommodate his actual experiences within his imaginative perspective, but it also enables him to include numerous extratextual issues through the multiple intercalated parodies of Menippean tradition.[13] Beginning with the first travel accounts produced in the New World by explorers, this form of discourse enjoyed continued success throughout the colonial period. Travel literature was especially in vogue during the Enlightenment as such Europeans as Frézier and La Condamine came to study the American ambience as well. Parodies of this discursive strategy also flourished during the eighteenth century, although the structure of the journey had long been associated with satire because of its rapid change of scene and its introduction of numerous character types. Swift's *Gulliver's Travels*, Voltaire's *Candide*, and Bougeant's *Voyage merveilleux du Prince Fan-Férédin dans la Romancie* are among the more famous works in which elements of travel literature are ridiculed,[14] and Carrió's work, in fact, must be added to this list as well. *El lazarillo* may parody aspects of the writings of Jorge Juan and Antonio de Ulloa, who also visited the Indies as a part of Spain's reassessment program.

Drawing upon both the tradition and popularity of the genre, Carrió de la Vandera uses the travelogue as a vehicle as well as a target of his satire. Travel has long been perceived as a metaphorical representation of human life, and Carrió's inclusion of satire in *El lazarillo* identifies this critical perspective as a continual undercurrent of one's very existence.[15] On the surface, he moves forward along a predetermined itinerary completing as he goes his assigned task of inquiry and investigation. Learning from his experiences, he offers his reader a detailed summary of facts and figures that provide an unusual portrait of prerevolutionary society. The common traveler, on the other hand, who represents the ordinary person, lacks his visibility and becomes caught up in a vicious circle brought about by problems that repeat themselves with monotonous regularity. For this individual the road is not a means of progressing but a series of obstacles that impedes advancement and is a source of interminable danger. Lame mules, impassable roads, and uncomfortable lodgings hinder and threaten the traveler and make the journey tedious. Few stretches of highway are completely safe and free from delay, but even when ostensibly optimum conditions can be found, they are ironically due to adversity. The road on the outskirts of Oruro, Bolivia, Carrió notes sarcastically, is virtually worry free because "los tambos están sin puertas" ("the inns have no doors") and "el país es esteril" (299) ("the country is barren") (184).

The inns, described in many travel accounts as locations of shelter where pilgrims can share their experiences with one another, are not given such favorable treatment in *El lazarillo*. Accommodations are frequently inadequate, and resting places are more often found on the ground with a tree or a bush for protection. Even when good inns are available, Carrió observes, they are abandoned in favor of a more relaxing atmosphere conducive to friendly association. Such is the case with a house called *Los baños* just outside of Potosí. Nude bathing there by both sexes evokes his moral indignation, which he stifles with understatement. Conduct, he quips, is extremely disorderly "hasta entre personas que no se han comunicado" (283) ("even among persons who are not acquainted") (170).

In addition to the traditional icons of travel, such as the road, the inn, and the cart and mule, Carrió includes the digestive upset, since it is, after all, an integral part of any trip. This predicament as well as their continual fleecing are the result of the travelers' own foolishness, since Spaniards, both European and American, insist on eating and drinking to excess regardless of the climate or the altitude.

> Es muy raro el pasajero que llega a esta capital por la costa de Arequipa que no contribuya a la facultad médica y botánica. Los de valles son más económicos porque se aplican más al método serrano, y aunque comen el cabrío, le pujan en el camino y llegan a esta capital sin la necesidad de pagar lanzas y media annata a médicos, cirujanos y boticarios; y los señores párrocos de esta capital no hacen concepto de los derechos de cruz alta y sepultura, por lo que los cancheros no tienen otro recurso que el de las promesas de misa que hicieron por el feliz tránsito de los formidables ríos. (114–115)

> (Rare is the passenger coming to this capital by way of the coast of Arequipa who does not make a contribution to medical and botanical science. Those coming through the valleys contribute less, because they make application of the mountaineers' methods, and although they eat goat, they rid themselves of it along the highways, and arrive in the capital without the necessity of paying *lanzas* and annates of a half year to the doctors, surgeons, and apothecaries; and the parish priests in this capital can put little hopes in the taxes on the high cross and the sepulcher, wherefore the alms priests have no source of income other than the promises of masses said for the successful crossing of the formidable rivers.) (39)

The emblem of the postal system is the robber, Carrió insists in *El lazarillo,* as he ironically demonstrates the high degree of professionalism encountered along the route from Buenos Aires to Lima. Although these confidence operators appear to have a wide range of occupations from *corregidor* (Indian agent) to mule driver, they all display a common talent, which is their competence at fraud and thievery. This is not unusual, the Inspector states, as crime is considered a craft. Unsuspecting travelers in general are these people's victims, but as Carrió illustrates, men with insight such as himself can also become victimized, and they along with society must suffer the consequences of the blindness of many (216).

Carrió's arrival in Lima, the final stop on his itinerary and his home, fails to bring a satisfactory conclusion to his mission or even shelter from adversity. The City of Kings is the epitome of all the problems he faced on the open road, and here he must contend not only with ignorance but also with rejection. Contrary to the allegedly superficial reports by such authorities as Juan and Ulloa, Carrió contends that crime and vice flourish in the viceregal capital and notes sarcastically that its overall unhealthy environment is rivaled only by Mexico City. His trip culminates, therefore, not with the promise of improvement and progress but in the destruction of a potentially rewarding experience, which has degenerated into a meaningless run of predictable occurrences.[16]

The satiric commentary in *El lazarillo* is channeled through the work's two principal characters, the Inspector and his guide, Concolorcorvo. Dialogue between literary figures of different cultures or beliefs is a common device used by satirists to identify and elaborate upon humanity's imperfections, and it generally follows a question-and-answer pattern designed to uncover the truth. Originating in the oral folk tradition of antiquity, the Socratic dialogue, as it was called, is a form of serio-comical literature and a manifestation of the carnivalesque.[17] The Greek Lucian used it in his *True History*, for example, and it appears in the works of Alfonso de Valdés, Cervantes, and Gracián in Spain. *El criticón* is particularly indicative of the character types and their relationship found in *El lazarillo*, as Gracián's literary figures, the sophisticated Critilo and the naïve Andrenio, share their opinions as they travel throughout various European countries.

Carrió uses the identities of both historico-literary characters to mask his role as a satirist. The Inspector is, indeed, much like Carrió in that the biographical profile provided to readers in *El lazarillo* corresponds to existing documention regarding the satirist's life and trip through South America. There is a crucial distance observed, however, in the transfer of the writer's other characteristics to his character, as the literary figure he creates is, in effect, a satirical portrait of himself as a model Spanish official before the failure of his mission. Although Carrió may have provided veiled identification of his enemies in the postal service in his so-called anecdote of the four P's, it is actually through his creation of the Inspector that he delivers his most forceful blow to government officialdom, and he even chides himself as well for having unwittingly contributed to the deception that this image perpetrated. On the surface, then, the Inspector is a serious and dedicated employee who bases his judgment on practicality, safety, and efficiency. A closer examination, however, clearly reveals that his loyalty is misguided as he recites self-incriminating statements that once seemed appropriate to the situation but now are not only unconvincing but farfetched as well.

Concolorcorvo is a more artistically and intricately formulated character than the Inspector and is generally the source of *El lazarillo*'s humor. He is a historical personage in name only, for he represents either the author himself or an aspect of his creativity. Controversial or sensitive statements are most frequently delivered by him, and thus he provides a safe outlet for Carrió's pent-up anger and resentment. Carrió also blames any errors in style on Concolorcorvo, since he is named as the author, in order to conceal any lack of his own rhetorical skills.

Because little is known about Concolorcorvo's early life, Carrió is at liberty to devise a personal history, which meets the needs of his narrative and reflects his satiric design.[18] Carrió invents a biography, or in this case autobiography, since Concolorcorvo purports to be the author of *El lazarillo*, and chooses a picaresque model. The *pícaro* had previously served to demythologize traditionally revered figures, such as the heroic conqueror and the saintly nun, and in colonial discourse Creoles and disfranchised Spaniards had generally assumed this role. Carrió, on the other hand, provides a twist to this, as he does so under the guise of portraying someone of native American ancestry as the persistent rascal, a clear indication that the time had come to dispel the myths about Indians and to reevaluate their place in society as well as their rhetorical representation. By juxtaposing the life of a picaresque Indian with views expressing the various postconquest attitudes taken toward the New World's indigenous population, Carrió establishes a dialogue between his satirical vision and those of the conqueror, the apologist, and the mestizo. Inviting his readers to reach their own conclusions, Carrió maintains his ambivalence on this issue by dutifully taking the position of the loyal official in *El lazarillo*.

Concolorcorvo's immediate association with such anti-heroes as Lazarillo, Pablos, and Guzmán is essential in the establishment of his character type, although this relationship is limited both in length and in scope.[19] Introducing himself as a typical *pícaro*, Concolorcorvo talks about his questionable family background and expresses his aspirations for attaining a comfortable life through facile means.

> Yo soy indio neto, salvo las trampas de mi madre, de que no salgo por fiador. Dos primas mías coyas conservan la virginidad, a su pesar, en un convento del Cuzco, en donde las mantiene el rey nuestro señor. Yo

me hallo en ánimo de pretender la plaza de perrero de la catedral del Cuzco, para gozar inmunidad eclesiástica. (116)

(I am an Indian pure and proud, except for the malpractices of my mother, for which I do not stand security. Two cousins of mine are preserving their virginity, to their sorrow, in a convent in Cuzco, where the King our lord supports them. I have in mind to try for the post of beadle [dogcatcher] of the Cuzco cathedral in order to enjoy ecclesiastical immunity.) (40)

While Carrió appears to parody the picaresque only in a revisionary sense here, by culturally elaborating upon the protagonist, he does perhaps chide the writers of such literature for wishing to send their main characters to the New World. According to his way of thinking, it is already overpopulated with *pícaros*, and he jestingly appears to discourage young misfits from Spain who are planning on striking it rich in the colonies.

After initially establishing Concolorcorvo's identity as that of the notorious rogue, who is generally lazy, irreverent, and quick to conform to a corrupt society in order to survive, Carrió then endows him with distinctive traits. These characteristics, however, do not appear to be based upon those of the historical personage of Calixto Bustamante Carlos Inca but purposely reflect a commonly held Spanish view of racially mixed people and demonstrate the author's skill at using satiric technique. Carrió's superimposition of a literary character upon an actual person is indicated in his assignation of an alias to his guide, and he reveals the Inspector's disparaging disposition toward him in the name "Crow Colored." The exact origin of the name is unknown, but it may have come from the Tale of the Crow in Ovid's *Metamorphosis* or been suggested by Quevedo's sonnet "Bodas de negros."[20] This, together with a number of other references to Concolorcorvo's size and facial features, indicates that he may have been either a mestizo, an Indian, a zambo, or a mixture of all three races converging in the New World. Concolorcorvo provides a humorous portrait of himself as a total incompetent whose appearance is suitable only for frightening children. Animal attributes continue to level his status, as he is reported to have hawklike eyes and to be as stupid as a mule (396).

Although Concolorcorvo mentions from time to time that he is a descendant of the Incas, he lacks cultural identity. He appears merely to recite opinions about people and issues without revealing any true comprehension of them.

En todo este país encontrarán en todos tiempos mis amados caminantes tambos sin puertas, mulas flacas y con muchas mañas, corderos y pollos

flacos y huevos con pollos nonatos o helados, porque las buenas indias
venden siempre los añejos. Sin embargo, se puede pasar decentemente
con alguna precaución y gasto, como nos sucedió a nosotros, por la prác-
tica y providencia del visitador. (306)

(In all of this country, in all seasons, my beloved travelers will find: inns
without doors, lank mules with many bad habits, skinny lambs and
chickens, and eggs that are frozen or contain unborn chicks, because the
fine Indians always sell the rancid ones. Nevertheless, with some precautions and expense one may proceed comfortably, as was the case
with us, aided by the experience and foresight of the Inspector.) (190)

Because of his failure to discern what is going on around him, the
darkness of Concolorcorvo's skin may be extended to signify the im-
penetrability and backwardness of his culture and his complete lack
of perception of his surroundings.[21]

While the Inspector continuously criticizes his native companion
and all that he represents, he also permits Concolorcorvo to chide
him, thus allowing the real author to make fun of himself. Latin
phrases, Concolorcorvo contends, were often used by his superior to
make him appear to be erudite, when in reality, he did not fully
understand them nor did he always know the source from which
they were taken (120).

The traveler has long been recognized as an invaluable source of
information for historians, and such historical issues as the conquest, conversion, and colonization are frequently drawn into the Inspector's conversations with Concolorcorvo. These discussions also
call into question the validity of diverse forms of New World historiography that had originated since the writing of Columbus' diary,
and their parodic integration into the text expands the Menippean
structure of *El lazarillo*. In order to cast doubt on the conquering
Spaniard's version of the conquest, Carrió creates controversy by
having the conqueror and the conquered agree. In keeping with his
official persona, therefore, the Inspector expresses his patriotism at
the outset of these exchanges through his support of the monarchy
and of Spain's policies in the New World. When portrayed as a *pícaro*, the native Indian guide is particularly instrumental in corrobo-
rating his viewpoint, as his slovenly nature is in itself part of the
justification for the Spaniards' aggression, and his speeches voice
Indian approval of the entire military takeover. Such confirmation
of the appropriateness and the benefits of the New World's subjugation
do not seem incongruous to Carrió's Inspector but simply the recognition and validation of the superior achievements of European
civilization.

Having reached such favorable conclusions about the encounter so quickly and apparently with the consent of both parties involved, Carrió then holds up to scrutiny accounts that conflict with militaristic discourse by apologizing for Spain's forceful measures in occupying American lands and by presenting the Indian as a "noble savage." Using understatement, the Inspector contends that the violent clash was greatly exaggerated and resulted over a misunderstanding. Any armed conflict could have been avoided if only the various Indian tribes, like the Tlascala, who aided Cortés, had sued for peace on realizing the strength of the Spaniards. Confronted with outrageously high figures of native mortality, the Inspector quips hyperbolically, "De cada indio de los que morían resucitaban mil" (335) ("From every Indian who died, a thousand more were resurrected!") (210). Colonization, too, has agreed with the Indians, he insists, although reports by observers in Peru indicate that they are diminishing. This is not due to their demise but simply to their cleaning up a bit and changing their shirts. This alteration in their appearance, therefore, qualifies them to be reclassified as *cholos* (mestizos) (385–386).

While the Inspector appears to condemn these historical accounts in general, he is adamant about the writings of churchmen, especially Father Las Casas, whose opinions fueled the "black legend" and aided Spain's enemies in denigrating its image abroad.[22] On a number of occasions, he uses role reversal in characterizing the conquered and the conquerors, and the Spaniards, consequently, become victims of the Indians' cruelty. Dating back to the arrival of the Spanish in the New World, natives sacrificed the sailors that Columbus left behind, and they have been robbing those who followed ever since, according to the Inspector's rewriting of history (331–332). After all, what could the Indians have that the Spaniards would have wanted. It was certainly not the exaggerated reports of gold and silver, for it was only through the introduction of European technology that the aborigines were able to tap their own mineral wealth.

As for the present condition of the Indians, the Inspector concludes, they cannot be too dissatisfied because they are so accustomed to misery. Just because they are rarely joyous around the Spaniards and fail to respond to even the funniest joke is not due to their unfortunate circumstances but to their lack of humor. "Los indios" ("We Indians"), as Concolorcorvo points out, "apenas nos reímos tres veces en la vida" (416) ("laugh scarcely three times in our lives") (269). Contrary to complaints about the harshness of the labor system instigated and supervised by the Spaniards in the Indies, the Inspector claims that the Indians could not survive without it. Those who die in the mines, for example, do so because of exhaustion from their all-night celebrating and other taxing excesses (390). With all of the advantages of the Spanish way of life, the assimilated Indians, like Concolorcorvo, should be grateful to the Spaniards, according to the Inspector, for imposing it upon them. Those who cannot conform, such as members of the Pampa tribes, should be shot.

Carrió also reflects critically on the works of writers who describe indigenous cultures in intricate detail stressing their relative merits and in some cases their greatness. Accounts by religious men such as Father José de Acosta's *Historia natural y moral de las Indias* exemplify this because while preserving an ethnographic profile of New World peoples, these authors often lessen the moral and ethical responsibility of the Indians for their actions.[23] The Inspector counters such thinking by claiming that the perpetuation of pre-Columbian stories and songs is unsettling to the Indians and disruptive to the Spaniards. Natives pine needlessly for their imaginary past because of them, and they instill hatred toward outsiders (369). Daily life before the arrival of the Spanish consisted of the acquisition of bad habits, many of which should provoke moral outrage among Carrió's readers as Christians. If, by chance, however, they have been tempted by any of these sins and find themselves sympathetic to the Indians, the Inspector resorts to a description of such stomach-turning practices as eating lice and mud to support his argument. Perhaps the only lasting reminder of their civilization rests with their production of artifacts, he contends ironically. They have been very successful at this, "porque no falta gente de mal gusto que se aplique a lo más barato" (386) ("because there is no lack of people of bad taste who are devoted to whatever is cheapest") (250).

A more specific target in Carrió's interrogation of early Spanish American writers who distort the capabilities and achievements of indigenous cultures is directed at the *Comentarios reales* by the Inca Garcilaso de la Vega.[24] In *El lazarillo* he appears to parody several features of the work and to mock the author for his creation of the myth of the mestizo as the representation of the best of two cultures. Carrió's intention, however, may have been more complex than that, as the Inca parodied utopian discourse in his presentation of the Incan Empire, a strategy that he hoped would accommodate an Amerindian civilization within Western tradition and thought. By juxtaposing the history of the New World with that of the Old, therefore, the Inca endeavored to raise the Spaniards' consciousness to a level of multicultural understanding.[25] Viewed in this light, then, *El lazarillo* is a parody of a parody. In contrast to his eighteenth-century critic's account, however, the Inca's *Comentarios reales* is an excellent example of a colonial work in which parody does not serve as a vehicle of satire but functions independently of it.

Carrió's formulation of the character of Concolorcorvo and his designation of the native guide as the narrator and author of *El lazarillo* are significant components of the parody of this distinguished mestizo writer's work. The Inca Garcilaso de la Vega was the illegitimate son of an Incan princess and an officer in Pizarro's army, and his account pays homage to the culture of each one of his parents. Part one of the *Comentarios*, which outlines the glorious history of the royal line of the Incas, is noted for its eloquence and creativity and is based upon the legends he heard as a youth growing up in Cuzco. The second part is a history of the civil wars that followed the conquest in Peru and places his father in a favorable light as both an able soldier and a loyal supporter of the Crown. The Inca sought to justify his condition as a mestizo in the *Comentarios reales* and hoped to gain respect and recognition for his family in Spain.[26]

After Carrió suggests the relationship between these two men of Incan descent, Concolorcorvo goes on to achieve precisely the opposite goals of those of the Inca, and he simply confirms the critical viewpoint that many Spaniards had of miscegenation. Born in Cuzco as the result of an unsanctioned union and, like other half-breeds, confronted with reconciling two very different cultures, Concolorcorvo pays lip service to an illustrious heritage. Appending the title of Inca to his real name, he boasts of being descended from the royal family "por línea tan recta como la del arco iris" (100) ("in a line as straight as a rainbow") (27) and insists that his genealogy would be verified if his papers were not so water-soaked and filled with erasures (394). His association with the Spanish *pícaro* reveals his sordid past, and he continues in this same vein to distinguish himself as a useless hybrid who is deserving of his low station. Focusing on the ordinary Indian and his struggle to survive, little attention is given to momentous historical events in *El lazarillo*. Manco Capac and Atahualpa are referred to, however, as being several of the last Incas to rule a unified empire before the conquest, but the Inspector demonstrates his lack of interest and disregard for native Peruvian history by confusing the identities of these two well-known men. If the Inca can favorably compare Tahuantinsuyo to the great Roman Empire, then the Spanish realm surpasses that of the Romans, according to the Inspector's way of thinking (338–340). Concolorcorvo, of course, cannot speak about his father, since he does not know who he was and indicates that his mother was probably unsure of his identity as well. Not only was his name a mystery, but his race also seems to have been an uncertainty.

Concolorcorvo, like the Inca, writes from his own memories as well as the recollections of others, but the overall impression given by the guide's account, after parodic procedures have been applied, is one of a rhetorical hodge-podge. Aware of some of the stylistic flaws in *El lazarillo*, the Inspector interrupts Concolorcorvo to remind him of his inarticulateness and his tendency to belabor a point. The Inspector also includes Quechua words in his narration from time to time, a characteristic of the Inca as well as other early chroniclers. On one occasion, he states that the need to define certain linguistic elements is not due to the Spaniards' lack of understanding but to the Indians' lack of clarity.

In an effort to establish additional causal factors for the Indians' inadequate participation in the colonial system of commerce—apart, that is, from the prevalent misconceptions about them—Carrió challenges a different type of order imposed upon the inhabitants of the New World. The assimilation of the Indian into early Spanish American society was a crucial part of Spain's colonization, and Carrió holds the Church responsible for the failure to successfully convert the Indians to Christianity and to educate them well enough to assume an economically productive role in society. He also contends that members of religious orders, especially the Jesuits, often kept their native charges isolated both geographically and linguistically because they viewed the Indian as a means to attain wealth and power.[27] Through the Inspector's satiric commentary, therefore, Carrió levels the utopian aspirations of the clergy and thus provides justification for the Jesuits' expulsion. Given these circumstances, the evangelization of the Indians was made to look not only superficial but also ridiculous.

With tongue in cheek, Concolorcorvo demonstrates in the prologue how well the first friars taught love and brotherhood to the Indians who proceeded to express them in the name of the wrong god. Just as the early Spanish religious viewed the Indians as the offspring of Adam and Eve, so, too, the Indians perceived the Spaniards as children of the Sun (100). Ironically, ordained men were also set up as role models for the natives, as representatives of the highest ideals of their profession. This is probably why Concolorcorvo aspires to the position of dogcatcher in the cathedral in order to enjoy the privileges and immunities granted to ecclesiastics. Feigning a defense of the clergy, however, the Inspector claims that their mistakes are not entirely their fault, for they themselves do not always possess the proper preparation for the task at hand. Even the Lord's

Prayer is not being taught with accuracy and is frequently even recited backward. On arriving at the line "Thy will be done on earth as it is in heaven," both Peninsular priests and Indian students alike threatened the firmament with terrestrial chaos (368–369).

In addition to religious instruction, the Church was responsible for the general education of its converts. Although many of the Indians learned to understand Spanish, and did so when it was convenient, few could actually speak it well, according to the Inspector. This type of training, however, should never have been entrusted to devotees of the Christian faith, but, he avers, to worshipers of a pagan deity. That Bacchus is the most effective instiller of languages is well known (370), and when the Indians are drunk, their fluency greatly improves. Since they are in an inebriated state most of the time, in the Inspector's opinion, a formidable obstacle has thus been overcome.

Despite the testimony of many early chroniclers, Carrió insists that the cross-cultural exchange that took place as a result of the encounter worked to the detriment of all who converged on the New World. This is exemplified by Concolorcorvo, whose goal was not to improve the existing system but to try to reap whatever gain possible from the disorganization and lack of morality created by the Spaniards. The gaucho, too, fell into this category, as life in the wilderness appealed to the adventurous who intended to live out their lives free from the responsibilities of ordinary citizens.

Although this outdoorsman would be hailed in the nineteenth century as a symbol of the truly American man who is independent, carefree, and in close contact with nature, Carrió sought to stop this myth at its inception by satirizing him in *El lazarillo,* and thus he hoped to ensure the gaucho's fruitful association with civilization in the future.[28] His description of the "gauderios" and their rustic way of life is the first in a literary work, and his use of the grotesque conveys his sharp criticism of them. In a humorous caricature Carrió presents these irresponsible and idle individuals as guitar-strumming horse lovers who live off the land in the most primitive fashion laying waste to all they encounter (134–135).

Carrió also presents the Argentine cowboy as a kind of Arcadian shepherd to parody elements of the pastoral eclogue.[29] Contrary to the idyllic locales described by Garcilaso and Lope where shepherds and shepherdesses tend their flocks and sing about the love they have for one another, Carrió describes a bunch of bumpkins at a raucous cookout in a setting littered with rotting carcasses and inhabited by hostile Indians. Their female companions often attend these gatherings, and although they have such mellifluous-sounding names as

Capracia, Clotilde, and Rudesinda, they are generally regarded as *machas*, to denote their masculinity, and resemble the rude *serranas* (hillbillies) of Juan Ruiz. Carrió's creation of a neologism, he admits, is not original but follows Quevedo, who had previously coined feminine nominalized adjectives in this manner (252). *El lazarillo*'s author may have additionally been criticizing the tendency of early chroniclers to ascribe manly traits to ideal frontierswomen.

As if their mere presence were not entertaining enough, these rustics proceed to perform for the travelers by having a man and a woman sing a duet. In this case, however, vulgarity replaces the wholesomeness and refinement of the bucolic ballad, and bad habits and excremental allusion oppose ennobling emotions as its theme.

Dama:	Eres una grande porra,
	sólo la aloja te mueve,
	y al trago sesenta y nueve
	da principio la camorra.
Galán:	Salga a plaza esa tropilla
	salga también ese bravo,
	y salgan los que quisieren
	para que me limpie el r... (250–251)

(Lady:	You are a big, boring dullard,
	Moved only to action by drink;
	At swallow number sixty-nine,
	You begin to raise a big stink!
Gallant:	Let the whole tribe here clear the way,
	Including that elegant male;
	Let all of them leave who wish to,
	So I can clean my t——!) (144)

After hearing these verses sung, the Inspector wisely retired his company, since he feared "las resultas del trago sesenta y nueve" (251) ("the results of the sixty-ninth drink!") (144).

In addition to his individual profiles of various sectors of colonial society, Carrió provides several scenes in which diverse groups converge and interact. The subsequent tension and confusion that these people create not only dominate these scenarios but serve as an ominous prelude to the eruption of violence as well. Festivals, which were unproductive observances, according to Carrió, were common occurrences in the Spanish American colonies and provided activities in which everyone could participate. In this carnival setting, each individual could behave in accordance with his or her capacity and mood, and Carrió's account of a procession in Lima clearly notes the diversity of those in attendance. The existing inequities and their potential to cause conflict are satirically dramatized, however, as animals are brought into the event. During the running of the bulls, those beasts with the most elaborate and expensive trappings are brutally ambushed and stripped before they can reach the ring (411–412).

That such desperation and hostility could easily be directed toward human beings is made amply apparent as Carrió focuses on another segment of the parade where lavishly dressed equestrians march before an audience of similarly attired ladies, who look on from their residences. In this crowded street scene, people of all classes congregate, but their social station is indicated by their physical relationship to the ground, as the few on horseback and on balconies become the targets of the mob on foot. Although this event is disguised by its presentation as a playful game, the breakdown of hierarchical barriers is clear as the vertical relationship of the characters to each other is reduced to a horizontal one by their similarly riotous actions.

> Estos caballeros forman sus cuadrillas . . . para saludar a las damas y recoger sus favores en grajeas y aguas olorosas, que arrojan desde los balcones, a que corresponden según la pulidez de cada uno, pero lo regular es cargarse de unos grandes *cartuchos de confite grueso* para arrojar a la gente del *bronce*, que corresponde con igual *munición* o *metralla*, que recoge del suelo la gente plebeya y vuelve a vender a la caballería. (412)

> (These gentlemen form their squads . . . to greet the ladies and to collect their favors in the form of sugarplums and scented water, thrown from the balconies, to which each responds according to his polish; but the usual thing is to supply oneself with a large bag of plump bonbons to throw at the people on the balconies, who respond with like ammunition or grapeshot, which the commoners pick up from the ground and sell back to the gentlemen.) (266–267)

A farcical finale appropriately ends this ludicrous spectacle, but Carrió's use of another ironic comparison divulges its fatal results.

> Al fin de la función, que es cuando suena la campana para la salutación angélica, sueltan dos o tres toros encohetados, y disparando varios artificios de fuego, y al mismo tiempo tremolando los pañuelos de las damas y varias banderas de los balcones, se oye un victoreo de una confusión agradable, aunque en parte semejante al *tiroteo* de los *gansos* de la Andalucía, porque del uno y otro resultan *contusiones* y heridas con pocas muertes. (412)

> (At the end of the function, which is when the bell is sounded for the Angelus, they turn loose three or four bulls with rockets attached and

shoot off fireworks; with the waving of ladies' handkerchiefs and several flags from the balconies, a *vitoreo* or cheer of pleasant confusion is heard—although it somewhat resembles the *tiroteo* or shooting of geese in Andalucía, since contusions, wounds and a few deaths result from both!) (267)

The portrait of the colonies painted by Carrió de la Vandera in *El lazarillo* distinguishes itself from those of previous satirists in its perspective, its ideological foundation, and its scope. Cultural, political, and social aspects of colonial life are presented from an economic point of view, and the author deliberately identifies abuses in trade, commerce, transportation, and communications. Although his focus is derived from the influence of the Enlightenment on Spain, it is unfortunately the failure of the colonial administration to apply its principles systematically to the New World that prompts Carrió's writing of *El lazarillo*. His enlightened approach to his initial assignment, however, is evident in the exposition of the many constructive observations that the Inspector makes. Taking a rational stance against an irrational society, he supports his recommendations with encyclopedic information, which he reports in the tradition of the eighteenth-century Spanish writer and philosopher Father Benito Jerónimo Feijóo y Montenegro.

Carrió's travels take him throughout South America at a time of transition during its history, and the lengthy narrative of his experiences clearly touches upon the underlying causes of the wars for independence. Using the postal service as an example of a government agency in Spanish America that stands for communication and exchange, the Inspector sees an immediate need for the reorganization of colonial administration to eliminate graft. Ironically, when government services were restructured and the position of Indian agent, or *corregidor*, was abolished, the animosity between *criollos* and *peninsulares* intensified, as it was one of the few lucrative offices that Spanish Americans held with regularity. The frequency with which the Inspector assailed the clergy also points to the increasing vulnerability of the Church, the state's most trusted ally in the Indies. Although criticism of churchmen is scattered throughout the writing of the colonial period, it culminates during the eighteenth century as ecclesiastics failed most notably to meet the intellectual requirements of a modern elite.

In dealing with other segments of colonial Spanish America's diverse and deeply divided population, Carrió singles out certain groups to point out their particular faults, and then in a reenactment of the encounter, he assembles them to disclose their collective volatility.

A more subtle revelation, however, becomes evident in the careful crafting of the character of the Inspector, as Carrió's placement of this rigid figure in a critical light is indicative of the internal struggle experienced by Creoles and disillusioned Spaniards alike, who had witnessed Spain's ambitious plans and good intentions come to naught in the New World.

While Carrió has a variety of satirical recourses at his command, his use of multiple parodies in the tradition of Menippean satire is the most striking strategy and provides a thorough critical review of early Spanish American discourse. Travel literature, New World histories and chronicles, and pastoral eclogues are among the discursive forms scrutinized in his work as well as specific accounts by such prominent colonial authors as Father Las Casas, Father Acosta, and the Inca Garcilaso de la Vega. Carrió's effective use of the Socratic dialogue, however, is the key to his introduction of these parodies, and his exploration of this mode of expression within the framework of the travelogue and the picaresque in *El lazarillo* links *menippea* directly to the early development of Spanish American narrative.

Esteban Terralla y Landa

Details of the life of the Spaniard Esteban Terralla y Landa remain obscure until his arrival in Peru in 1787. His residence in the viceregal capital, however, is remembered by the public outcry that greeted his poem *Lima por dentro y fuera* ("Lima Inside and Out"),[30] which resulted in the confiscation and burning of numerous copies of the work. According to Ricardo Palma, his only biographer, he was originally lured from New Spain by mining prospects in Cajamarca and Huamachuco, but he soon became disenchanted by the state of the industry and made his way to the City of Kings. There he became a member of the viceregal court, under the protection of Viceroy Teodoro de Croix, where he wrote commemorative pieces for affairs of state. After the Spanish official's return to Spain, Terralla y Landa was forced to suffer financial hardships back in Lima. Because he composed riddles that he sold during these periods of poverty, he is also referred to as "el poeta de las adivinanzas."[31]

Apart from *Lima por dentro y fuera*, Terralla y Landa is known to have written several other works containing satire. His *Lamento métrico general*, though written on the occasion of Charles III's death in 1788, provoked some protest with its humorous tone and various satiric passages ridiculing lawyers, scribes, and members of the Royal Audiencia. In 1790 he became a collaborator in the writing of the *Diario Erudito*. Notable among his contributions to this journal is his prose work *Vida de muchos* ("The Life of Many") or *Una semana bien empleada por un currutaco* ("A Week Well Spent by a Dandy"), a satiric *cuadro de costumbres* about life in Lima. Luis Alberto Sánchez also attributes to him the unpublished satiric dialogue "Azote de mentecatos y bolonios" ("The Scourge of Fools and Ignorant People").[32]

Lima por dentro y fuera, appearing under the pseudonym Simón Ayanque, was by far Terralla y Landa's most popular work, and his most controversial, and it has been published in at least six editions. Attempting to explain the poet's bitterness toward the capital, which led to the controversy, Palma conjectures that he may have felt rejected after his protector's departure for Spain in 1790 and after the shunning he received from Lima's society because of his critical views. A case of venereal disease contracted in Peru may also have contributed to his resentment and probably caused his death, though the exact details and date of his demise are unknown.

By the time Terralla y Landa wrote *Lima por dentro y fuera*, the exposure of a colonial city's ills had established its own tradition as a topic of early Spanish American satire. The City of Kings was a prime target for satirists throughout Spain's three-hundred-year domination, and its institutions, customs, and residents had already been attacked unmercifully by Mateo Rosas de Oquendo, Juan del Valle y Caviedes, and Alonso Carrió de la Vandera. Terralla y Landa reiterates many of the same warnings expressed by his predecessors, when he takes a fictitious friend on a tour of the downtown area, but the sheer length of his poetic description permits a more extensive presentation of the lively setting through the inclusion of meticulous and copious detail. Such realistic grounding, however, does not prevent his trip from being an imaginative projection and a prophetic vision of the viceregal capital.

The time period in which *Lima por dentro y fuera* was written is of particular importance both for the empire and for Terralla y Landa because it corresponds to the final stage of Spain's rule of Peru and, apparently, to the last years of the poet's life. The earthquake-torn city with its materialistically motivated society reveals the depths to which a colonial capital had sunk, and Terralla y Landa considers the ramifications of its physical and moral deterioration for humanity and society. Personal precaution rather than enlightened reform stirred him to express his criticism, and he advocates avoidance, not change.

In *Lima por dentro y fuera* Terralla y Landa not only announces the failure of the Spaniards to impose their ideology on the New

World but also decries the inability of their traditional rhetoric to communicate it. Parodying the hegemonic vision set forth in official discourse, therefore, it is the last confrontation between Spanish and American cultures that the poet describes, and he relies heavily on the spectacle, rather than the event, to convey the complete collapse of all established hierarchies. Money is the most powerful influence in this new order, and women and racially mixed people control society. Privileged Peninsular Spaniards have been completely marginalized, and ultimately defeated, and their attitude toward recovery is one of utter desolation. According to the poet, retreat is the only way to avoid extinction in this cataclysm in which colonial society self-destructs.

Terralla y Landa's use of the grotesque dominates his poem, and its various expressions from the macabre to the monstrous appropriately capture the carnivalesque atmosphere of a city riddled with decay. As the cutting edge of the poet's satire, it adds a sense of urgency and gravity to his message,[33] and its continual utilization portrays life as a form of dying and Lima as hell on earth. By juxtaposing a satiric vision of eighteenth-century Lima with the worst nightmares of a society initially dedicated to utopian ideals, Terralla y Landa confirms that the Spaniards not only fell far short of their intended goals in the New World but also created a full-scale dystopia in the process. As he begins his infernal tour of Lima, he notes ironically that the city designated for "Kings" has become a center of vice and a haven for sinners. Before entering, he stops at the bridge over the Rímac River where many have been hanged, and in Dantesque fashion he welcomes his readers to a South American underworld:

Que ves sus ojos llorando,
que ves sus niñas corriendo,
muchos perdidos que entraron
y otros muchos que salieron. (7)

(You see crying eyes,
You see running children,
Many lost souls who entered
And many more who left.)

The structure and thematic development of *Lima por dentro y fuera* most directly resembles Quevedo's *Sueños*, inspired initially by the medieval *Danza de la Muerte*. The imaginary journey to or through the netherworld, however, may be traced to antiquity, when it was considered a favorite scenario for writers of *menippea*. Humanity's greatest fantasies and deepest fears have often manifested themselves during sleep or during a dreamlike state, and their literary expression permits the author to synthesize and exaggerate without explanation and to project himself or herself into the unknown.[34] Satirists have long recognized the potential of the *visio,* or dream vision, for dispelling illusion and presenting moral lessons, and it may include a look into the future or beyond the grave, where a person's life is reviewed and judged. The Greek satirist Lucian was the first to use the dream framework successfully in his dialogues, and his influence on Spanish writers may be traced through Erasmus' *Praise of Folly.*[35] Works written on the Peninsula that are Erasmian and contain as well the systematic adjudication of social types for passage to another world include Gil Vicente's *Barcas* trilogy and Alfonso de Valdés' *Diálogo de Mercurio y Carón.*[36]

Among Quevedo's *sueños,* "El mundo por de dentro" stands out as the principal model for Terralla y Landa's lengthy poem.[37] The title, structure, characters, and themes were recontextualized by the Andalusian poet, although he chose to change the generic mode of his vision. Lima replaces the world as the setting for his imaginary excursion, and much of the activity he describes is centered around a street named Peligro (Danger) rather than Hipocresía (Hypocrisy). Terralla y Landa also fills in as a friend's guide for Quevedo's character El Desengaño (The Undeceiver). Numerous types are targeted for ridicule by both satirists, but women, they agree, are particularly deserving of their criticism.[38]

Although Terralla y Landa's major influence can be identified as that of Quevedo, the contributions of his eighteenth-century disciple, Diego de Torres Villarroel, are significant. In his *Visiones y visitas,* Torres Villarroel takes the seventeenth-century satirist on a tour of Madrid to see the changes that had occurred in that city since his death. Torres Villarroel combines the visionary structure of the *Sueños* with his own pictorial vividness, and both are reiterated by Terralla y Landa in *Lima por dentro y fuera.*[39] Switching his attention to the New World, then, the latter mentions recognizable landmarks of eighteenth-century Lima as well as aspects of daily life involving food, dress, and forms of entertainment. Current attitudes regarding race, foreigners, and women are also expressed in Terralla y Landa's poetic account, and he provides convincing testimony about the social unrest of the prerevolutionary period.

Terralla y Landa exposes the disparity between appearances and reality in a long poetic monologue directed toward a silent companion, who is also the center of the numerous episodes that he narrates. Autobiographical elements loosely associate the poet with the speaker, but he is clearly related to his mute creation as well because the misadventures of this character are probably based on his own experiences soon after his arrival in Lima. The poet-narrator's omniscience, acquired through his capabilities as a daydreamer, enables him to peer into people's lives as well as their future. He hypothesizes about his friend's prospects and destiny and links his observations and advice to the fate of the common person. The familiar pronoun *tú* (you) is the only form of address that identifies this individual, and the intimacy it implies draws the reader into the situations narrated in the poem. In a paternalistic manner, Terralla y Landa reassures and even flatters his protégé about his goodness and refinement but continually points out that not everyone possesses such exceptional personal qualities and all-around preparation. Steps, therefore, should be taken to protect oneself from being taken in by others, according to the poet, and so suffering an unhappy lot.

The advice Terralla y Landa gives his friend is both short-term and long-range. For the moment, he recommends that anyone faced with the chaotic circumstances of Lima should stay home and not let anyone in the house. Such precautions would eliminate once and for all the multitude of social, economic, and political problems he describes in his poem. Departing from the immediate practicalities, however, the poet takes a moral and spiritual stance toward the debauchery in the viceregal capital. Heaven is the farthest point from the hellish city of the damned and the only orderly and peaceful realm accessible to humankind. Preparations should consequently be made to provide for one's eternal salvation, and this can only be secured through belief in God.

The topsy-turvy world that is eighteenth-century Lima is reflected in the overall organization of the poem and the paradoxical and contradictory content of episodes and imagery. Characters and themes are introduced in a haphazard manner and resemble the chance encounters one might experience while ambling about the downtown area. Divisions are observed in the poem as rest stops during the excursion and are designed to permit the reader to absorb the moral lessons of a particular section. Terralla y Landa concludes *Lima por dentro y fuera* when he feels that he has presented enough evidence to convince his reader that Lima is just as he says it is and a harbinger of worse things to come.

Of all the types ridiculed in *Lima por dentro y fuera*—which include members of diverse professions, races, age groups, and sexual orientations—women, especially prostitutes, are the most frequently and harshly criticized by Terralla y Landa. Not only are they emblematic of the physical and moral decay besetting the city, but they are indicative of its carnivalesque cover-up as well. His approach is much like that of Rosas de Oquendo in his *Sátira a las cosas que pasan en el Pirú, año de 1598* in that he parodies traditional visions of femininity in his presentation of them. The *limeñas*, however, had brought additional controversy upon themselves in the intervening years because they typically wore an opaque veil to conceal their identity during Terralla y Landa's time. Although viceregal legislators had attempted to prohibit the use of such concealment in the seventeenth century, this attire grew in popularity during the 1700's until the *tapada* was indeed the symbol of colonial Peru.[40] Summing up his advice to his young friend, Terralla y Landa warns him against complimenting a cloaked woman "que puede ser una negra / o algún horrible esqueleto" ("because she could be a negress / or some horrible skeleton") (67). Older women and those of color are especially repugnant to him because they represent other contemptible elements of Lima's society and are the embodiment of death and the devil.[41]

Having firmly established a woman's nature as deceptive, Terralla y Landa, like Caviedes, considers her anatomy in detail. Instead of focusing on lower bodily functions, however, he concentrates on portraying her as a monstrous creature composed of replaceable parts, many of which are unnatural and incompatible with human form. The resultant image is that of a contemporized harpy from Greek mythology, an ancient symbol of destruction. If she is to represent Lima, however, her numerous "repairs" may also resemble the patchwork done on the city's buildings after so many earthquakes. Makeup and padding were used by women of all ages to enhance their favorable features while concealing their imperfections. As Terralla y Landa points out, however, the results may be completely contrary to their intended purpose. Such a conspicuous cover-up can be more hideous than the original condition and totally repelling to men. Quevedo proved to be a master of grotesque female portraiture, and his presentation of Dueña Quintañona in "Sueño de la muerte" may have served as a model for Terralla y Landa's representation of the dregs of womanhood.[42]

In the following passage, Terralla y Landa exposes the facade created by cosmetics and prostheses, and the phrase "false front" passes graphically from the figurative to the literal. Altering a woman's physical appearance, he contends, can be as easy as changing her clothes.

Verás muchos albayaldes,
dientes postizos y pelos,

cejas de aceite de moscas
y de tizne de un caldero,
pantorillas de algodón,
de la misma especie pechos,
los zapatos embutidos
y los carrillos rellenos. (48–49)

(You will see a lot of makeup
False teeth and hair,
Eyebrows painted with flies' oil,
And kettle soot.
Cotton calves,
Breasts of the same kind,
Tight-fitting shoes
And full cheeks.)

Feature by feature, the poet dissects his victim and reassembles her in random fashion with artificial substitutions. From wigs to under-sized shoes, womanhood appears to be a mere illusion composed, in many cases, of materials that are ironically not thought of as contributing to personal attractiveness. While the addition of cotton padding here and there does not immediately evoke a reaction of repugnance, only laughter, the reader must recoil at the application of crushed insects and a carbon residue to the face, a startling indication not only of ugliness but of a lack of cleanliness as well.

In keeping with the general premise of the grotesque, Terralla y Landa paints a vivid portrait of this woman that is both comic and horrible, and it not only constitutes an example of decay but also outlines its destructive process of erosion. Her state of physical decline is an expression of stark reality yet a reminder of a lost past and the prefiguration of a bleak future, which inevitably approaches with time. Women are condemned for their moral and physical weaknesses, and they must ultimately pay for their greed and vanity. Age, alcoholism, and venereal disease serve as punishments for these *limeñas* in *Lima por dentro y fuera*.

The other principal element of Lima's social spectrum, whose status Terralla y Landa presents as a symptom of decline, is the presence of various dark-skinned peoples. Indians, zambos, mulattoes, mestizos, and blacks are crowded into many scenes of the poem, and they clearly outnumber the Spaniards and residents of Spanish descent. Concerned about this racial imbalance, he remarks "que tal cual blanco es el blanco / y el lunar de todos ellos" ("that the white person is becoming the white spot, / and the beauty mark of all the rest") (21). Hyperbole is again used by the poet in his description of nonwhites, just as it was in the portrayal of women. In the case of the former, however, he inflates their importance in the community rather than diminishing it by literally tearing his target apart. While women are disgusting and therefore a nuisance, the poet contends, blacks, Indians, and half-breeds pose a far more serious threat to the social order. Terralla y Landa's prejudice no doubt originated with the Spanish concept of racial purity, but his intolerance was fueled by the increasing economic power gained by Lima's blacks, mulattoes, mestizos, and so forth, which in turn brought them a modicum of social equality with Hispanics.[43] The Crown may have even encouraged this, in fact, in order to lessen the advancement of Creoles.

Terralla y Landa deplores the upward mobility of the lower classes and fears that they will ultimately dominate, and he envisions a society turned upside down.

> Que los negros son los amos
> y los blancos son los negros
> y que habrá de llegar día
> que sean esclavos aquéllos. (21)

> (The blacks are the masters,
> And the whites are the blacks,
> And it is possible that the day may arrive
> In which the former are the slaves.)

The power of money, Terralla y Landa concludes, should not be underestimated in Lima's society, and it is even capable of lightening a person's skin.[44]

Although Terralla y Landa provides sketches of particular societal types, it is in his creation of numerous tableaux that he discloses the real diversity and dissension within Lima's population, and the frequency with which he employs such settings may be indicative of the increased threat of conflict in the viceregal capital. In these lively scenes certain groups, while pursuing their own individual interests, are ironically portrayed as working in concert toward their own downfall. Using the Royal Coliseum as a microcosm of a topsy-turvy Lima, Terralla y Landa exposes a pretentious and ignorant community by presenting life, as well as the evening's entertainment, as a farcical comedy. The dramatic arts flourished in the City of Kings during the eighteenth century, from the viceroyship of the marquis of Castell dos Rius to that of Don Manuel de Amat y Junient. Lima boasted numerous accomplished theatrical productions and a large theatergoing public.[45] Even Terralla y Landa's description of the building itself, however, is a blow to the capital's image of cultural sophistication. Introducing the theme of the theater, he advises his friend that "corral" is a more appropriate name for the Coliseum (50). In accordance with its obsolete meaning, this Spanish word was used in reference to Peru's early colonial theaters, but it also means an enclosure for livestock just as it does in English. This fleeting impression is not reiterated in the poem but quickly equates the undisciplined behavior of the people and the filthy conditions in which they live with those of animals.

Masks are figuratively worn on both sides of the footlights, according to Terralla y Landa's satirical description, and because of this confusion, it is hard to determine who is giving the performance. Stripping the disguises from those on stage, Terralla y Landa finds inept, racially mixed extras only posing as actors.

> Verás unos comediantes
> sin acciones, movimientos,
> piso, gracia, compostura,
> propiedad, voces ni afectos . . . (50)
>
> . . .
>
> Verás . . . cómicas y cómicos . . .
> que representan mascando,
> que repiten dos mil yerros
> y que hay tres apuntadores
> lo mismo que pregoneros. (51)
>
> (You will see some comedians
> Without any animation, movements,
> Timing, grace, composure,
> Voices or feelings. . . .
>
> . . .
>
> You will see . . . male and female comics . . .
> Who play their parts mumbling,
> Who repeat two thousand mistakes,
> And there are three prompters
> Who sound like town criers.)

Just a few feet away, however, the masquerade is being carried on in the audience with a real flare. The chaotic scene is one of an outrageous *entremés* that spills out into the auditorium to become a spectacle.[46] The spectators are then transformed into the real participants, as they are interested only in themselves and not in the original players. They are the ones who are wearing elaborate costumes, making exaggerated gestures, and speaking loudly. Just as in many dramatic pieces, love motivates the action, and prostitutes and eager customers assume the roles of *damas* and *galanes*.[47] With all this action and emotion at the Coliseum, the evening can only be a resounding success for any common person, but the entire experience leaves the discriminating individual wondering why it is desirable to go to the theater at all.

In addition to providing a view of Lima through his comical description of the theater world, Terralla y Landa also includes a list of the types of dramatic works that were performed at the Coliseum. Among them are the satirical pieces put on in honor of court-days, and he indicates that the viceroy may have been the target of some of them.

> Verás, cuando entra un virrey,
> escena de luto y muerto
> que acaba en danza de diablos
> que salen de los infiernos. (51)

> (You will see when a viceroy enters
> A scene of mourning and death,
> Which ends in a dance of devils
> That come out from the infernal regions.)

Another activity, which reveals the interaction of Lima's types and their participation in the process of social breakdown, is Terralla y Landa's version of the dinner party, a frequent pretext for the presentation of Menippean satire. Festive reunions have historically been held to celebrate the heroic and have found representation in such forms of literature as the Homeric epic.[48] Satirists, however, have used these occasions as a mechanism through which to mock literary tradition, local customs, and individuals as well, and they generally do this by confusing the gustatory with the excremental, and culture with nature. Ennius, the father of Latin poetry, employed prandial imagery in his *Hedyphagetica*, and dining subsequently drew the attention of other writers of antiquity. Horace's treatment of the theme in the eighth satire of his second book served as the model for Lucian's *Feast of Lapithae*, and the latter was followed by Petronius' *Cena Trimalchionis*, a portion of the *Satyricon*, and Juvenal's fifth satire.[49]

Food and eating become the focus of descriptive and episodic passages of *Lima por dentro y fuera*, and the poet's silent companion supposedly takes part in several of these meals both as the guest and as the host. The gatherings begin in a carnivalesque atmosphere, but the gaiety and merriment quickly give way to shocking indications of a deteriorating society forced to feed on itself. These two dinners in which the young man is involved are designed to formally initiate a courtship, although the relationship has already demonstrated itself to be unconventional and a reversal of customary courting procedures. The man, in this case, is the one pursued, and he is lured by flattery into meeting a woman who he hopes will be his true love. In reality he is taken in by a persuasive pimp who represents a group of ravenous prostitutes who are after his money.

The event that unfolds at the table is unmasked by the poet through his use of the grotesque in which animal appetites and bodily functions are stressed. The digestive system from the mouth to the anus comes to the forefront of the description, and references to feces, vomit, and flatulence are not uncommon. In this manner Terralla y Landa exposes the local cuisine and table manners of the *limeños* to ridicule and points out the adverse effects of overeating.[50]

The first course on one occasion is a soup containing tripe, which the poet remarks "a veces viene relleno" ("at times comes stuffed") (22), and such an aside sets the tone for the appearance, smell, and consistency of the other delicacies to follow. After viewing the next two dishes, which he labels as "vomitaduras de perro" ("dog puke") (22), he makes it clear that the food is not fit for human consumption and, in fact, may have been forcefully ejected by the household pet or eliminated as waste by a farm animal. In addition to this, he also uses the form of the grotesque in which incompatible parts are assembled to describe a popular stew. Referring to the mixture of vegetables and meat known as "ropa vieja" ("old clothes") (27), he not only evokes a sensorial image of a stale smell, a faded color, and a leathery perhaps shredded appearance but notes that it contains a number of unrecognizable and inedible items that are either discarded or leftover.

The effects of sampling this allegedly delectable fare are suffered by the young man who must pay the consequences of his excesses. The overriding sensation in his alimentary canal is an unnatural one that brings to mind such inanimate objects as a blacksmith's bellows or a bagpipe to describe them. Not only does he vividly capture the bloated feeling caused by gas, but he suggests the resultant sound it produces as well.

The people attending these affairs are as disgusting as the menu, and their behavior changes from overly patronizing to repulsive and even hostile. To get the food to their stomachs as quickly as possible, they stick their fingers in their mouths all the way to their windpipes and in the process smear their faces with grease and *ají*, a favorite regional condiment. They then wipe their hands on the bread and toss it about the table. The young woman and her "relatives" begin to lose their human qualities and are described by the poet as devouring their meal with more fervor than vultures. As the eating continues, however, Terralla y Landa's friend replaces the food as the main course, and the poet observes reprovingly:

Te cenaron, te comieron,
Te almorzaron, merendaron,
Y luego te digerieron. (28)

(They dined on you, they ate you up
They lunched on you, they snacked on you,
And then they digested you.)

This figurative and repetitive description of anthropophagy reveals the inherent violence and lack of morals in the poet's projection of the city of Lima. Such expressions as "comiéndote vivo" ("eating you alive") (55) and "royéndo(te) los huesos" ("chewing on your bones") (68) appear scattered throughout the poem and graphically signify the loss of money, property, self-esteem, or dignity through trickery. Terralla y Landa implies that this cannibalism even continues beyond the grave. Again turning the figurative into the literal in his last will and testament, he uses black humor to express the fear that he, like Pablos' father in Quevedo's *Buscón*, could ultimately wind up in a meat pie.[51]

As Terralla y Landa guides his companion through the city of Lima, he simultaneously takes him through various periods in the life of an average *limeño*. Courtship is only the first phase of a man's progression through adulthood that Terralla y Landa describes in *Lima por dentro y fuera*. Marriage, child rearing, and the last rites are also divested of their dignity and meaning. While broadening the focus of his poem to scrutinize these stages of a man's life, the poet continues his condemnation of a materialistic society and again notes the disruption of traditional hierarchies. A husband is no longer the head of the household and receives very little respect from either his wife or his children. A sick slave, Terralla y Landa contends using inversion once more, merits more attention than he does because good servants are hard to find and represent a considerable economic investment. Mothers, too, are involved in social upheaval as they like the habit of using familiar address with their offspring because it makes them feel young. The real problem with this, the poet insists, arises when the sons and daughters use the *tú* form when playing with the children of colored domestics. Summing up the relationship among family members as well as conveying a racial slur, Terralla y Landa states that they get along like blacks and Indians, that is, with total hatred for one another (43).

The most devastating blow and the culmination of a long series of humiliating and degrading experiences is death itself. Its finality, however, is questioned by Terralla y Landa as he returns to the theme of anthropophagy and the macabre grotesque. Funeral customs especially draw his reproof as he points out that they are a sham and an observance for the wealthy only. While a rich man can afford a ceremony befitting a king, a poor man is lucky if a couple of candles mark his passing (47–48). Ironically death can be a very lucrative business, and people survive by living off the dead. Funeral services constitute one way in which the deceased still has to pay, and his relatives and the Church stand to benefit from the rest of his estate.

Terralla y Landa uses black humor to complete his lengthy poem by presenting his own last will and testament. While admitting to having made a number of mistakes in his life, he is consoled by the fact that at least he, unlike many others, recognized his own faults and has confessed his sins. Because of the world's disarray, however, he is happy to be leaving this earthly existence behind, and he attests to having no material possessions of value because they had all been previously pilfered. His soul, of course, is all that remains of his being, and it ultimately belongs to God.[52]

In the final instructions to his survivors, he is still intent upon taking jabs at old targets. With tongue in cheek, he asks that twelve black men be engaged for his funeral. The racial makeup of these attendants is of particular importance, since they are already dressed in mourning for the occasion (74). Dividing up a few of his remaining personal effects, he states with feigned resignation:

Mando mi espadín, que es bueno,
al que me robó mi capa,
con condición que se dé
con él muchas estocadas. (75)

(I give my sword, which is a good one,
To the person who stole my cape,
On the condition that he be given
A multitude of thrusts.)

As Terralla y Landa ends his work ostensibly to face the end of his life, he echoes the *Danza de la Muerte*. Just as he and the others must face the consequences of their actions, so, too, must the reader. Death comes to everyone, and its effects are ultimately the same.

The comprehensiveness of Terralla y Landa's *Lima por dentro y fuera* provides a virtual compendium of all previous criticism of the City of Kings and portrays a colonial society that is not only upside down but also out of control. Untouched by the ideas of the Enlightenment that had influenced Carrió, the poet sees only the failure and loss of the utopian dream in a present that he likens to a vision of hell. Spain's presence in the New World began dramatically on an island paradise in the Caribbean to be concluded not on a battlefield with heroic dignity or grandeur but on a street in Lima crowded with prostitutes, half-breeds, and thieves. It is a tragic chapter in the history of the Spanish Empire that culminates in the death of culture and even civilization, according to Terralla y Landa, and he transforms this national tragedy into a grotesque spectacle.

In the last years of Spain's domination, before isolated outbreaks of rebellion had spread throughout Spanish America, Terralla y Landa captures with extraordinary vividness the growing tensions in a large colonial metropolis, and the intensity with which he conveys them sets the stage for violent upheaval. Unlike several other satirists who took up residency in the Indies, Terralla y Landa did not develop a sympathy for Americans in general, and his repetition of the theme of xenophobia is significant and sheds light on the intensifying conflict between *criollos* and *peninsulares*. Although the poet makes no real comparison between the situation in eighteenth-century Lima and that faced by other great empires, historical parallels become evident in the direct influence of Petronius' *Satyricon*,[53] for example, and Quevedo's *Sueños*. Both of these other satirists found themselves confronting difficult and uncertain times with a spirit of pessimism and even a sense of doom. Irony and the grotesque are imperative in the presentation of a society consuming itself amid carnivalesque frivolity, and they, like Terralla y Landa, used it with frequency and force in their works.

The scene rather than the distorted characterization of a particular type or individual is the set piece of Terralla y Landa's poem, and each one reflects the themes of the whole work by imparting the confusion and contradiction of a society without restraints. Each tableau is teeming with life, and readers are disoriented by the continuous bombardment of information about aspects of daily existence through technical devices such as anaphora and the enumeration of unaccompanied nouns, adjectives, and verbs. Social struggle is characteristic of Lima, according to the poet, and he approaches it from two levels. From the point of view of the individual in society, he presents humankind's universal fight against adversity, and from a more specific perspective, he portrays this turmoil in the context of colonial Lima and outlines the imminence of class conflict based upon race and national origin.

While depicting the comicality and chaos of life in general and of a viceregal capital in particular, Terralla y Landa systematically devalues every aspect of life by dwelling on its evidence of decay and underscores the finality of the grave. His outlook on life as a preview of death, therefore, is the most pessimistic of the satirists considered in this volume. His view is apocalyptic, and his timing is significant. In a moment of truth, for both the poet and the empire, Terralla y Landa effectively blends the destiny of humanity with the ominous fate of Spain in the New World predicted by the collapse of social structure in Lima, the heart of Spanish America's wealthiest viceroyalty. Although spiritual guidance may be able to save the individual, he infers, little hope is held out for the progress or the preservation of colonial society in the New World.

Francisco Javier Eugenio de Santa Cruz y Espejo

The satire of Francisco Javier Eugenio de Santa Cruz y Espejo has scarcely been considered by scholars in spite of the political importance that he achieved during his lifetime. Today he is recognized as a pivotal figure of early Ecuadorian history whose unusual foresight and constructive programs shaped the destiny of modern Quito. His monumental treatise on communicable diseases in the viceroyalties is credited with saving countless lives from the scourge of smallpox in that city, and he was the founder and editor of Quito's first newspaper and the director of its first public library.[54] Confident in the ability of his fellow citizens to grow and progress, he became a relentless advocate of change in Spain's colonial administration, and thus a precursor of Ecuadorian independence. Espejo is recognized as an important writer of the eighteenth century who heightened America's nationalist consciousness by introducing European, especially French, modes of thought into Quito's intellectual circles, and his numerous works, ranging in subject from the scientific to the pedagogical, contain a detailed program for the revitalization of his birthplace. Satire, he envisioned initially, was an important vehicle for his protest against the status quo, and he considered it to be a good way to bring his philosophy of reform before the public.

Eugenio Espejo's background and the goals he aspired to achieve sharply distinguish him from the other satirists of the colonial period. As a mestizo with his sights set on a role of leadership in his community, he was forced to overcome formidable social barriers to attain recognition and prominence. A physician by profession, with a profound dedication to serve the welfare of humankind, he sought to improve the lot of disadvantaged *quiteños* by drawing upon the undercurrent of liberal thinking in the colonies as a source for possible solutions, an endeavor that would later establish him as a true man of the Enlightenment. Imbued with the innovative ideas that would bring significant social and political change on both sides of the Atlantic, Espejo formulated a comprehensive vision for Spanish America, not just for his own remote Andean metropolis, and devised the practical means for its realization. When his writing failed to bring about the proposed changes, however, he was compelled to take another course of action and one that would bring him into direct conflict with royal officials. Seeking to rid Quito of its oppressors, Espejo became involved in a conspiracy against the government, and as a result of the punishment he received, he ultimately paid with his life for the cause of freedom.

Born in 1747 to a full-blooded Indian and his mulatto wife,[55] Espejo grew up in Quito amid poverty. As a youth, he was very bright and inquisitive, and he regularly accompanied his father to work at La Misericordia, the city's only hospital, which was then run by the Bethlehemite priests. During these formative years, he gained considerable insight into the medical profession and the problems of hospital administration, and he questioned the critical inadequacies of both the physicians and their facilities. Determined to become a doctor himself, he learned the basic subjects on his own before entering the medical school of the Dominican College of San Fernando, where he graduated in 1767. Although he studied to be a lawyer as well and received degrees in both civil and canon law, he continued his medical training and became licensed to practice medicine in 1772.[56]

The social and professional obstacles confronted by Espejo during his youth and the years of his preparatory training, together with the deplorable conditions he had witnessed at the hospital, left an indelible impression on him, and he became determined to bring Quito out of its perpetual state of backwardness. Looking beyond the ignorance of doctors and members of the clergy, he endeavored to identify the real source of society's problems. Concluding that the insufficient knowledge of these men was due to the irresponsible instruction they had received under the auspices of the Church, he demanded that the course of study as well as the qualifications for teachers be changed. Ultimately, he recommended the secularization of schools on the grounds that the education provided by ecclesiastics only served to perpetuate the existing system of standards and values.

The Jesuits were primarily responsible for education in Quito, and for that reason, they were the target of Espejo's more forceful attacks. By the time he wrote his first complete satires, however, the

Jesuits had been expelled from Spanish America and hardly posed a threat to Quito's future generations. Using them simply as an example, therefore, Espejo sought to warn other religious orders that aspired simply to fill the void created by their departure. His focus on the Jesuits could also underscore the gravity of the educational crisis in the colonies resulting from their absence, as they were considered to be among the better teachers of any of the members of the New World's religious communities and were, in fact, attempting to apprise themselves of the latest achievements in scientific investigation.

Espejo's first experience at writing satire probably came from his composition of pasquinades that frequently appeared on Quito's public buildings.[57] Although the authorship of these satirical protests was never proven, it is a generally accepted assumption that he participated in this form of dissension, as he alludes to it in his later literary production.[58] In 1779 Espejo began to write a series of satiric works, which included dialogues, defenses, and letters. Many of them, which circulated in manuscript form, appeared anonymously or under a pseudonym.[59] By using satire in expressing his complaints, he hoped to alert the public to the urgent need for economic, political, social, and educational reforms without causing alarm. Although royal officials were not as strict as once thought with regard to the circulation of enlightened literature, they did take precautions to limit the flow of materials that could prove to be seditious. Their concern, however, centered mainly on protecting their wealthier viceroyalties of New Spain and Peru, and Espejo may have taken advantage of the less-restrained atmosphere of New Granada to read prohibited books, organize other intellectuals with similar concerns, and write satirically about current issues that would affect Quito's future.[60]

Espejo's preparation as a writer and social reformer is indicative of the education of the enlightened thinker of eighteenth-century Spanish America, as the works of Bacon, Newton, and Descartes were among those he consulted in the formulation of his educational programs. He also relied closely upon Father Luis Antonio Verney's *Verdadeiro método de estudar*, a treatise used throughout Europe that was designed to bring teaching in Portugal up to date with more modern techniques, and Father Benito Jerónimo Feijóo y Montenegro's writings regarding a new method for the training of physicians. As for his plans to bolster Quito's economy, he drew upon the theories of Adam Smith, Quesnay, and Jovellanos, and for his political changes, upon the concepts of Locke, Montesquieu, and Rousseau, among others. He also kept abreast of the progress of the Enlightenment in Spanish America by reading such periodicals as the *Mercurio Peruano* that reflected the spread of liberal ideas among colonial intellectuals.[61]

Although authorities were concerned about Espejo's liberalism, they did not consider him to be subversive until 1781 when *El retrato de golilla* ("Portrait of a Magistrate"), a work satirizing Charles III and José de Gálvez, the colonial minister of the Indies, began to circulate. Hoping to rid themselves of such a troublemaker, officials appointed him medical director of the Requena boundary expedition. Although he managed to get out of this assignment by going into hiding, he was eventually arrested, and in 1788 he was finally sent to Santa Fe de Bogotá to appear before the viceroy, Joaquín de Ezpeleta.[62] Fortunately, his trip to New Granada's capital did not result in any further detention at that time, and his presence there brought him into contact with a number of the region's youth who would later become revolutionaries. Among them was the twenty-three-year-old Antonio Nariño. Espejo must have impressed the young man on this occasion, as some years later, when Nariño himself was under investigation by authorities, a work by Espejo was found among the books confiscated from his library.[63]

Inspired by his meeting with Bogotá's young liberals, Espejo returned to Quito where he founded the patriotic society, the Amigos del País, whose organizations were being started in various parts of the viceroyalties. This group also sponsored the establishment of the first newspaper in Ecuador, *Las Primicias de la Cultura de Quito*, and in 1792 Espejo served as editor of all seven of the issues the press was permitted to produce. With increased government suppression of both the organization and its journal, Espejo again became the subject of official investigation. When news leaked out about his involvement in a plot to overthrow the government, he was arrested, and this time he spent most of the remainder of his life in prison. In 1795, when officials again failed to prove his guilt, he was released from custody but died in December of that same year. Espejo, of course, would not see the emancipation of Spain's colonies in America, but there is no doubt that his dedication and perseverance hastened the arrival of independence to his area.[64]

Although government officials considered Espejo to be a real threat to the stability of Quito during the later years of his life, his ideas were not as revolutionary as they envisioned, as he consciously sought to blend tradition with the newly devised concepts of a modern society. His goal was to create happiness and prosperity for his fellow citizens, and he proposed to do this by developing the region's natural resources and by offering a wide range of social services to its inhabitants. Under a republican form of government with the modified participation of the Catholic church, information would be allowed to circulate freely, and the populace at large, including such disfranchised groups as Indians, mestizos, and women, would have access to a secular school system and public libraries. Education, he concluded, was the key to the success of his plan and the only way to create an informed citizenry, the foundation for a moral and ethical society.[65]

In assessing the particular situation confronting Quito, Espejo placed the blame for the backwardness and suffering of the city's residents on two sectors of society, the clergy and the medical profession.[66] Members of both groups received extensive preparation and training from the Church, and according to Espejo, they shared the dubious honor of embodying the inadequacies of the parochial educational system. During the colonial period, the Church was instrumental in producing some of the more outstanding intellectuals in the viceroyalties, but as Carrió de la Vandera had also noted, this accomplishment was often marred by clergymen at the lowest levels of the ecclesiastical hierarchy, who were barely literate and were ill equipped to teach their parishioners. Given the trust and respect traditionally accorded representatives of the Church, however, few steps were taken to improve the competence of village priests, and their pronouncements were generally accepted without question by their devout followers.

An example of how the crisis besetting the clergy profoundly influenced other sectors of society is reflected in the dilemma facing Quito's physicians. Many doctors, Espejo felt, lacked a basic understanding of medicine as a result of the cursory schooling they had received, but they were licensed to practice anyway because superficial examinations failed to detect their deficiencies. Although it is difficult to determine whether or not Caviedes inspired him to satirize doctors, it is probable that he was acquainted with the Peruvian satirist's poetry through his reading of the *Mercurio Peruano*. As a doctor, Espejo had extensive knowledge of the abuses within the medical profession, and he possessed irrefutable evidence of the malfeasance suggested by Caviedes' scathing caricatures of Lima's physicians as the conspiring cohorts of death. With both the body and the soul of Quito's residents at risk, therefore, Espejo made clergymen and physicians bear the brunt of his criticism, and he uses their spreading of moral confusion and physical distress as a basis for his topsy-turvy view of life in that city.

On March 20, 1779, Dr. Sancho de Escobar delivered a sermon on the sorrows of the Virgin Mary in observance of Lenten activities in Quito's cathedral, and his use of pompous and incomprehensible rhetoric on this occasion provided Espejo with the pretext for writing his first satire. Communication, in the latter's view, had improved little since the days of the conquest, when the *requerimiento* was read to the newly conquered Indians, who were hearing Spanish spoken for the first time, and even Christianity had failed to provide a common ground for understanding among faithful Hispanics. That same year *El Nuevo Luciano de Quito o Despertador de los ingenios quiteños en nueve conversaciones eruditas para el estímulo de la literatura* ("The New Lucian; or, The Awakener of the Clever Citizens of Quito in Nine Erudite Dialogues as an Incentive to Literature"), a work that would precipitate the composition of his other major literary *obras,* began circulating in manuscript form under the name Don Javier de Cía, Apéstegui y Perochena.[67] His use of a pseudonym was designed to protect him from any reprisals but was also an attempt by the author to distance himself from his autochthonous background.[68] Under a veil of personal secrecy and under the guise of attacking pulpit oratory, Espejo addresses the very real issue of education in Quito and thus challenges the intellectual foundation of Hispanic thought on which Spain's colonialism was based.[69]

The sermon is the constant target of Espejo's satire, and the examination of various aspects of it lends thematic unity to his dialogues. This important instrument of communication, which was used by the first friars to arrive in the New World, was designed to impose Spanish culture on that of native America by introducing a new mode of thinking and comportment to the aborigines. Ironically, Espejo's dismantling and subsequent demystification of it mark the advent of another cultural transition, which also claimed to open channels of expression and to provide access to the truth. By breaking down the various literary conventions of Escobar's sermon and by focusing more specifically on the traditional method of thought that informed the composition of his speech, Espejo exposes the inadequacies of both the spoken and the written word used by the clergy as a way of interacting with the public, maintaining its confidence, and providing for its welfare. Viewed in this light, the sermon creates doubts and misunderstandings that lead to the confusion and isolation of its listeners, and he censures clergymen who communicate with their followers using only outmoded and affected language.

Because the sermon was at its peak during the evangelization and conversion of America's natives and the early years of colonization,

Espejo indirectly casts a shadow over the very essence of Christianity as it was practiced in the New World and brings into question the sincerity of its practitioners. Instead of assimilating the Indians into Spanish society and culture with their teaching, Espejo infers, early priests and friars used it to deny them entrance into the system in a participatory sense and to keep them dependent upon the role of the clergy to serve as an intermediary between the masses and officials of both Church and state. The power of the Church, therefore, and subsequently that of the state, was reliant not upon the skill with which these institutions imparted knowledge and integrated the Other but upon their ability to keep knowledge subject to their manipulation.[70] In this respect the conquest was less the result of a series of successful military campaigns than a consequence of purposely devised rhetoric in a virtual war of words.

As the title of Espejo's work indicates, Lucian's dialogues served as a model for his examination of Escobar's sermon and the discussion of such related themes as rhetoric and poetry, good taste, philosophy, Scholastic theology, and Christian oratory. Lucian of Samosata (b. ca. A.D. 125) was the first writer of *menippea* to have his satires preserved in their entirety, and he followed the basic satiric concept established by Menippus and Varro. Although Lucian's concern for the quality of language and its use in literature are probably what initially drew Espejo to his works, the structural simplicity of his dialogues, unencumbered by descriptive passages and character development, must have attracted the colonial Ecuadorian writer as well.[71]

In keeping with his intention of modernizing tradition, as he had done in proposing nonrhetorical reforms, Espejo adapted aspects of Lucian's literary strategy to assist him in solving current problems of language and style. This, he hoped, would bridge the current gap between words and their meaning by reverting to their origins. Antiquity represented a simpler, more vital time of life, both satirists contended, and an era guided by reason rather than emotion. By juxtaposing an earlier epoch with the present, as Lucian had done, Espejo hoped to preserve the meaningful thought and practical wisdom of the ancients and to use these fundamental components as a means of identifying the negative aspects of contemporary society and proposing workable alternatives to replace them. With obscurantism so prevalent in Quito, Espejo has one of his characters muse at how ironic it is that the eighteenth century could possibly be called the Age of Enlightenment. According to his experience, it is "la época del idiotismo y . . . el siglo de ignorancia" ("the era of idiocy and . . . the century of ignorance") (27).

Apart from following Lucianesque dialogical structure in the composition of *El Nuevo Luciano,* Espejo also models his interlocutors on those of the classical satirist. These speakers generally represent societal types, and at least one is designated to voice the point of view of the author. Their exchange is usually conversational in tone, and those who participate condemn themselves with their own opinions. The absence of extensive setting or plot development in Lucian's dialogues facilitates the adaptability of this literary form to Espejo's purpose, and it also leads the reader to believe that this discussion is just the spontaneous interaction of several ordinary people who could have met by chance any time, any where.

Contrast, which is the key to Lucian's exposure of the discrepancies between appearances and reality, is also utilized by Espejo, as he, too, mixes high and low styles and prose and poetry and frequently alludes to various other literary compositions within *El Nuevo Luciano.* By the end of the conversation, therefore, those who present themselves as authorities are revealed and a new, less defined yet provocative view of how things could be unfolds.

Espejo was also influenced by major Spanish writers of his time, and he incorporates aspects of their works in the process of renewing Lucian's fundamental literary model. Father Feijóo, for example, introduced various elements of the Enlightenment into Hispanic culture, and Espejo greatly admired his initiative as well as the diversity of his talents as a philosopher, scholar, and theologian. Feijóo was a firm believer in education and was highly critical of his country's educational system, especially the methods employed by its teachers. He deplored the continuing predominance of Scholasticism in the schools to the exclusion of other more current approaches to investigation, and he vowed to instigate reform in Spain's institutions of learning. In addition to attacking educators and the pedagogy of his time, he also derided doctors, a favorite target of Espejo, and devised a workable plan to provide them with adequate training. From a literary standpoint, Espejo may have also endeavored to imitate Feijóo's style of writing in which a high level of erudition is attained without diminishing a work's clarity or didacticism.[72]

Perhaps a more obvious model for Espejo's *El Nuevo Luciano,* which contains a prototype of Father Escobar, was Father Francisco de Isla's *Historia del famoso predicador, Fray Gerundio de Campazas, alias Zotes.* Although the Inquisition tried to stop its publication, the first part of this work came out in 1758 under the pseudonym Francisco Lobón de Salazar. While Father Isla was concerned about education as well, he was outraged more specifically by the preaching style of his time, which he deemed as an unfortunate holdover of the baroque age.[73] The novel involves the experiences of a young man who studies religion and philosophy under the direction of Friar Blas, a proponent of the Gongorist school of exposition. Imitating his teacher, therefore, Fray Gerundio, as he was called, becomes famous for his ornamentative sermons based upon nonsensical concepts. Friar Prudencio is one of his few colleagues to speak out on the youth's bombast, and Father Isla uses this opportunity to present a lesson on how to be a good orator.

Using aspects of both classical and contemporary literature, therefore, Espejo writes nine dialogues in which two characters represent opposing sides of the controversy surrounding the 1779 sermon delivered by Father Escobar. One allegedly imitates the attitude and rhetoric of the preacher, and the other espouses the opposite point of view and fulfills the author's desire to criticize the Jesuit's extravagant performance. Both of them were, indeed, historical personages, but Espejo's cursory treatment of their personal characteristics reduces them to types. Dr. Miguel Murillo y Loma is a physician and pseudointellectual who defends the teaching of the Jesuits, and his speech patterns immediately establish him as a product of their instruction. Dr. Luis Mera, on the other hand, is a former Jesuit who, like Espejo, has come to understand the importance of the Enlightenment and to view his ecclesiastical education critically by pointing out the flaws in the system of communication it imparted. Because he is a former member of the Society, his elucidative comments on the ineffectiveness of Jesuit teaching appear to be authenticated, therefore lending particular credence to them. His clear, concise remarks contrast sharply with the pedantic expression of Murillo, and in a professorial tone, he begins the process of reeducation by stressing the importance of presenting the truth as a crucial way of confronting the pressing problems of one's existence.

Espejo also clarifies the changing role of a satirist, in a succinct and open declaration of *El Nuevo Luciano*'s critical purpose in his dedicatory preface to the president of the Audiencia of Quito, when he presents himself as a patriot. After referring to his position as that of a "Procurador y Abogado de Causas desesperadas" ("Solicitor and Advocate of Desperate Causes") (3), he assures this official that his satiric protest is an expression of "sincero amor por la patria" ("sincere love for his country") (6). Skepticism and interrogation, he infers, should not be associated with disloyalty and sedition but with a genuine outpouring of patriotism.

At the outset of *El Nuevo Luciano*, Espejo defines his characters boldly, making Murillo appear to be mired down in an abyss of Latin phrases and Scholastic methodology and Mera to be the authorially inspired voice of truth and reason. The choice of Dr. Murillo to imitate Escobar is an important one as it unifies Espejo's targets into one. Physicians, like Murillo, were noted for their Latin phraseology, just like members of the clergy, and their retreat into their own world of authoritative sources and specialized jargon frequently left their patients puzzled about the true state of their health. As the dialogues progress, however, the distinctions between the two characters become somewhat clouded as Mera also cites sources he has not read or not fully understood and finds it virtually impossible to abandon all aspects of the training that had become ingrained in his very being. Murillo contributes further to this convergence as his articulation becomes more lucid and less florid when he fully understands major points of Mera's argument. Such ambivalence subsequently blocks the expeditious and facile adoption of any single approach to the issue and forces the reader to be more discerning.

As Murillo mimics the bombastic, or gerundian, oratory of Escobar, Mera tries unflaggingly to convince his opponent that a good speech is a reflection of sound judgment and the embodiment of clarity, ingenuity, and scholarship, and he holds up the eloquent yet accessible sermons of Fray Luis de Granada as excellent examples of these attributes. The contrast between the viewpoints of the two interlocutors is too sharp at the outset of their discussions, however, and when neither is able to penetrate the seemingly incomprehensible rhetoric of the other, they decide to examine their individual differences.

Language is the first matter taken up by Murillo and Mera, and they address both the tendency to view rhetoric monologically and the inclination to assign importance and mystery to esoterica and bilingualism. Viewed in this light, therefore, words and phrases may function to obscure and twist just as easily as they can serve to clarify and inform. Because Murillo is a physician, he often interprets reality in terms of human anatomy and physical conditions. Tradition is associated with normalcy, or wellness, and any deviation from it is diagnosed by him as a malady that must be treated and cured. After Mera quotes a verse from Petronius in which the Roman writer warns how deceptive appearances can be, ostensibly referring to Escobar, Murillo replies indignantly:

> Blasfemó Vm., y perdonándome la licencia que asumo de hablarle con ingenuísima apertura de corazón, me ha de oír, que Vm. manifiesta mu-

cha dosis de humor bilioso, y pateface un colmillazo córneo, nigricante de adusta envidia. ¿No ve Vm., ha sabido que este Doctor sapientísimo lo es realmente, y por consiguiente orador plusquamperfecto, porque fue de la eximia sociedad de los sabios, de los doctos, de los literatos, en quienes únicamente, como en su apacible regácico seno, se reclinaba la señora Domina Sabiduría? Basta decir que es ex-jesuita, para decir que sabe todo lo que debe, y debe todo lo que sabe a la doctísima Compañía. Así Vm., Señor Doctor, es un maldiciente malédico, es un individuo gárrulo, es un atrevido, osático igno . . . (8)

(Your Grace has blasphemed, and pardoning the license that I take by speaking to you with extremely candid openness of heart, you have to hear me out, because Your Grace shows a high degree of bitter humor and inflicts the puncture wound of a hardened fang producing black swells of sullen envy. Don't you see, Your Grace, it is known that this doctor is really extremely knowledgeable, and consequently a more than perfect orator, because he was from a most eminent Society of wise, learned, literary men, in whom uniquely, as in your gentle bosom, Lady Wisdom rested? It is enough to say that he is an ex-Jesuit, in order to say that he knows everything that he should and that he owes everything he knows to the extremely learned Society. Therefore, doctor, you are a bad-mouth slanderer, a chatterer, an insolent, ossified ignoramus . . .)

Mocking his adversary's limited perspective and his use of anatomical references, Mera sarcastically ladens his answer with feigned praise.

Poco a poco, Dr. Murillo. ¿Qué insultos son ésos? ¡Oh! mas perdónolos desde luego, por Vm. mismo, y por todo el conjunto de hombres que hablan como Vm. y de quienes es Vm. perfectísimo órgano. (8)

(One step at a time, Dr. Murillo. What kind of insults are those? Oh! But I forgive them, of course, for Your Grace's sake and for the entire group of men who speak as Your Grace does and of whom you are an extraordinarily perfect member.)

At first Murillo diagnoses Mera as having a fever, but later when he notes the number of gallicisms in the former Jesuit's speech, he declares that he must be suffering from the "mal francés" (venereal disease) (43). With all this talk of infirmities, together with Murillo's stubbornness, Mera finally admits that he is, indeed, feeling a bit queasy.

Fearing anything that is new and different, Murillo ridicules Mera for looking to the French for guidance and for advocating the teaching of modern foreign languages, currently viewed as dangerous steps that could lead to the establishment of cross-cultural and multinational affinities. Frenchmen, the former imagines, are frivolous and effeminate, an attitude that was not uncommon among xenophobic Spanish Americans, and he attacks the definition of "buen gusto" formulated by Father Domingo Bouhours in his *Entretiens d'Ariste et d'Eugène*.[74] Referring to Bouhours as Father Domingo "Burros," Murillo decides to interpret the concept of "good taste" quite literally and takes it to mean simply the physical satisfaction of the gustatory sense. In this respect, then, the French do produce works of that description, he admits, and he mentions their cookbooks containing recipes for "ocho mil fricasés y ochenta mil especies de cremas" ("eight thousand fricassees and eighty thousand sauces") to illustrate his point (41). This is one of the many examples of Murillo's resistance to influences from any national origin other than Spain, and in this way, he directly opposes the Creole segment of the population that traveled to London and Paris for its education and that kept a watchful eye on social and political developments occurring in the former British colonies to the north.[75]

The Scholastic method was another major obstacle to clear, relevant communication, according to Mera, and Murillo thwarts any suggested changes to this pedantic tradition. Scholasticism, according to Mera, was based upon untested ideas, and its application to any problematic situation only served to confirm previous speculation. Just as supposedly educated people recited Latin phrases randomly, so, too, they cited numerous authoritative sources from classical antiquity and the Bible without knowing anything about them. This type of name-dropping was a commonly accepted way of demonstrating one's erudition, and in many cases the speaker did not know who these authorities were, not to mention how to pronounce their names. When Mera refers to "El Grocio, el Seldeno, Cumberland, Coringio, Heinecio," in support of one of his statements, Murillo repeats them comically as "El Huevo Grueso, el Salcedo, el Cumbresaltas, el Chorizo y el Incienso." ("Mr. Bulky Egg, Mr. Willow Garden, Mr. Cummerbund,[76] Mr. Sausage, and Mr. Incense") (51).

As an alternative approach to the traditional problem solving inherent in the Scholastic method of inquiry, Mera proposes a more active means of uncovering the truth. Assuming the role of a teacher, he stages a demonstration on how to read, an excellent way for the reader to learn to scrutinize the ideological foundations of any text and to entertain change in its formulation in the face of appropriate evidence. Tricking Murillo by asking him to evaluate an ostensibly authoritative text, he shows the doctor a book that will obviously impress him because it is in Latin.

Dr. Mera.
Aquí dice: *sufficit et non sufficit.* Más allá: *potest et non potest.*
Dr. Murillo.
Válgame Dios, ¡qué prodigio! Este autor es mucho hombre, ¿qué digo? es
un ángel. Voltee, voltee Vm. más y más. ¡Ah, buena cosa! *Excusat et
non excusat.* Acá, *infert et non infert.* (99)

(Dr. Mera.
It says here: *sufficit et non sufficit.* Further on: *potest et non potest.*
Dr. Murillo.
Good Lord, what a prodigy! This author is a real man. What am I saying?
He is an angel. Keep turning, keep turning, farther and farther. Ah! This
is great! *Excusat et non excusat.* There, *infert et non infert.*) [77]

Upon looking more closely, however, in compliance with the exercise, Murillo announces a surprising discovery:

Dice: *Si sufficit mane collatiunculam sumere et vesperi coenare, teneturne ad id?* Estamos en la pregunta del caso. Veamos la respuesta. Dice:
*Non tenetur: quia nemo tenetur prevertere ordinem refectionum. Ita
Filiucius.* ¡Jesús! ¡Jesús! ¡Qué ángel es éste? *Quis est hic qui etiam peccata dimittit?* ¿Quién es éste que hasta los pecados perdona? (100)

(It says: *Si sufficit mane collatiunculam sumere et vesperi coenare,
teneturne ad id?* Now we're at the heart of the matter. Let's see the answer. It says: *Non tenetur: quia nemo tenetur prevertere ordinem refectionum. Ita Filiucius.* Jesus! What kind of angel is this? *Quis est hic qui
etiam peccata dimittit?* Who is this person who even pardons sins?)

Mera, who is also trying to get Murillo to challenge the authority
represented by the written text, and thus to question the Church as
an infinite repository of the truth, abruptly demystifies the puzzling
Latin phraseology by changing its frame of reference from the divine
to the infernal.

"Qué demonio es éste? debía Vm. preguntar: porque éste y sus seme-
jantes son peores que los mismos demonios, corruptores autorizados de
la moral cristiana, destructores de la Ley y del Evangelio. (100)

(What the hell is this? You should ask. Because this person and those
like him are worse than demons themselves, [they are] the authorized
corruptors of Christian morality and the destroyers of the Law and of
the Gospel.)

Approaching the text in this confrontational manner, then, Mera
forces his fellow interlocutor to believe not only that rigorous questioning is natural and healthy but that it is the duty of every receiver

of information as well. What the reader brings to the text in reading, therefore, will determine its final form and essentially make him a writer of the work.

Conversing about Christian oratory in the final dialogue of *El Nuevo Luciano*, Murillo concedes that Mera's criticism is justified because he has provided sufficient proof in support of his argument, and he subsequently changes his mind in accordance with his companion's proposed revisions in both spoken and written communication. What Mera, or perhaps Espejo, fails to do here is to illustrate through his own expression the goals of good writing and speaking that he so adamantly espouses. Espejo is capable of following his own advice, but the reader must look to texts other than *El Nuevo Luciano* for confirmation of this. Espejo's own sermons offer specific models of effective religious writing, and his secular *Reflexiones acerca de las virelas* ("Reflections about Smallpox") not only exemplifies a lucid style for scientific investigative reporting but reveals that Espejo was indeed an extraordinary physician for his time.

The issues raised in *El Nuevo Luciano*, together with the additional matter of the circulation of the manuscript itself, would be taken up again in Espejo's two other literary works, *Marco Porcio Catón, o Memorias para la impugnación del Nuevo Luciano de Quito* ("Marco Porcio Catón, or, Memoirs for a Debate about the New Lucian of Quito") (1780) and *La Ciencia Blancardina* ("Blancardine Science") (1780). The former, which appeared under the pseudonym Moisés Blancardo, is a satiric defense of Quito's status quo, especially the role of that city's religious members, in which Espejo pretends to be a sharp critic of *El Nuevo Luciano's* author. By appearing to find fault with his own arguments, Espejo cleverly denied his real adversaries the opportunity of censuring his dialogues, and at the same time he perpetuated the principle of viewing all texts with skepticism. While this was probably not done by any other colonial satirist, the idea is not original and was used by Horace and Boileau-Despréaux to stave off attacks by their opponents.[78]

The satire of Eugenio Espejo presents one of the more practical responses of a colonial satirist to the utopian vision imposed upon Americans by Europeans, and his *El Nuevo Luciano* strikes at the very philosophical and ideological foundations of Spain's empire in the New World. In his determination to bring profound substantive change to so many aspects of society, however, his satiric purpose becomes secondary to his goal of actual reform, and he consequently fails to maintain a balance between satire's most important elements of wit and criticism. The humor of Espejo's early dialogues diminishes as the contrast between Murillo and Mera fades, and his tendency to be too didactic and utilitarian contributes to the work's monotonous rhythm and its repetition of themes. With his limited utilization of satiric technique and its lack of variety, the later dialogues of *El Nuevo Luciano* cease to be amusing and lapse into tedium. Hampered by his uneven satiric treatment of themes and the absence of an elaborate literary framework, therefore, Espejo denies himself the opportunity of exploring the creative potential of Menippean satire pursued by Carrió de la Vandera. Although the latter's adaptation of the Socratic dialogue in *El lazarillo de ciegos caminantes* is a much more imaginative composition than *El Nuevo Luciano*, and an important step in the development of early Spanish American narrative, Espejo chooses to open up another dimension of *menippea*'s creativity. By constructing a revisionary parody of Lucian's dialogues, he not only advocates social transformation but also proposes the vehicle to bring it about. In so doing, he makes clear the place of satire in the process of questioning and reform and underscores its necessity and significance in a changing world. The role of the satirist, then, is not only that of mentor but of patriot as well. Focusing principally on addressing the more pressing cultural issues of his time, he designates the open exchange of informed argumentation, or the combative dialogue, as a means of testing authority and convention and providing answers to society's problems. Such debate is a form of persuasive oratory, and it consequently contributes to the emergence of the essay in Spanish America. Difference of opinion within this forum is viewed as an essential and valuable developmental component of society, not a heresy or a crime against the state, and this truth-seeking mechanism encourages the common person or minority member to speak out and to take part in the decision-making process formerly imposed upon him or her. A society that remains static ultimately destroys itself, but one that has the freedom to change in order to meet the needs of all of its citizens will endure and prosper.

When evaluating *El Nuevo Luciano*, it is also necessary to place the work within its historical context, and from Espejo's point of view, it was a time in which the written expression of raucous humor and the recitation of routine complaints were not appropriate. Plans for definitive action were required, and constructive proposals were imperative to their success. Espejo's use of satire, therefore, is only a point of departure for the fulfillment of the practical purpose of his dialogues, which is to initiate the social realignment of Quito's population. Moving from the strictly subversive to the pragmatic, he hoped to incorporate groups of people previously excluded from active participation in their own governance, thus creating an informed citizenry that would spread reform to every aspect of life in Quito. For this reason, his dialogues encourage the production of oral forms of communication whose public does not necessarily have to be literate.[79]

The erudite discourse of *El Nuevo Luciano,* however, was not directed toward a general audience but specifically toward the Creole segment of Quito's society. They, Espejo realized, would be the next leaders, not the mestizos or Indians whose attempts to defy authority would fail, most notably with the quelling of the Tupac Amaru rebellion in 1781.[80] Because they were the apparent heirs to power in the viceroyalties, he appealed to Creoles for support and cooperation and deliberately avoided the radicalism often associated with a revolt of the masses. Unlike the other satirists considered in this volume, Espejo hoped that other sectors of the population, in addition to the Creoles, would be the beneficiaries of his recommended reforms.

Espejo's parody of Escobar's sermon and his subsequent dismantling of Scholastic tradition emphasize the social responsibility of the writer and the orator to address the problems of the common person in a manner that can be understood by everyone. The successful transmission of useful knowledge would lead to the betterment of human existence, and this new accessibility to communication, he felt, would encourage average *quiteños* to consider the uniqueness of their identity and to contribute to its general formulation. They would then seek to exercise their right to forge their own destiny, an objective that Espejo sincerely believed would ensure a bright and prosperous future. As Espejo indicates in his *El Nuevo Luciano,* however, his program of social reform could not be realized without altering the course of literary history. His neoclassic approach, designed to combat the stylistic excesses of previous periods and outmoded methods of inquiry, serves as a model for the general review of discourse as a whole, and he advocates that only those forms that are characterized by clarity and reason be revived and renewed to depict the particular reality of Quito's residents as well as that of the other inhabitants of the viceroyalties. If, as Todorov writes in his study *The Conquest of America,* Western civilization triumphed in part over that of native Americans because of "its superiority in human communication,"[81] it is appropriate, then, that Espejo, as a representative of the New World's cultural and racial mixture, clearly call this form of expression into question during the waning years of Spain's empire and that he demand both rhetorical and ideological change to reflect the expectations of a new and independent Spanish America.

5. A Reappraisal of Colonial Satire

The prevalence and commonality of dystopian visions of the New World establish satire as a principal countercurrent within colonial literature that subsequently lends insight into the ideological debate engendered by the differences between American reality and its representation. As a protean mode, it was capable of penetrating all forms of discourse, and it ultimately provides a link between Western tradition and the destiny of creative writing in twentieth-century Spanish America. Satire is a discourse of the Other, and it was cultivated principally by Creoles and other like-minded individuals who endeavored subversively to disassemble the hegemonic vision of the New World projected by the Peninsular Spaniard. The critical tension satirists produced by juxtaposing the past with the present, rather than imposing one upon the other, created a cultural and historical visibility for Americans that was both edifying and amusing, and this new perspective highlighted quotidian life and encouraged many residents to think constructively about themselves and their relationship to authority.

Considering tradition critically within the context of a present consciousness, writers of satire set out to rediscover the New World through self-reflection and rhetorical experimentation. Writing and reading became key processes in their opposition to utopianism, and the successful reorientation of these procedures broke the repetitive and degenerative patterns of its ideology. While attempting to de-mythologize Spanish American culture and to expose the continual interrelationship between history and literature during the colonial period, however, satirists clearly acknowledged the importance of creative writing in the interpretation of reality by consistently advocating the presentation of truth within an imaginative framework, unencumbered by excessive factual detail. The process of telling, therefore, became the focus of these authors rather than what is told, and by encoding their texts satirically, they created numerous literary possibilities that would have particular influence on the development of the novel, the essay, and autobiography.

Without competent readers, however, the ironic perspective is easily lost, and colonial satirists undertook the task of reeducating a literate public. Getting their readership to question the authority presented by the text was their principal objective, and teaching them to uncover complex, stratified levels of meaning embedded within it was essential to their mission. Even before the first sentence of the text appeared on the page, the lesson could begin with the title or other information given on the frontispiece of a book, and these clues often unlocked the secret of authorial point of view, and thus facilitated the appropriate decoding of the work.

By the nineteenth century the cult of nature replaced utopian ideas, and the search for the true American to symbolize the intimate bond of humankind to the land would be crucial to its development. This new ideological concept substituted the previous mythology with its own and witnessed as well the continued alliance between documentation and creativity, a tendency enhanced by colonial satirists themselves.

The reflection of reality presented in colonial satire is a startling profile of Spain's dominions in the New World that documents, in retrospect, the cracking and crumbling of the empire's foundations. Satire served as a diagnostic tool in its attempts to identify society's ills, and satirists ultimately made an effort to influence existing social and political powers by using it as an agent of change. Because Spain's government was the source of absolute authority over life in the colonies and because it intended to sustain that power through the initiation and perpetuation of myth in Spanish American history and culture, satirists frequently leveled their attacks at colonial administration. Their initial attempts to break its powerful hold rhetorically seem fitting, as the Crown had endeavored to promote the vision of an idealized America in the mainstream of early colonial writings. Although the viceroy and members of the Audiencia were caricatured by a few satirists, many more, out of fear of reprisals, chose to divulge the results of official ineptitude in their descriptions of the decline and decay of Spanish America's cities, the foundational unit of imperial Spain and the alleged realization of utopian dreams in the New World. Early nineteenth-century writers retreated to the countryside and relied on nature to provide them with new themes and imagery, and the gradual disintegration of the metropolis during the colonial period contributed to this refocusing of American life and art.

The role of the Church in the fulfillment of the imperialistic designs of the state exposed it to severe criticism as well. Strictly religious issues were carefully avoided by satirists, who concentrated principally on the Church's ineffectuality in the educative process as a result of its outdated methods of teaching and investigation and its dissemination of politically motivated and socially expedient ideas. Education was vital to the foundation of a stable and progressive society, and for this reason writers of satire chided members of the ecclesiastical hierarchy for using it to support existing authority rather than to speak out for justice and equality. Although Church officials were only occasionally singled out as targets, the criticism of entire religious communities was more prevalent and intensified during the eighteenth century. Of the orders in the New World, the Society of Jesus was most often charged with placing its interests before those of the people. Critics advocating changes within the ecclesiastical system hoped for the expanded participation of Creoles, and in the case of Sor Juana the increased role of women, and those who wanted to separate Church from state espoused the secularization of the educational process, thought to be a positive step in the creation of clear and impartial communication.

In satiric works of the colonial period, viceregal society is portrayed as multiracial and multilingual, and deeply divided along social, political, and economic lines. Such diversity was the source of daily tension, and the failure to address it on a wide scale unleashed the inherent violence instilled in Spanish American life by the Spaniards at the time of the conquest. Of the many groups alienated from the Peninsular-oriented viceroyalties, the Creoles, together with other Hispanics excluded from participating in the system, formed the most powerful coalition. They were the most outraged at being denied the rights and privileges guaranteed them by their Spanish heritage, and they possessed the linguistic and literary skills to make their resentment known. They were the only group to rely on satire as an important way of conveying their opposition to Peninsular dominance, and when their verbal efforts failed to bring about a solution, armed intervention and revolution became inevitable. The schism between *criollos* and *peninsulares* that began shortly after the arrival of the first Europeans in the New World widened dramatically by the end of the eighteenth century as evidenced by the proliferation of satire focusing on their differences, and these writings more than any other form of discourse produced in the colonies document the emergence of a national consciousness in Spanish America.

While a number of Creoles ventured to protest, Indians, blacks, and interracial mixtures had little recourse, and documentation of their resistance to the Spanish yoke, therefore, is not as copious, nor does it consistently contain the satiric elements of the works examined in this volume. Histories, chronicles, and treatises produced by indigenous authors, however, constitute an important part of the subversive discourse written in the Indies, and the combination of Western and native codes in these accounts provides a more authentically American perspective on the conquest and colonization of their lands by Europeans than that of the Creoles. Eugenio Espejo was a rare example of a member of a racially mixed group who was able to rise to prominence and sought to bring current issues to the attention of the public through works of satire. While being concerned about the problems of other disfranchised groups, however, he was completely Europeanized in his approach to them, as he looked to France rather than Spain as his model, and viewed Creoles as being the only segment of the population strong enough to deal effectively with the Spaniards. Creoles and Americanized Spaniards, however, while looking to the American autochthonous population for a cultural foundation to serve as an original and authentic backdrop for their new identity, could be just as prejudicial in their treatment of other races as the dominant Spaniard. Although Spaniards adamantly pursued the issue of *limpieza de sangre,* Creoles and their allies were hesitant to embrace these fellow Americans.

Women, too, were excluded from any prominent role in the Peninsular-oriented patriarchy, and the men who supervised them seemed unwilling to reconsider their traditionally inferior status in society. There was little chance of establishing a dialogue either, as women were generally barred from the educative process, a means by which they could have gained access to positions of importance and prestige. They were without a doubt members of the Other, as they were looked upon by male Spaniards as among the submissive segments of the world's population like Indians and blacks. Sor Juana Inés de la Cruz was the only woman to speak out at length on woman's place in colonial society, and she used satire to express her feminist views. Being a woman, however, was not Sor Juana's only reason for feeling the isolation she describes in her many *obras;* she was also a Creole and an intellectual, which put her in other spheres of conflict with the prevailing ideology. This made her task of protest a more complicated one and her goals of attaining a measure of freedom insurmountable.

Like *peninsulares,* however, *criollos* were unsympathetic to the plight of women, as they continually denigrated them in satiric works of the colonial period. From the sixteenth century to the eighteenth, misogyny emerged as a principal theme of early Spanish

American satire, and it even overshadowed the criticism of political figures as a more popular and less risky topic. In satiric discourse, the prostitute came to represent the effects of the long-term exploitation of America and the distressing decay so prevalent in the cities. Women were also resented because of their association with racial integration, as marriage often afforded them a modicum of upward social mobility.

Even though a political separation from Spain was achieved in most regions of Spanish America by the first quarter of the nineteenth century, the former New World viceroyalties were ill prepared for independence, and dictatorship moved in, in most cases, to occupy the void left by colonialism. Satirists had carefully analyzed colonial society and identified its problems, but few real solutions ever resulted from their literary deliberations. Education was the most important area in which they advocated constructive change, and had educational reforms been implemented on a grand scale, they would indeed have changed the destiny of Spanish America. While early satirists had seen the need for additional consciousness training, they had directed their initial efforts more at the reeducation of existing readers and writers. During the eighteenth century, however, there was an attempt to transform the satirically based dialogue, in which current issues were debated, into a pedagogical tool that emphasized oral communication for the masses. In addition to the creation of dialogues for public presentation, newspapers experienced considerable growth at the end of the colonial era and the beginning of the independence period. They, too, were noted for their plain language, topical content, and accessibility to the public.

Although colonial satire could not change the course of history or alter the social structure in Spain's viceroyalties, this critical art form, which originated in the carnivalesque spirit of antiquity and was nurtured by the subsequent growth of serio-comic literature, emerged from three centuries of development in the New World as an influential mode of literary expression. It had effectively challenged convention, especially with regard to the writing of history, and then, using its regenerative powers, facilitated the creation of new and original forms of discourse. Colonial satire's greatest impact, however, was felt in the realm of fiction where early satirists hastened the exploration and expansion of creative narrative in Spanish America.

Of the mechanisms used by colonial satirists to restructure literary production, parody was the most prevalent, and it, indeed, served as the basic foundation for satiric writing in the New World. It had the ability to oppose any strategy or code simply by reversing the original model, and it could be applied to a single aspect of any target or to the sum total of its components. Epic poetry, the history of the Indies, courtly love poetry, pastoral literature, sermons, travelogues, and correspondence were among the more frequent targets of satirists in the New World. Multiple parodies such as those characteristic of Menippean satire were often devised during the colonial period, and parodic elements were also used in conjunction or simultaneously with other satiric recourses.

The grotesque, which is saturnalian in nature and therefore related to the carnivalesque and to satire, is often an integral part of parody, as it violated conventional sensibilities in the extreme. A dehumanized or evil world fashioned by this radical distortion was designed to offend readers through the vicarious exposure to degradation, which distanced or alienated them from their allegedly objectionable surroundings and thus incited them to protest.

The most influential literary apparatus, however, to disassemble tradition and to reconstruct aspects of it in an innovative way during the colonial period was Menippean satire. Although the representation of entities and ideas had the same carnivalesque relationship to the world in *menippea* as it did in other forms of the serio-comical, it was distinguished from them by its almost complete disassociation from a legendary past. Aside from being grounded in the present, it also offered satirists in the New World a chance to delve creatively into fantasy, and they took advantage of forms such as the trip to hell, the dream framework, the banquet scenario, and numerous other ways of placing scandal, eccentricity, and incongruity in a critical light within an atmosphere generally permeated by comedy. Perhaps the most significant characteristic of this complex satiric vehicle for writers in the colonies, however, was its intricate involvement in the testing of ideas and the search for truth. Crucial to this intention was *menippea*'s assimilation of other forms of the serio-comical, such as the Socratic dialogue, a device used by early Spanish American satirists to present timely ideological and philosophical debate. Lucian and Erasmus probably provided the most complete models of this heterogeneous aggregation of literary forms for colonial writers to follow, and the adaptation of such diverse media to the colonial context opened up creative possibilities for nineteenth-century authors whose works ran the gamut from the realistic to the fantastic. In the process of reevaluating written communication and its representation of reality, however, a compendium of literary criticism was created as well, and it critically reviewed every form of literature introduced into the New World by the Spaniards and advanced a synthesis formulated upon their more vital aspects.

Working in conjunction with Menippean satire for the transformation of colonial discourse was the Spanish picaresque. Human life, rather than the world, was upside down in this novelistic subgenre, and works with picaresque elements became principally a form of Creole-oriented expression. The popularity of the picaresque during the colonial era may indeed be tied to the emergent *criollo* middle class, and in this respect it is not surprising to find a *pícaro* as the protagonist of Spanish America's first novel written during the early independence period.

The subverted hero of the picaresque provided for the complete demythologizing of the conqueror/chronicler, and his disadvantaged state and amusing misadventures provided an appropriate framework for someone who was on the social periphery. Assuming picaresque characteristics themselves, satirists could also ostensibly claim to be righting wrongs in a comical knightly fashion by presenting negative examples of behavior. The *pícaro* was also successful in demythologizing the ideal model of femininity represented by the saintly woman and proved effective in the reevaluation of emergent myths such as those surrounding the Indian and the mestizo. But the picaresque offered much more to colonial satirists than the chance to present events from the perspective of the Other; it afforded them the opportunity of inventing a self and creating, as it were, an identity. Writers of satire were compelled in most cases to conceal themselves to some degree while voicing controversial opinions, and through the discursive vehicle of fictional autobiography, they were able to strike the desired balance between documentation and fiction. A view of the Other and one of the self, therefore, were presented simultaneously, and the delineation of the point of view of the Other served as affirmation of the self.

The first-person picaresque narration dramatized the role of the narrator in the unfolding events and captured quite clearly the feelings of one who has lost something of value and who no longer belongs to the social and cultural milieu in which he or she exists. This crucial separation permits the narrator to analyze his or her own situation from the vantage point of an outsider yet with the knowledge of an insider, the unique position of one who is alienated or exiled. Although often repelled by the circumstances confronted by the *pícaro*, colonial readers were drawn into events by this familiar figure, and they found it easy to identify with his predicament. In this respect, the picaresque complies with the process of reeducation at work in the viceroyalties. The *pícaro* often began with the narration of his early life when he was an impressionable and naïve individual. These traits soon disappeared, however, as adversity forced him to learn quickly in order to survive. By observing his surroundings closely, then, he discovered how to separate appearances from reality, and he proceeded throughout life by testing and weighing the results of his experience in search of a practical solution, characteristics typical not only of colonial satirists but also of other self-conscious Americans.

Although the new images and innovative ideas resulting from the efforts of New World satirists influenced works produced in Spanish America during the nineteenth century, the formulative process that they set in motion during the three-centuries-long colonial period continues to the present day. Satire, in fact, has had particular impact on Spanish American literature since the 1940's with the occurrence of the Boom in narrative production, and it has endured principally because the very real social and political changes advocated by Americans during the viceregal era have never been fully achieved. Dictatorship replaced colonial administration as the absolute authority, and efforts to incorporate the masses through education failed to raise their level of participation in the social, economic, and political destiny of Spanish America's modern republics.

Just as in the colonial period, however, political oppression has aroused the critical spirit and inspired the creativity of contemporary writers, who continue to assault authoritarianism and demand social justice in their works. Satire is a constant recourse of theirs, and after benefiting from centuries of experimentation in this hemisphere, it still provides one of the more effective means of subverting and dismantling convention. Its continued usage reflects the ceaseless questioning that tradition must still undergo and emphasizes the current role that criticism plays in literature. Twentieth-century works in which satire is employed often present the point of view of those alienated from society or those exiled from their own countries and capture as well the changeability of the Spanish American identity as its culture evolves. Chaos and confusion are features of the world many writers project, and they reflect the instability of their times in the expression of their concerns and fears. While numerous ideologies have come and gone since the colonial period, Spanish American writers have never again turned solely to Europe for their inspiration and have maintained their central focus on America as a source of the originality and artistic creativity they so desired.

As the quincentennial of Columbus' landfall is commemorated, readers of modern Spanish American literature reap the benefits of colonial satire's lengthy development and experience the vitality of its rich legacy. Wit and criticism in their satiric mode contribute in no small measure to the inventiveness of contemporary writers and ensure for generations to come the continual review of ideologies and rhetoric in order to maintain their validity and relevance. Viewed in this light, therefore, viceregal satire cannot be perceived simply as a marginal art form, solely based upon an ironic perspective of life or born out of hostility or morality, but as a vital force in the meta-morphic process that leads to the creation of a truly unique Spanish American identity and then provides for its continual reassessment and renewal.

Notes

1. Origins of Satire in the Old World and the New

1. Edmundo O'Gorman, *The Invention of America*, pp. 4, 17, 20. See also Luis Weckmann, "The Middle Ages in the Conquest of America," *Speculum* 26.1 (1951): 130–141.

2. Mircea Eliade, "Paradise and Utopia: Mythical Geography and Eschatology," in *Utopias and Utopian Thought*, ed. Frank E. Manuel, pp. 262–263.

3. Edmundo O'Gorman, *La invención de América*, p. 31; O'Gorman, *The Invention of America*, p. 79.

4. Christopher Columbus, *The Diario of Christopher Columbus's First Voyage to America, 1492–1493*, trans. Oliver Dunn and James E. Kelley, Jr., pp. 70–71.

5. Columbus, *Diario*, pp. 66–69. See also O'Gorman, *The Invention of America*, pp. 96, 97, 99.

6. Rosa Perelmuter Pérez, "El paisaje idealizado en *La Araucana*," *Hispanic Review* 54.2 (1986): 129–146.

7. Harry Levin, *The Myth of the Golden Age in the Renaissance*, p. 143.

8. Margarita Zamora, *Language, Authority, and Indigenous History in the "Comentarios Reales de los Incas."* See esp. Chapter 6, "Nowhere Is Somewhere: The *Comentarios reales* and the Utopian Model." For further discussion of utopianism, see Stelio Cró, *Realidad y utopía en el descubrimiento y la conquista, 1492–1682*.

9. Stephen Gilman, "Bernal Díaz del Castillo and *Amadís de Gaula*," in *Studia Philologica, Homenaje a Dámaso Alonso* 2: 99–114.

10. Irving A. Leonard, *Books of the Brave*, pp. 59–60.

11. Antonio Antelo, "El mito de la Edad de Oro en las letras hispanoamericanas del siglo XVI," *Thesaurus* 30.1 (1975): 106. This article contains the indigenous Americans' conception of the Golden Age as well. Levin, pp. 93, 156.

12. Northrop Frye, "Varieties of Literary Utopias," in *Utopias and Utopian Thought*, ed. Manuel, p. 37. For a discussion of early colonial texts and how they were used to dominate the conquered, see René Jara and Nicholas

Spadaccini, "Allegorizing the New World," *1492–1992: Re-Discovering Colonial Writing,* ed. René Jara and Nicholas Spadaccini, pp. 15–18.

13. The perspective of the Other, that is to say any member of a group that is not dominant, has been the focus of considerable scholarship in recent years and is of particular importance to the study of colonialism regardless of its historical context. See Homi K. Bhabha, "The Other Question: Difference, Discrimination, and the Discourse of Colonialism," in *Literature, Politics, and Theory,* ed. Francis Barker, et al.

14. Among the important studies of subversive discourse written by native Americans are Rolena Adorno's *Guaman Poma: Writing and Resistance in Colonial Peru, From Oral to Written Expression: Native Andean Chronicles of the Early Colonial Period,* and "El sujeto colonial y la construcción cultural de la alteridad," *Revista de Crítica Literaria Latinoamericana* 14.28 (1988): 55–68; Raquel Chang-Rodríguez' *La apropiación del signo: Tres cronistas indígenas del Perú,* and *Violencia y subversión en la prosa colonial hispanoamericana, siglos XVI y XVII,* pp. 1–18; and Margarita Zamora's previously mentioned study on the Inca.

For recently published investigations on subversive discourse written by women, see Electa Arenal and Stacey Schlau's *Untold Sisters: Hispanic Nuns in Their Own Works.*

15. Because critics of satire do not agree on its precise definition or on a clear set of terminology to assign to its various aspects and components, I have described it here and in the following pages from an eclectic standpoint by noting its more commonly stated characteristics that are applicable to satiric writings of the colonial period. General works on satire consulted in the preparation of this discussion are listed separately in the Bibliography. Of particular significance to my study, however, are Frank Palmeri's *Satire in Narrative* and Linda Hutcheon's *Theory of Parody: The Teachings of Twentieth-Century Art Forms.*

16. Palmeri, pp. 1–10. Although Palmeri refers to Cabrera Infante and discusses the works of Borges, he does not mention the development of satire in narrative written during the colonial period.

17. Palmeri, pp. 10–20, 32–34.

18. The Latin word *satura,* from which the term satire is derived, refers to a full plate of a medley or mixture of things. The extent to which satiric elements may be found in any composition depends upon the author's personal preference and artistic design. At the very least, satire may influence the tone of a work and may be confined to a single description or anecdote, or at the other extreme, it may permeate the entire piece from its fundamental structure to its individual tropes.

19. Nancy Vogeley, "Defining the 'Colonial Reader': *El Periquillo Sarniento,*" *Publications of the Modern Language Association* 102 (1987): 785. Although Vogeley uses Fernández de Lizardi's picaresque novel to formulate her definition of the colonial reader, many of her observations may be applied to a readership that existed before its 1816 publication.

20. Hutcheon's study of parody in twentieth-century art and literature is the most thorough of its kind to date, and she makes a convincing argu-

ment for calling it a principal mode in the construction of contemporary texts. Unlike Margaret A. Rose in her *Parody/Meta-fiction*, for example, she does not define parody as a form of satire, and she distinguishes it from satire by the nature of its focus. Parody, she contends, deals strictly with textual matters, while satire concerns itself with social and moral issues that are extratextual. Parody and satire frequently interact, however, and the former, in fact, has proven to be an effective vehicle for satirists; Hutcheon, pp. 32, 51; 19, 43.

21. Margaret A. Rose, *Parody/Meta-fiction*, pp. 25–28.

22. Hutcheon, pp. 6, 15, 52.

23. Michel Foucault, *The Order of Things*, pp. 47–50. For a detailed discussion of Cervantes' use of parody's power to transform narrative within a satiric framework, see James A. Parr's *Don Quixote: An Anatomy of Subversive Discourse*.

24. Hutcheon, p. 35.

25. Richard E. Greenleaf, *The Mexican Inquisition of the Sixteenth Century*, p. 183. See also Henry Charles Lea, *The Inquisition in the Spanish Dependencies*, pp. 265, 444–446.

26. The first book to be printed on this press was the *Breve y más compendiosa doctrina christiana en lengua mexicana y castellana*, produced in 1539. Its printing antedates the earliest book published in the British colonies by nearly one hundred years. Julie Greer Johnson, *The Book in the Americas: The Role of Books and Printing in the Development of Culture and Society in Colonial Latin America*, p. 5.

27. Vogeley, pp. 784–785.

28. Newspapers, however, had to submit to censorship too, and those printing unsuitable material according to royal officials were forced to close. Such was the case of the *Mercurio Peruano*, Lima's second newspaper, which was shut down by orders of the government after only five years of publication; Johnson, *The Book in the Americas*, p. 65.

29. Dorothy Schöns, *Book Censorship in New Spain*, ix–xviii. See also Stephen C. Mohler, "Publishing in Colonial Spanish America: An Overview," *Inter-American Review of Bibliography* 28.3 (1978): 259–273.

30. Leonard, *Books of the Brave*. This is the thesis of Leonard's excellent study.

31. Schöns, p. xv.

32. Anthony M. Pasquariello, "The *Entremés* in Sixteenth-Century Spanish America," *Hispanic American Historical Review* 32.1 (1952) 44–48.

33. Irving A. Leonard, *Baroque Times in Old Mexico*, p. 103.

34. Mohler, pp. 266–268. In discussing the effects of censorship on the nineteenth-century press, Mohler mentions that Joaquín Fernández de Lizardi was imprisoned in Mexico for his controversial contributions to newspapers and journals.

35. Leonard, *Baroque Times in Old Mexico*, p. 107.

36. Francisca Josefa Castillo y Guevara, *Obras completas*, ed. Darío Achury Valenzuela, 1 : 10.

37. For a general discussion of similar circumstances in Mexico, see Jean

Franco's "La heterogeneidad peligrosa: Escritura y control social en vísperas de la independencia mexicana," *Hispamérica* 12 (1983): 3–34.

38. In his introduction to *Deconstruction in Context*, Mark C. Taylor discusses the nature of Western philosophy and acknowledges a similar countercurrent evident from its beginning in Greece, which was intended to subvert its "privileged oneness and unity." By focusing on differences rather than similarities, therefore, some philosophers offered an alternative expression that elucidated the position of the Other and established for it a new identity; Taylor, ed., *Deconstruction in Context: Literature and Philosophy*, p. 4.

Bakhtin's lengthy discussion of the grotesque in his *Rabelais* is also important to my investigation, as he considers it to be synonymous with the carnivalesque; Mikhail Bakhtin, *Rabelais and His World*, trans. Helene Iswolsky, pp. 30–53.

39. Although some objections to Bakhtin's theories have been raised by such notable critics as Tzvetan Todorov, few theoreticians have recognized the vitality of satire as Bakhtin has done or have been able to trace it so convincingly from antiquity to modern times; Todorov, *Mikhail Bakhtin: The Dialogical Principle*, trans. Wlad Godzich, p. 79. Palmeri, in fact, by reevaluating the importance that Bakhtin accords the carnivalesque as officialdom's opposite, focuses not on carnival itself but on the process it initiates by confronting the official order; Palmeri, p. 16.

40. Mikhail Bakhtin, *Problems of Dostoevsky's Poetics*, trans. R. W. Rotsel, pp. 87–90.

41. Emir Rodríguez Monegal, "Carnaval/antropofagia/parodia," *Revista Iberoamericana* 108–109 (1979): 408.

42. Among the types of fantasy mentioned by Bakhtin are dreams and trips to the netherworld, which will be discussed later in this study; Bakhtin, *Problems of Dostoevsky's Poetics*, pp. 94–96.

43. *Problems of Dostoevsky's Poetics*, Bakhtin, pp. 93–97, 110. According to Bakhtin: "This carnivalized genre [Menippean satire], extraordinarily flexible and as versatile as Proteus, and capable of penetrating other genres, has had enormous, but as yet underestimated significance for the development of European literatures. The "Menippean satire" became one of the chief carriers and implementors of the carnival attitude toward the world and has remained so up until the very present" (93).

44. In this brief profile of satire written in Spain, I have mentioned the more important works of this critical mode of expression and those that will influence in some way satirical writings produced in the viceroyalties. For a general overview of early Peninsular satire, see Kenneth R. Scholberg's two studies, *Sátira e invectiva en la España medieval* and *Algunos aspectos de la sátira en el siglo XVI*. Studies on specific satirists or satiric works are referred to in later chapters of this book as the impact of Peninsular satire is felt in colonial Spanish America.

45. Among the many notable studies on picaresque literature are Stuart Miller, *The Picaresque Novel*; Richard Bjornson, *The Picaresque Hero in European Fiction*; Alexander Blackburn, *The Myth of the Picaro*; and Clau-

dio Guillén, "Toward a Definition of the Picaresque" and "Genre and Countergenre: The Discovery of the Picaresque," in *Literature as System*, pp. 71–106, 135–158.

2. The Sixteenth Century: The Conquest and the Years That Followed

1. Bernal Díaz del Castillo, *Historia verdadera de la conquista de la Nueva España*, pp. 577–578.

2. Francisco de Terrazas, *Poesías*, ed. Antonio Castro Leal, p. 90. Other poets, such as Pedro de Trejo and Antonio de Saavedra Guzmán, voice similar discontent in their epics.

3. See Castro Leal's introduction to Terrazas' *Poesías*, p. ix and Baltazar Dorantes de Carranza, *Sumaria relación de las cosas de la Nueva España*, pp. 18–23; Díaz del Castillo, p. 376.

4. Alfonso Méndez Plancarte, ed., *Poetas novohispanos: Primer siglo (1521–1621)* p. 137.

5. Joaquín García Icazbalceta, ed., *Obras*, p. 279.

6. Méndez Plancarte, pp. 136, 20–22.

7. Francisco A. de Icaza, "Cristóbal de Llerena y los orígenes del teatro en la América española," *Revista de Filología Española* 8.2 (1921): 121–130. Other references to this article appear in the text. Icaza was the first scholar to publish Llerena's *entremés*. It was reprinted, however, in Pedro Henríquez Ureña's *La cultura y las letras coloniales en Santo Domingo*, pp. 153–157.

8. Pasquariello, "The *Entremés*," p. 55.

9. Max Henríquez Ureña, *Panorama histórico de la literatura dominicana*, p. 38.

10. Christopher Columbus, *The Journal of Christopher Columbus*, trans. Cecil Jane, p. 92.

11. Ronald Paulson, *The Fictions of Satire*, p. 110.

12. José Juan Arrom, *El teatro de Hispanoamérica en la época colonial*, p. 61.

13. For a definition of the grotesque and its use in Spanish literature, see Henryk Ziomek, *Lo grotesco en la literatura española del siglo de oro*, pp. 7–18.

14. Julie Greer Johnson, *Women in Colonial Spanish American Literature: Literary Images*, pp. 85–109.

15. Fray Toribio de Benavente (Motolinía), *Historia de los indios de la Nueva España*, pp. 66–67.

16. Eliade, "Paradise and Utopia," in *Utopias and Utopian Thought*, ed. Manuel, pp. 262–263.

17. Fernán González de Eslava, *Coloquios espirituales y sacramentales* 1:228. See also Juan del Valle y Caviedes, *Obras completas*, ed. Daniel R. Reedy; Pedro de Peralta Barnuevo, *Obras dramáticas*; and Guillermo Lohmann Villena, *El arte dramático en Lima durante el virreinato*.

18. Dorantes de Carranza, pp. 150–154. Two comprehensive compilations of Rosas de Oquendo's poetry have been published since 1604. See

A. Paz y Melia: "Cartapacio de diferentes versos a diversos asuntos compuestos ó recogidos por Mateo Rosas de Oquendo," *Bulletin Hispanique* 8 (1906) 154–162; "Sátira hecha por Mateo Rosas de Oquendó á las cosas que pasan en el Pirú año de 1598," *Bulletin Hispanique* 8 (1906): 255–278; "Cartapacio de Oquendo," *Bulletin Hispanique* 9 (1907): 154–185; and Rubén Vargas Ugarte, *Rosas de Oquendo y otros*. In 1990 a new critical edition of Rosas de Oquendo's most famous poem appeared that contains the latest study on the satirist and his work. See Pedro Lasarte, ed., *Sátira hecha por Mateo Rosas de Oquendo a las cosas que pasan en el Pirú, año de 1598*. References to Rosas de Oquendo's *Sátira* have been taken from this edition and will appear hereafter in the text.

Additional information about the poet may be found in the following sources: Alfonso Reyes, "Rosas de Oquendo en América," in *Obras completas* 6:25–53; Fernando Cabrices, "Mateo Rosas de Oquendo, poeta y escritor satírico de la conquista," *Revista Nacional de Cultura* 5.40 (1943): 10–16; and C. Flores Franco, "Andanzas de Mateo Rosas de Oquendo," *Sustancia* 2.5 (1940): 90–93.

19. In a recent article, Pedro Lasarte warns against taking what Rosas de Oquendo says about himself at face value and cites several studies in which scholars have formulated his biography on allegedly autobiographical elements in his poetry; Lasarte, "Apuntes bio-bibliográficos y tres inéditos de Mateo Rosas de Oquendo," *Revista de Crítica Literaria Latinoamericana* 14.28 (1988): 91–94. Unfortunately, little information is currently available from other sources about Rosas as well as other satirists of the colonial period, and investigators have had to rely on literary portraits to suggest in some way the life of these elusive authors.

20. In his "Romance" ("Ballad"), Rosas de Oquendo laments this situation.

Muxer es quien me persigue,
por muxer perdi mi patria
y por muxer pierdo agora,
Mexico, tus bellas damas. (171)

(It is the women who follow me,
for women I lost my country
and for women I am losing now,
Mexico, your beautiful ladies.)

Paz y Melia, "Cartapacio de diferentes versos," p. 171.

21. Lasarte, *Sátira*, p. xiii. Reyes has published what he believes to be Rosas de Oquendo's account of his journey to the New World; Reyes, pp. 27–29.

22. Emilio Carilla, "Rosas de Oquendo y el Tucumán," in *Estudios de Literatura Argentina (Siglos XVI–XVIII)*, pp. 87–88, 100.

23. Dorantes de Carranza, p. 150.

24. Percy G. Adams, *Travel Literature and the Evolution of the Novel*, pp. 78, 173.

25. Juan Ruiz, *Libro de buen amor*, ed. Joan Corominas (Madrid: Gredos, 1967).

26. Luis Leal, "Picaresca hispanoamericana: De Oquendo a Lizardi," in *Estudios de literatura hispanoamericana en honor a José J. Arrom*, ed. Andrew P. Debicki and Enrique Pupo-Walker, pp. 47–48.

27. For a lengthier discussion of Rosas de Oquendo's grotesque female portraiture as well as his presentation of sexual allegory, see Pedro Lasarte, "El retrato y la alegoría satírico-burlesca en Rosas de Oquendo," *Lexis* 10.1 (1986): 81–93.

28. The Hurtado de Mendoza family openly favored the accounts written by other members of the Araucan expedition such as Pedro Mariño de Lovera and Alonso de Góngora Marmolejo: Mariño de Lovera, *Crónica del reino de Chile*, vol. 6 of *Colección de historiadores de Chile y documentos relativos a la historia nacional* (Santiago, Chile: Imprenta del Ferrocarril, 1865); Góngora Marmolejo, *Historia de Chile desde su descubrimiento hasta el año de 1575*, vol. 2 of *Colección de historiadores de Chile y documentos relativos a la historia nacional*. Among the tributes written in the colonies were Christóval Suárez de Figueroa's *Hechos de don García Hurtado de Mendoza, Quarto Marques de Cañete* (Madrid: Imprenta Real, 1613); Belmonte Bermúdez' *comedia* entitled *Algunas hazanas de las muchas de D. García Hurtado de Mendoza, Marqués de Cañete;* and Pedro de Oña's *Arauco domado.*

29. Rubén Vargas Ugarte, *Historia general del Perú, Virreinato (1551–1596)* (Lima: Carlos Milla Batres, 1966) 2:311–313.

30. Ercilla remembered his flamboyant commanding officer and his part in the highly successful campaigns only as a formality and point of historical accuracy in *La Araucana*. During the Chilean conflict, Don García had sentenced Ercilla to death for allegedly provoking a fight with another soldier. The sentence was commuted, however, when several of his admirers intervened on his behalf; José Toribio Medina, *Vida de Ercilla* (Mexico City: Fondo de Cultura Económica, 1948), pp. 78–79.

31. Félix Lope de Vega Carpio, *La dragontea* (Burgos, Museo Naval, 1935), pp. 79, 83. Further homage is paid to Oña's work by Lope in his creation of the *comedia* entitled *Arauco domado* in which the youthful governor of Chile is again the main character. Félix Lope de Vega Carpio, *Arauco domado por el excellentisimo señor don García Hurtado de Mendoza* (Santiago, Chile: Sociedad de Bibliófilos Chilenos, 1963). Don García is also the protagonist of lesser works by Gaspar de Avila and Francisco González de Bustos.

32. For Oña's description of Don García, see pp. 57–61. Even the Chilean poet mentions his sickly condition during his viceroyship; Oña, p. 621. Don García was so ill, in fact, that he wrote to the king for a replacement shortly after assuming his post in Lima.

33. James A. Williamson, *The Age of Drake* (London: Adam and Charles Black, 1965), pp. 347–352.

34. The only remaining ship was *The Dainty*, or *La Linda* as the Spanish called it, which had been named by Queen Elizabeth I.

Richard Hawkins' threat to Lima was the subject of a fifteen-page pamphlet printed in 1594 by Antonio Ricardo, who brought the printing press to South America from Mexico. The distribution of this account probably marked the first occasion in which news was circulated in printed form on the continent; Johnson, *The Book in the Americas*, p. 65.

35. Philip Ainsworth Means, *Fall of the Inca Empire and the Spanish Rule in Peru, 1530–1780*, p. 233. Hawkins remained in Peru until 1597 when he was sent to Spain to spend an additional five years in prison before returning to England in 1602.

36. References to Rosas de Oquendo's *La victoria naval peruntina* have been taken from Vargas Ugarte's edition of his works and will appear hereafter in the text. For a comprehensive discussion of Oña's work, see Salvador Dinamarca, *Estudio del "Arauco domado" de Pedro de Oña.*

37. Oña's account of the sea battle, the last episode of *Arauco domado*, is much more detailed, but it, too, is incomplete. In the final lines of the poem, he expresses the desire to continue it in a sequel; however, his continuation was never written. Oña, pp. 682–683.

38. According to the Inca Garcilaso de la Vega, *pacha* means "the world, or universe"; el Inca Garcilaso de la Vega, *Comentarios reales*, in vol. 133 of Biblioteca de Autores Españoles (Madrid: Ediciones Atlas, 1960), book 2, chap. 2, p. 43.

39. For the Chilean poet's mention of Venus, see Oña, pp. 52–53.

40. See Oña, p. 63.

41. Oña, pp. 57–64.

42. Oña, p. 193.

43. See Oña's cantos 5 and 6.

44. Oña portrays Hawkins as a worthy adversary; Oña, p. 623.

45. Oña, p. 34.

46. Vargas Ugarte, *Historia general*, pp. 318–319, 358–360.

47. Doña Teresa died in Cartagena during her return trip to Spain; Fernando Campos Harriet, *Don García Hurtado de Mendoza en la historia americana* (Santiago, Chile: Editorial Andrés Bello, 1969), pp. 126–171.

48. Oña, p. 1.

49. For a discussion of the portrayal of women in *Arauco domado*, see Johnson, *Women*, pp. 41–44.

50. Francisco J. Santamaría, *Diccionario general de americanismos*, 2: 223.

51. Oña, pp. 250, 424.

52. Oña, pp. 634–635, 647–682. Another description in which Don Beltrán is portrayed as a great hero in his encounter with Hawkins appears in the Count of La Granja's epic poem to Lima's patron saint; Luis Antonio de Oviedo y Herrera, *Santa Rosa de Lima* (Lima: Imprenta de Aurelio Alfaro, 1867) 254, 258, 265–266.

53. Rosas de Oquendo's disparaging image of Galicians is a reflection of the *criollos'* opinion of *peninsulares* from that region of Spain; Francisco A. Encina, "The Basis of Spanish American Independence," in *The Origins of*

the Latin American Revolutions, 1808–1826, ed. R. A. Humphreys and John Lynch, p. 246.

54. Leal, pp. 47–58.

55. Leonard, *Books of the Brave,* pp. 258–259. Leonard mentions that the picaresque was a parodic interpretation of chivalric fiction and that the *pícaro* was an Amadís upside down.

3. The Seventeenth Century: The Growth of Colonial Society

1. Juan Rodríguez Freire, *El Carnero,* ed. Miguel Aguilera, pp. 53, 129–130, 110. Other references to *El Carnero* correspond to this edition as well and are noted hereafter in the text of the chapter. The spelling of the author's name is not constant and appears as Freire, Fresle, Freyle, and Freile in both documentation and criticism.

2. Chang-Rodríguez, *Violencia y subversión,* pp. 43–44.

3. Chang-Rodríguez, *Violencia y subversión,* pp. 44–45. Other important studies of Rodríguez Freile's life and work are Esteban Pavletich, "El código del honor de Juan Rodríguez Freyle," *Boletín Cultural y Bibliográfico* 10.7 (1967): 1508–1520; Pedro Lastra, "Sobre Juan Rodríguez Freyle (Notas de lectura)," *University of Dayton Review* 16.2 (1983): 35–41; and Alessandro Martinengo, "La cultura literaria de Juan Rodríguez Freyle," *Thesaurus* 19.2 (1964): 274–299.

4. The most recent research on Rodríguez Freile's work focuses on its contribution to the early development of the novel in Spanish America and not on its importance to the emergence of satire in the colonies. Three valuable studies in which its novelistic qualities are discussed are Raquel Chang-Rodríguez, "Las máscaras de *El Carnero,*" in *Violencia y subversión,* pp. 41–61; Enrique Pupo-Walker, "La historia como pretexto: Formas de la invención literaria en *El Carnero,*" in *La vocación literaria del pensamiento histórico en América, desarrollo de la prosa de ficción: siglos XVI, XVII, XVIII y XIX,* pp. 123–155; and Roberto González Echevarría, *Myth and Archive: A Theory of Latin American Narrative,* pp. 67, 87–92.

5. Although the application of Hayden White's theories on historiography has recently come under fire in scholarship related to the colonial period, he does address the use of irony in writing history and discusses its role in the creation of "metalogical" discourse. Such an arrangement of textual elements, he contends, is done "in the interest of resituating consciousness with respect to its environment, of redefining the distinction between self and environment or of reconceptualizing the relation between self and other in specifically nonlogical, more nearly imaginative ways"; Hayden White, *Tropics of Discourse: Essays in Cultural Criticism,* p. 10.

6. Although the meaning of the popular title *El Carnero* is still not precisely understood, it probably refers to a repository for refuse rather than a leather binding or a cuckolded husband; Susan Herman, "Conquista y descubrimiento del Nuevo Reino de Granada," *Boletín Cultural y Bibliográfico* 20.1 (1983): 83.

7. Johnson, *Women*, p. 46.

8. This period in New Granada's history is covered in Chapters 11–14 of *El Carnero*. For more details on the mayhem during this administration, see my article "A Satiric View of Colonization: Rodríguez Freile's History of New Granada," *North Dakota Quarterly* 55.3 (1987): 166–174.

9. Eliade, "Paradise and Utopia," in *Utopias and Utopian Thought*, ed. Manuel, pp. 262–263.

10. Palmeri, p. 67.

11. A discussion of the Fall and its relationship to the Chibcha civilization was presented by Susan Herman in her paper "Conquest and Discovery: Subversion of the Fall in *El Carnero*."

12. Fernando de Rojas, *La Celestina*, ed. Bruno Mario Damiani (Madrid: Cátedra, 1976), p. 63. For the English translation, see Lesley Byrd Simpson, trans., *The Celestina*, by Fernando de Rojas (Berkeley and Los Angeles: University of California Press, 1955), p. 8.

13. Under the guise of protecting the New World's women, who were viewed as being as impressionable as the Indians, men restricted their access to the reading materials generally available to the literate public; Adorno, "El sujeto colonial y la construcción cultural de la alteridad," p. 60. For a longer discussion of Rodríguez Freile's treatment of female characters, see my study *Women*, pp. 92–95.

14. Juan Rodríguez Freile, *The Conquest of New Granada*, trans. William C. Atkinson, p. 72. This translation is abridged, as much of Rodríguez Freile's moralistic commentary has been omitted by the translator; Rodríguez Freire, *El Carnero*, p. 206.

15. Ruth Behar, "Sexual Witchcraft, Colonialism, and Women's Powers: Views from the Mexican Inquisition," in *Sexuality and Marriage in Colonial Latin America*, ed. Asunción Lavrin, p. 179.

16. Palmeri, p. 67.

17. For a discussion of Rodríguez Freile's use of Rojas' masterpiece, see my article "Three Celestinesque Figures of Colonial Spanish American Literature," *Celestinesca* 5.1 (1981): 43–44. Chang-Rodríguez discusses the influence of the picaresque in her book *Violencia y subversión*, pp. 43, 47–48.

18. Robert C. Elliott, *The Power of Satire: Magic, Ritual, Art*.

19. Sor Juana's date of birth as given by her first biographer is 1651; however, in recent years it has been cited as 1648.

20. Sor Juana's life and works continue to intrigue scholars and are the subject of a number of outstanding, recent studies. Among them are Octavio Paz, *Sor Juana; or, The Traps of Faith*, trans. Margaret Sayers Peden; Georgina Sabat de Rivers, ed., *Proceedings of the Symposium on "Sor Juana Inés de la Cruz y la cultura virreinal," University of Dayton Review* 16.2 (1983); and Stephanie Merrim's collection of essays, *Feminist Perspectives on Sor Juana Inés de la Cruz*.

21. The burlesque poetry of Sor Juana has frequently been dismissed as being too frivolous and absurd, and the satiric elements of her most famous works have often been overlooked for other aspects of their composition.

For these reasons, Sor Juana's considerable talent as a satirist has never been evaluated in detail.

22. The failure of women to live up to this image may be responsible in part for their recurring presentation as targets of colonial satire.

23. Johnson, *Women*, pp. 166–168.

24. Georgina Sabat de Rivers, "Sor Juana: Diálogo de retratos," *Revista Iberoamericana* 120–121 (1982): 706–707.

25. Sor Juana Inés de la Cruz, *Obras completas*, ed. Alfonso Méndez Plancarte and Alberto G. Salceda, vol. 4, pp. 38, 65–74. See also Anthony M. Pasquariello, "The Seventeenth-Century Interlude in the New World Secular Theater," in *Homage to Irving A. Leonard*, ed. Raquel Chang-Rodríguez and Donald A. Yates, pp. 106–107.

26. Méndez Plancarte, vol. 1, pp. 320–330. All of Sor Juana's satirical works may be found in this edition, and references to them are cited hereafter in the text.

27. Frederick Luciani, "El amor desfigurado: El ovillejo de Sor Juana Inés de la Cruz," *Texto Crítico* 34–35 (1986): 17–18. This study carefully examines the metaphorical language of Sor Juana's poetry and places her *ovillejos* within the context of Renaissance and baroque tradition.

28. Luciani, "El amor desfigurado," pp. 21–22.

29. Although the fact that Sor Juana wrote both Petrarchan and anti-Petrarchan poetry appears to be contradictory, other famous poets such as Quevedo and Caviedes indulged in this literary exercise as well. See Frederick Luciani, "The Burlesque Sonnets of Sor Juana Inés de la Cruz," *Hispanic Journal* 8.1 (1986): 85–95.

30. For the translation of "Hombres necios," see Elias L. Rivers, ed., *Renaissance and Baroque Poetry of Spain*, pp. 322–324. For a more comprehensive translation of Sor Juana's works, see Alan S. Trueblood, *A Sor Juana Anthology*.

31. Translations of Sor Juana's *Respuesta* have been taken from *A Woman of Genius: The Intellectual Autobiography of Sor Juana Inés de la Cruz*, trans. Margaret Sayers Peden. References to them appear hereafter in the text of the chapter.

32. David S. Wiesen, *St. Jerome as a Satirist*, pp. 235–240.

33. For discussions of the rhetorical structure of Sor Juana's *Respuesta* that focus on nonsatirical elements, see Constance M. Montross, *Virtue or Vice? Sor Juana's Use of Thomistic Thought*, and Rosa Perelmuter Pérez, "La estructura retórica de la *Respuesta a Sor Filotea*," *Hispanic Review* 51.2 (1983): 147–158.

34. Jean Franco, *Plotting Women: Gender and Representation in Mexico*, p. 45; Kathleen A. Myers, "Sor Juana's *Respuesta*: Rewriting the *Vitae*," *Revista Canadiense de Estudios Hispánicos* 14.3 (1990): 459–468. Myers notes nonsatirical revisions.

35. Arenal and Schlau, *Untold Sisters*, pp. 11–16.

36. Because of her amazing New World exploits, Catalina de Erauso became the subject of several Golden Age plays, among them Juan Pérez de Montalbán's *La monja alférez* ("The Nun Ensign"). She also allegedly wrote

an account of her adventures, which contains numerous picaresque elements; Erauso, *Historia de la Monja Alférez Doña Catalina de Erauso, escrita por ella misma.* In addition to her interest in the theater and the picaresque, Sor Juana may have also felt an affinity for her because both women shared Basque origins and heritage.

37. Caviedes, p. 454.

38. Sor Juana's reference to Aristotle as a traditional authority is particularly sarcastic, as he was a firm believer in the inferiority of women; Vern L. Bullough, *The Subordinate Sex: A History of Attitudes toward Women,* pp. 61–64.

39. Dorothy Schöns, "Some Obscure Points in the Life of Sor Juana Inés de la Cruz," *Modern Philology* 24.2 (1926): 151–159.

40. Mabel Moraña, "Barroco y conciencia criolla en Hispanoamérica," *Revista de Crítica Literaria Latinoamericana* 14.28 (1988): 248.

41. Shortly after the beginning of the nineteenth century, both Joaquín Fernández de Lizardi and Anastasio María Ochoa became noted for the use of satire in their works. The former's satiric writing is voluminous and merits an individual study of its own.

42. Palma was inspired by Caviedes' creativity, and satire consequently became an important aspect of his own literary production; Roy L. Tanner, *The Humor of Irony and Satire in the Tradiciones peruanas.*

43. Caviedes, pp. xiv–xv. This edition by Daniel R. Reedy is the first complete one of Caviedes' works, and it supersedes those of Rubén Vargas Ugarte, *Obras,* and Ricardo Palma, *Flor de Academias, y Diente del Parnaso.* All references to Caviedes' poetry have been taken from Reedy's edition and are cited hereafter in the text. See also Guillermo Lohmann Villena, "Un poeta virreinal del Perú: Juan del Valle y Caviedes," *Revista de Indias* 33–34 (1948): 778.

44. Daniel R. Reedy, *The Poetic Art of Juan del Valle Caviedes,* pp. 23–26.

45. Because of their visual qualities, Caviedes' verbal caricatures could have served as the forerunner of cartooning in Peru.

46. Mary Claire Randolph, "The Medical Concept in English Renaissance Satiric Theory," in *Satire: Modern Essays in Criticism,* ed. Ronald Paulson, p. 135.

47. Glen L. Kolb, *Juan del Valle y Caviedes: A Study of the Life, Times, and Poetry of a Spanish Colonial Satirist,* p. 17.

48. Kolb, pp. 16–17.

49. Several general studies have been written that deal with the definition and the theoretical development of the grotesque. Among the initial ones contributing to its establishment as an aesthetic category are Wolfgang Kayser, *The Grotesque in Art and Literature,* trans. U. Weisstein; Arthur Clayborough, *The Grotesque in English Literature;* and Frances Barasch, *The Grotesque: A Study in Meanings.* For an excellent discussion of the grotesque and its place in the history of humor and satire, see Bakhtin, *Rabelais,* pp. 19–29. Although his view of the grotesque has been criticized for

overstating its positive value, Bakhtin's concept of this radical distortion in literature is presently the most clearly defined.

An extensive review of Quevedo's use of the grotesque may be found in James Iffland's two-volume study, *Quevedo and the Grotesque.*

50. Francisco de Quevedo y Villegas, *Obras completas* 1:175–176; Palmeri, p. 15.

51. Kolb, p. 27.

52. Translations of fragments of Caviedes' feminine satire have been taken from my study, *Women,* pp. 96–99.

53. For an overview of the *mujer varonil* in colonial literature, see Johnson, *Women,* pp. 9–59.

54. Because they were originally designed to emulate the rhythm of a funeral dirge, verses written in *pie quebrado* can, indeed, sound like a dragging or broken foot.

55. In contrast to this, Caviedes takes a lighter and even frivolous approach to illness in his short dramatic works, as he describes pangs of love as physical symptoms, a frequent device of the courtly poet and lover. For a discussion of satire in Caviedes' dramatic works, see Julie Greer Johnson, "Three Dramatic Works by Juan del Valle y Caviedes," *Hispanic Journal* 3.1 (1981): 59–71. See also Frederick Luciani, "Juan del Valle y Caviedes: *El amor médico,*" *Bulletin of Hispanic Studies* 64 (1987): 337–348 for specific commentary on Caviedes' presentation of love as an infirmity.

56. Susan Sontag, *Illness as Metaphor,* pp. 63–65.

57. Sontag, p. 38.

4. The Eighteenth Century: A Prerevolutionary Setting

1. Alonso Carrió de la Vandera, *El lazarillo de ciegos caminantes,* ed. Emilio Carilla; Alonso Carrió de la Vandera, *El Lazarillo: A Guide for Inexperienced Travelers between Buenos Aires and Lima,* trans. Walter D. Kline. All references to Carrió's work come from this edition and appear hereafter in the text.

2. Walter B. L. Bosé, *El lazarillo de ciegos caminantes y su problema histórico,* pp. 219–287.

3. For additional information regarding Carrió and his creative travelogue, see Félix Alvarez-Brun, "Noticias sobre Carrió de la Vandera (autor del *Lazarillo de ciegos caminantes),*" *Caravelle* 7 (1966): 179–188; Marcel Bataillon, "Introducción a Concolorcorvo y su itinerario de Buenos Aires a Lima," *Cuadernos Americanos* 19 (1960): 192–216; Emilio Carilla, "Carrió de la Vandera y Quevedo," *Quaderni Ibero-Americani* 47–48 (1976–1977): 329–335; Raúl Castagnino, "Concolorcorvo, enigma aclarado," in *Escritores hispanoamericanos,* pp. 117–131; José M. Gómez-Tabanera, "En el bicentenario de Alonso Carrió de Lavandera, Concolorcorvo, autor de *El lazarillo de ciegos caminantes, " Boletín del Instituto de Estudios Asturianos* 108 (1983): 3–36; and José M. Gómez-Tabanera, "Nueva luz sobre el gijonés don Alonso Carrió de Lavandera, *Concolorcorvo:* Su estirpe, hidal-

guía, nacimiento y relaciones," *Boletín del Instituto de Estudios Asturia-nos* (1984): 227–236.

More recent views on Carrió's contribution to the history of prose fiction may be found in Pupo-Walker's *La vocación literaria*, and Karen A. Stolley's *"El lazarillo de ciegos caminantes": Un itinerario crítico.*

4. Emilio Carilla, *El libro de los "misterios,"* pp. 12–13.

5. Carilla, *El libro de los "misterios,"* pp. 13–14.

6. Bosé, p. 270.

7. Carilla, *El libro de los "misterios,"* p. 15.

8. Carilla, *El libro de los "misterios,"* p. 16.

9. José Real Díaz, "Estudio preliminar," in *El lazarillo de ciegos cami-nantes,* by Concolorcorvo, ed. Juan Pérez de Tudela, vol. 122 of Biblioteca de Autores Españoles, p. 271.

10. The Inspector praises the viceroy for his contributions to the cultural and recreational facilities of the city of Lima (445–446). There is a certain irony to this tribute, however, as Don Manuel de Amat is most notably remembered for his love affair with the famous actress Micaela Villegas, La Perricholi.

11. Carilla, *El libro de los "misterios,"* pp. 18–20.

12. Adams, pp. 52, 156–158. Adams relates travel literature in general to historiography as well as to particular literary forms such as the picaresque and the pastoral in his extensive work. These relationships will be discussed later in relation to Carrió's use of the travelogue as a structural device for his account.

13. Pupo-Walker frequently mentions Carrió's use of parody in *El laza-rillo,* but a detailed discussion of it falls outside the scope of his study; Pupo-Walker, *La vocación literaria,* pp. 156–190. *El lazarillo* may also be considered a work of Menippean satire because of its mixture of prose and poetry and its use of the dialogue in ideological discussion, for example; Evaristo de Souza Penha, *La función ideológica de la ironía en "El lazarillo de ciegos caminantes,"* pp. 205–222.

14. Ferdinand's instructions to Columbus were followed by numerous New World explorers who wrote travel accounts, and Swift pokes fun at the Spanish king's advice; Adams, p. 78.

Lucian's satiric travel book served as the Hellenic model for works ridi-culing aspects of the genre.

15. Adams, p. 184.

16. The best description of Lima written from a critical yet nonsatirical point of view is found in the *Noticias secretas* of Jorge Juan and Antonio de Ulloa, who visited Peru in the 1740's on the orders of Philip V. That *El lazarillo* may be a parody of the writings of Juan and Ulloa is suggested by Irving Leonard in his foreword to its English translation.

17. Bakhtin, *Problems of Dostoevsky's Poetics,* pp. 89–90. The Socratic dialogue is an early form of serio-comical literature that later becomes in-corporated into Menippean satire.

18. Bosé proves that Calixto Bustamante Carlos Inca was a real person

but raises questions about such details of his life as the authenticity of his letters of recommendation presented for the position of guide; Bosé, p. 283.

19. According to Adams, the picaresque "mode" is "one of the closest to the literature of travel in *persona*, theme, and structure"; see his discussion, pp. 199–203.

Richard A. Mazzara, "Some Picaresque Elements in Concolorcorvo's *El lazarillo de ciegos caminantes*," *Hispania* 46.2 (1963): 323–327; María Casas de Fauce, *La novela picaresca latinoamericana*.

20. Stolley, chap. 5; Quevedo y Villegas, *Obras completas* 2:242–243.

21. Alan Soons, "An Idearium and Its Literary Presentation in *El lazarillo de ciegos caminantes*," *Romanische Forschungen* 92 (1979): 92–95.

22. Father Bartolomé de Las Casas, as the defender of the New World's Indians, called for their protection in his numerous works. His *Brevísima relación de la destrucción de las Indias*, which vividly presents the atrocities committed by the Spaniards during the conquest, helped to deal a blow to the *encomienda* labor system with the passage of the 1542 New Laws. The portrayal of the Spaniard as cruel and ruthless, however, was quickly utilized by England, France, and Holland, Spain's more powerful adversaries.

Despite the pleas of members of both the clergy and the laity, the condition of indigenous peoples did not improve to any great extent over the next 150 years, and their treatment is again a matter of protest in accounts written by Juan and Ulloa during the first half of the eighteenth century.

23. José de Acosta, *Historia natural y moral de las Indias, en que se tratan las cosas notables del cielo, y elementos, metales, plantas y animales dellos: y los ritos y ceremonias, leyes y gobierno, y guerras de los indios*, ed. Edmundo O'Gorman (Mexico City: Fondo de Cultura Económica, 1940).

24. El Inca Garcilaso de la Vega, *Obras completas*, vols. 132–135 of Biblioteca de Autores Españoles (Madrid: Ediciones Atlas, 1960).

25. For a discussion of the use of the utopian model in the *Comentarios reales*, see Zamora's *Language, Authority, and Indigenous History*, pp. 129–165.

26. Enrique Pupo-Walker, *Historia, creación, y profecía en los textos del Inca Garcilaso de la Vega* (Madrid: Ediciones J. Porrúa Turanzas, 1982).

27. The Jesuit missions, established in Paraguay during the eighteenth century, are a good example of this.

28. The best example of *literatura gauchesca* is considered to be *Martín Fierro* by José Hernández. The tendency to satirize the gaucho, however, persisted in the nineteenth century as well. In his humorous play *Fausto*, Estanislao del Campo portrays a gaucho who comes to Buenos Aires for the first time and attends Gounod's opera *Fausto* without realizing it is a performance. Del Campo also used the pseudonym Anastasio el Pollo (Anastasio the Chicken) to poke fun at his contemporary Hilario Ascasubi, Aniceto el Gallo (Aniceto the Rooster), for writing works of this type.

29. Several excellent examples of pastoral literature from Spain are Garcilaso's *Egloga primera* and Lope de Vega's *Arcadia*.

30. Esteban Terralla y Landa, *Lima por dentro y fuera*, ed. Alan Soons.

All quotations have been taken from this edition of Terralla y Landa's poetry and are cited hereafter in the text. The translations are mine.

31. Ricardo Palma, "El poeta de las adivinanzas," in *Tradiciones peruanas completas,* ed. Edith Palma, pp. 711–724.

32. Luis Alberto Sánchez, *Los poetas de la colonia y de la revolución,* pp. 282–287. See also his introductory note "Dos palabras," in *Lima por dentro y fuera,* by Simón Ayanque, pp. 5–6.

33. For references to the definition and theoretical development of the grotesque, see Chapter 3 on Caviedes. Examples of the grotesque from Quevedo's works have been taken from Iffland's extensive study, *Quevedo and the Grotesque.*

34. Another good example of this strategy may be found in Fernández de Lizardi's description of an oneiric tour of Mexico City in *Noches tristes y día alegre.*

35. Suzanne Dolores Valle-Killeen, *The Satiric Perspective: A Structural Analysis of Late Medieval, Early Renaissance Satiric Treatises,* pp. 48–49.

36. In these three plays, passengers debark in hell, purgatory, and heaven, respectively. The first two dramatic pieces were written in Portuguese and the last in Spanish.

37. Quevedo y Villegas, *Obras completas* 1:163–172.

38. Ilse Nolting-Hauff, *Visión, sátira, y agudeza en los "Sueños" de Quevedo,* trans. Ana Pérez de Linares; José Antonio Castro, "Estructura y estilo de *Los Sueños* de Quevedo," *Anuario de Filología* 1 (1962): 73–85.

39. Diego de Torres Villarroel, *Visiones y visitas de Torres con Don Francisco de Quevedo por la corte,* ed. R. P. Sebold (Madrid: Clásicos Castellanos, 1966). *La barca de Aqueronte,* which is set in the underworld, was later added to the *Visiones.*

40. Raquel Chang-Rodríguez, *Cancionero peruano del siglo XVII.* See also her article "Tapadas limeñas en un cancionerillo peruano del siglo XVII," *Revista Interamericana de Bibliografía* 28.1 (1978): 57–62.

41. Sabino Sola, *El diablo y lo diabólico en las letras americanas (1550–1750),* p. 66.

The transformation of two beautiful *tapadas* into a black woman and a dowager by Cupid posing as a spectre initiates the action in Jerónimo de Monforte y Vera's short dramatic piece *El amor duende;* Lohmann Villena, *El arte dramático,* pp. 540–553.

42. Quevedo y Villegas, *Obras completas* 1:189–190.

43. Leon G. Campbell, "Racism without Race: Ethnic Group Relations in Late Colonial Peru," in *Racism in the Eighteenth Century,* ed. Harold E. Pagliaro, p. 329. See also John D. Browning, "The Periodical Press: Voice of the Enlightenment in Spanish America," *Dieciocho* 3.1 (1980): 5–17.

44. Members of the lower castes were permitted to buy *cédulas de gracias al sacar* (certificates of whiteness) from the Crown to enable them to enter the upper echelons of colonial society; Campbell, p. 326.

45. The Coliseum was rebuilt after the earthquake of 1746. Lohmann Villena discusses the variety and splendor of Lima's theaters during the eighteenth century in the third part of *El arte dramático.*

46. A very similar scene occurs in *El Buscón* when Pablos plays the king in a school pageant; Quevedo y Villegas, *Obras completas* 1:325–326.

47. *Comedias* of Spain's Golden Age, in which ladies and gentlemen appear, were still very popular in the colonies during the eighteenth century.

48. George de Forest Lord, *Heroic Mockery.*

49. Palmeri, pp. 34–35; Gilbert Highet, *The Anatomy of Satire,* p. 39; Bakhtin, *Rabelais,* pp. 226–228.

50. A similar banquet scene is depicted by Quevedo in his poems "Descubre Manzanares secretos de los que en él se bañan" (2.266–267) and "Describe el río Manzanares cuando concurren en el verano a bañarse en él" (2.333–335).

51. Quevedo y Villegas, *Obras completas* 1:342–343. See also Emir Rodríguez Monegal, "Carnaval/antropofagia/parodia," *Revista Iberoamericana* 108–109 (1979): 401–412.

52. The last will and testament may not have been an original part of *Lima por dentro y fuera.*

53. Michael Seidel, *Satiric Inheritance: Rabelais to Sterne,* pp. 57–59.

54. By order of Charles III, many of the Jesuit libraries became public domain after the Society's expulsion in 1767. Espejo was appointed to the directorship of one of Quito's two confiscated collections in 1791. For a complete description of his library, see Alfonso Lastra Espín, "Biblioteca General de la Universidad Central: Sección de libros coloniales que pertenecen a la Universidad de San Gregorio Magno y luego a la biblioteca del doctor Eugenio Espejo," *Cuadernos de Arte y Poesía* (Quito) 9 (1960): 107–147.

55. Espejo was a mixture of all three of the New World's principal races. His father, Luis Santa Cruz y Espejo, who was also referred to as Chusig (Chuzhill or Chuzhig), was a Quechua Indian from Cajamarca, Peru. Although Espejo was apparently the name his father used, it is especially appropriate for his son who, as a satirist, is a mirror that reflects the problems of society in his writing. María Catalina Aldaz y Larraincar, Espejo's mother, was the daughter of a slave from Quito. Her maternal ancestry, it appears, was of Basque origin. José María Vargas, *Biografía del Dr. Eugenio Espejo,* pp. 14–16; Philip L. Astuto, "Eugenio Espejo: A Man of the Enlightenment in Ecuador," *Revista de Historia de América* 44 (1957): 370–371, 374. Scholars have found it difficult to piece together a completely accurate biography because of the numerous contradictions in the information given by Espejo's early critics.

56. Vargas, pp. 47–48; Astuto, "Espejo: Man of the Enlightenment," p. 372.

57. Espejo may have been influenced by Juan Bautista Aguirre (1725–1786), one of his teachers who wrote the satirical *Breve diseño de las ciudades de Guayaquil y Quito.* This poetic letter provides an early model of protest in Quito and portrays that city as one in stagnation.

58. In *La Ciencia Blancardina* Espejo apparently refers to himself as having a talent for writing a form of satire that was well received by the public.

59. Espejo's literary works were published in 1912 at the insistence of Federico González Suárez, one of the writer's more notable biographers. His prologue and notes to the two-volume *Escritos del doctor Francisco Javier Eugenio Santa Cruz y Espejo* are still considered to be a valuable source of information. He is the first of Espejo's critics to note his great appreciation for literature but lack of literary skill in *El Nuevo Luciano.*

60. John Tate Lanning, "The Reception of the Enlightenment in Latin America," in *Latin America and the Enlightenment,* ed. Arthur P. Whitaker, pp. 71–73; Gonzalo Rubio Orbe, *Francisco Eugenio Javier de Santa Cruz y Espejo, biografía,* pp. 59–60.

61. Philip L. Astuto, "Eugenio Espejo: Crítico dieciochesco y pedagogo quiteño," *Revista Hispánica Moderna* 34.3–4 (1968): 515–519.

62. Germán Arciniegas, "Francisco Javier Espejo o el del golilla," *Letras del Ecuador* 11.105 (1956): 1. Details of this incident are still sketchy.

63. Nariño was arrested by royal officials because he translated and published the *Declarations of the Rights of Man* in New Granada.

64. Isaac J. Barrera, "Prólogo," in *El Nuevo Luciano de Quito,* by Francisco Javier Eugenio de Santa Cruz y Espejo, pp. xvi–xxi.

65. Espejo's comprehensive plan is fragmented throughout his individual works as well as the articles he wrote for his newspaper, *Las Primicias de la Cultura de Quito;* Astuto, "Espejo: Man of the Enlightenment," pp. 379, 386–387.

66. Espejo occasionally criticized lawyers, scholars, and dandies, and in his *Defensa de los curas de Riobamba,* he staunchly defended the priests of Riobamba to the detriment of the Indians.

67. Eugenio de Santa Cruz y Espejo, *Obra educativa,* ed. Philip L. Astuto. References to three of Espejo's literary works, *El Nuevo Luciano, Marco Porcio Catón,* and *La Ciencia Blancardina,* have been taken from this edition and appear hereafter in the text. Translations are mine.

Some of his other satirical works, such as his *Cartas riobambenses,* will not be considered in this study because of their vituperation, an expression of his desire to get even with those who opposed him.

68. Espejo's use of this particular pseudonym, together with the over-documentation of sources in his works, may reveal the inferiority complex that he had because of his mixed blood. He tried on numerous occasions to prove his nobility by using the Basque surnames of his mother's family, and he even succeeded in getting a certificate of *limpieza de sangre;* Astuto, "Espejo: Man of the Enlightenment," p. 374.

69. The *Ratio studiorum* was a course of study devised by the Jesuits during the sixteenth century to provide a student with a basic education. Because it had not been revised by the eighteenth century to incorporate new fields of knowledge, it became a point of contention for Espejo.

70. Tzvetan Todorov, *The Conquest of America: The Question of the Other,* trans. Richard Howard, pp. 107, 121, 123. See also Adorno, "From Story to Sermon," in *Guaman Poma,* pp. 57–79. In the latter study, the author discusses the importance of the sermon in cross-cultural communi-

cation and explores the possibility that sixteenth-century indigenous writers used it as a literary strategy of resistance to colonialism.

71. Hardin Craig, "The Vitality of an Old Classic: Lucian and Lucianism," in *The Written Word and Other Essays*, pp. 26–30; Douglas Duncan, *Ben Jonson and the Lucianic Tradition* (Cambridge: Cambridge University Press), pp. 9–25. See also Peter Gay's *Bridge of Criticism: Dialogues among Lucian, Erasmus, and Voltaire on the Enlightenment*, pp. 156–157.

Lucian's ideas may have been introduced to Espejo through the works of Erasmus, who was also an admirer of Lucian and who, like Espejo, targeted education and the clergy for satirical attacks.

72. Espejo was especially influenced by Feijóo's *Teatro crítico* and his *Cartas eruditas*. Although Espejo praises him highly in *El Nuevo Luciano*, his legal *Defensa de los curas de Riobamba* contains some severe criticism of the Spaniard. Lanning, p. 73.

73. As a Jesuit, Father Isla was forced to go to Italy after the expulsion of the Society of Jesus from Spain.

74. Espejo borrows extensively from Bouhours' works as well as from those of other French authors, a practice that has led his critics to charge him with plagiarism. His contribution to colonial letters, however, does not lie in the originality of his ideas but in his application of them to life in New Granada.

75. See Clarence H. Haring, "The 'Reception' of the Enlightenment," p. 35, and Charles C. Griffin, "The Enlightenment and Latin American Independence," pp. 39–40, in *Origins of Latin American Revolutions*, ed. Humphreys and Lynch.

76. It is very difficult to translate satire and convey the original meaning intended by the author. Most of these names translate humorously into English; however, the fact that Murillo chose them because of their similar sound is lost. Instead of literally translating "el Cumbresaltas," therefore, I selected a nonsensical name with a comparable sound.

77. Latin was the official language of the Church during the colonial period, and for this reason, many ecclesiastics opposed the translation of the Bible and other religious works into Spanish and native American languages. Because of the controversy surrounding this matter, it was one of the first issues taken up by the Inquisition in Mexico City; Johnson, *The Book in the Americas*, p. 16.

Espejo has chosen these particular quotations in order to mock the ambiguity of medieval, ecclesiastical Latin and the inherent contradictions in the philosophy of that period.

78. Astuto, "Espejo: Man of the Enlightenment," p. 375.

In *La Ciencia Blancardina*, a series of seven dialogues, the discussion between Mera and Murillo resumes. This time, however, they are joined by Moisés Blancardo, a character who represents Juan de Arauz y Mesia, one of Quito's censors. Espejo again criticizes the educational system that could have produced such a closed-minded individual, and he is especially critical of a piece that Arauz wrote praising the funeral oration of Ramón Yépez, a preacher who appears to demonstrate all the gerundian tendencies of Father Escobar.

79. Fernández de Lizardi, for example, successfully addresses a general audience in his dialogues, *El hermano del perico que cantaba la victoria* and *Conversaciones del Payo y el Sacristán*.

80. This uprising was led by José Gabriel Concorcanqui, who symbolically took the name of the Inca Tupac Amaru. For a discussion of this rebellion, see Steve J. Stern, "The Age of Andean Insurrection, 1742–1782: A Reappraisal," in *Resistance, Rebellion, and Consciousness in the Andean Peasant World: Eighteenth to Twentieth Centuries*, ed. Steve J. Stern, p. 39.

81. Todorov, p. 251.

Selected Bibliography

Primary Sources—Spanish Texts

Carrió de la Vandera, Alonso. *El lazarillo de ciegos caminantes.* Edited by Emilio Carilla. Barcelona: Editorial Labor, 1973.

García Icazbalceta, Joaquín, ed. *Obras.* Mexico City: Biblioteca de Autores Mexicanos, 1896.

González de Eslava, Fernán. *Coloquios espirituales y sacramentales.* 2 vols. Mexico City: Porrúa, 1976.

Juana Inés de la Cruz, Sor. *Obras completas.* Edited by Alfonso Méndez Plancarte and Alberto G. Salceda. 4 vols. Mexico City: Imprenta Nuevo Mundo, 1955; Fondo de Cultura Económica, 1957.

Lasarte, Pedro, ed. *Sátira hecha por Mateo Rosas de Oquendo a las cosas que pasan en el Pirú, año de 1598.* Madison, Wis.: Hispanic Seminary of Medieval Studies, 1990.

Méndez Plancarte, Alfonso, ed. *Poetas novohispanos: Primer siglo (1521–1621).* Mexico City: Universidad Autónoma de México, 1964.

Palma, Ricardo, ed. *Flor de Academias, y Diente del Parnaso.* Lima: Oficina Tipográfica de El Tiempo por L. H. Jiménez, 1899.

Paz y Melia, A. "Cartapacio de diferentes versos a diversos asuntos compuestos ó recogidos por Mateo Rosas de Oquendo." *Bulletin Hispanique* 8 (1906): 154–162.

———. "Cartapacio de Oquendo." *Bulletin Hispanique* 9 (1907): 154–185.

———. "Sátira hecha por Mateo Rosas de Oquendo á las cosas qué pasan en el Pirú año de 1598." *Bulletin Hispanique* 8 (1906): 255–278.

Rodríguez Freire, Juan. *El Carnero.* Edited by Miguel Aguilera. Bogotá: Imprenta Nacional, 1963.

Santa Cruz y Espejo, Eugenio de. *Obra educativa.* Edited by Philip L. Astuto. Caracas: Biblioteca Ayacucho, 1981.

Terralla y Landa, Esteban. *Lima por dentro y fuera.* Edited by Alan Soons. Exeter: University of Exeter Press, 1978.

Terrazas, Francisco de. *Poesías.* Edited by Antonio Castro Leal. Mexico City: Porrúa, 1941.

Valle y Caviedes, Juan del. *Obras completas.* Edited by Daniel R. Reedy. Caracas: Biblioteca Ayacucho, 1984.

————. *Obras.* Edited by Rubén Vargas Ugarte. Lima: Talleres Gráficos de la Tipografía Peruana, 1947.

Vargas Ugarte, Rubén, ed. *Rosas de Oquendo y otros.* Lima: Clásicos Peruanos, 1955. (This is volume 5 of the series.)

Primary Sources—English Translations

Carrió de la Vandera, Alonso. *El Lazarillo: A Guide for Inexperienced Travelers between Buenos Aires and Lima.* Translated by Walter D. Kline. Bloomington: Indiana University Press, 1965.

Columbus, Christopher. *The Diario of Christopher Columbus's First Voyage to America, 1492–1493.* Translated by Oliver Dunn and James E. Kelley, Jr. Norman: University of Oklahoma Press, 1988.

————. *The Journal of Christopher Columbus.* Translated by Cecil Jane. London: Anthony Blond, 1968.

Juana Inés de la Cruz, Sor. *A Woman of Genius: The Intellectual Autobiography of Sor Juana Inés de la Cruz.* Translated by Margaret Sayers Peden. Salisbury, Conn.: Lime Rock, 1987.

Rivers, Elias L., ed. *Renaissance and Baroque Poetry of Spain.* New York: Dell, 1966.

Rodríguez Freile, Juan. *The Conquest of New Granada.* Translated by William C. Atkinson. London: Folio Society, 1961.

Trueblood, Alan S. *A Sor Juana Anthology.* Cambridge: Harvard University Press, 1988.

Secondary Sources

Adams, Percy G. *Travel Literature and the Evolution of the Novel.* Lexington: University Press of Kentucky, 1983.

Adorno, Rolena. *From Oral to Written Expression: Native Andean Chronicles of the Early Colonial Period.* Syracuse: Maxwell School of Citizenship and Public Affairs, Syracuse University, 1982.

————. *Guaman Poma: Writing and Resistance in Colonial Peru.* Austin: University of Texas Press, 1986.

————. "El sujeto colonial y la construcción cultural de la alteridad." *Revista de Crítica Literaria Latinoamericana* 14.28 (1988): 55–68.

Alvarez-Brun, Félix. "Noticias sobre Carrió de la Vandera (autor del *Lazarillo de ciegos caminantes*)." *Caravelle* 7 (1966): 179–188.

Antelo, Antonio. "El mito de la Edad de Oro en las letras hispanoamericanas del siglo XVI." *Thesaurus* 30.1 (1975): 106.

Arciniegas, Germán. "Francisco Javier Espejo o el del golilla." *Letras del Ecuador* 11.105 (1956): 1.

Arenal, Electa, and Stacey Schlau, eds. *Untold Sisters: Hispanic Nuns in Their Own Works.* Albuquerque: University of New Mexico Press, 1989.

Arrom, José Juan. *El teatro de Hispanoamérica en la época colonial.* Havana: Anuario Bibliográfico Cubano, 1956.

Astuto, Philip L. "Eugenio Espejo: Crítico dieciochesco y pedagogo quiteño." *Revista Hispánica Moderna* 34.3–4 (1968): 513–522.

―――. "Eugenio Espejo: A Man of the Enlightenment in Ecuador." *Revista de Historia de América* 44 (1957): 369–391.

Barrera, Isaac J. "Prólogo." In *El Nuevo Luciano de Quito*, by Francisco Javier Eugenio de Santa Cruz y Espejo. Quito: Imprenta del Ministerio de Gobierno, 1943.

Bataillon, Marcel. "Introducción a Concolorcorvo y su itinerario de Buenos Aires a Lima." *Cuadernos Americanos* 19 (1960): 192–216.

Behar, Ruth. "Sexual Witchcraft, Colonialism, and Women's Powers: Views from the Mexican Inquisition." In *Sexuality and Marriage in Colonial Latin America*, edited by Asunción Lavrin, pp. 178–206. Lincoln: University of Nebraska Press, 1989.

Benavente, Toribio de (Motolinía). *Historia de los indios de la Nueva España*. Mexico City: Porrúa, 1969.

Bhabha, Homi K. "The Other Question: Difference, Discrimination, and the Discourse of Colonialism." In *Literature, Politics, and Theory*, edited by Francis Barker et al. London: Methuen, 1986.

Bjornson, Richard. *The Picaresque Hero in European Fiction*. Madison: Wisconsin University Press, 1977.

Blackburn, Alexander. *The Myth of the Picaro*. Chapel Hill: University of North Carolina Press, 1979.

Bosé, Walter B. L. *El lazarillo de ciegos caminantes y su problema histórico*. La Plata: Publicación de la Universidad Nacional de La Plata, 1941.

Browning, John D. "The Periodical Press: Voice of the Enlightenment in Spanish America." *Dieciocho* 3.1 (1980): 5–17.

Bullough, Vern L. *The Subordinate Sex: A History of Attitudes toward Women*. Urbana: University of Illinois Press, 1973.

Cabrices, Fernando. "Mateo Rosas de Oquendo, poeta y escritor satírico de la conquista." *Revista Nacional de Cultura* 5.40 (1943): 10–16.

Campbell, Leon G. "Racism without Race: Ethnic Group Relations in Late Colonial Peru." In *Racism in the Eighteenth Century*, edited by Harold E. Pagliaro, pp. 323–333. Cleveland and London: The Press of Case Western Reserve University, 1973.

Carilla, Emilio. "Carrió de la Vandera y Quevedo." *Quaderni Ibero-Americani* 47–48 (1976–1977): 329–335.

―――. *Estudios de Literatura Argentina (Siglos XVI–XVIII)*. Tucumán: Facultad de Filosofía y Letras, 1968.

―――. *El libro de los "misterios."* Madrid: Gredos. 1976.

Casas de Faunce, María. *La novela picaresca latinoamericana*. Madrid: Alianza, 1977.

Castro, José Antonio. "Estructura y estilo de *Los Sueños* de Quevedo." *Anuario de Filología* 1 (1962): 73–85.

Castagnino, Raúl. "Concolorcorvo, enigma aclarado." In *Escritores hispanoamericanos, desde otros ángulos de simpatía*, pp. 117–131. Buenos Aires: Nova, 1971.

Chandler, Richard E., and Kessel Schwartz. *A New History of Spanish Literature*. Baton Rouge: Louisiana State University Press, 1974.

Chang-Rodríguez, Raquel. *La apropiación del signo: Tres cronistas indígenas del Perú*. Tempe: Center for Latin American Studies, Arizona State University Press, 1988.

————. *Cancionero peruano del siglo XVII*. Lima: Pontificia Universidad Católica del Perú, Fondo Editorial, 1983.

————. "Tapadas limeñas en un cancionerillo peruano del siglo XVII." *Revista Interamericana de Bibliografía* 28.1 (1978): 57–62.

————. *Violencia y subversión en la prosa colonial hispanoamericana, siglos XVI y XVII*. Madrid: Studia Humanitatis, 1982.

Craig, Hardin. "The Vitality of an Old Classic: Lucian and Lucianism." In *The Written Word and Other Essays*, pp. 18–31. Chapel Hill: University of North Carolina Press, 1953.

Cró, Stelio. *Realidad y utopía en el descubrimiento y la conquista, 1492–1682*. Troy, Mich.: International Book Publishers, 1983.

Díaz del Castillo, Bernal. *Historia verdadera de la conquista de la Nueva España*. Mexico City: Porrúa, 1970.

Dinamarca, Salvador. *Estudio del "Arauco domado" de Pedro de Oña*. New York: Hispanic Institute in the United States, 1952.

Dorantes de Carranza, Baltazar. *Sumaria relación de las cosas de la Nueva España*. Mexico City: Imprenta del Museo Nacional, 1902.

Erauso, Catalina de. *Historia de la Monja Alférez Doña Catalina de Erauso, escrita por ella misma*. Paris: Imprenta de Julio Didot, 1829.

Flores Franco, C. "Andanzas de Mateo Rosas de Oquendo." *Sustancia* 2.5 (1940): 90–93.

Foucault, Michel. *The Order of Things*. New York: Vintage, 1973.

Franco, Jean. "La heterogeneidad peligrosa: Escritura y control social en vísperas de la independencia mexicana." *Hispamérica* 12 (1983): 3–34.

————. *Plotting Women: Gender and Representation in Mexico*. New York: Columbia University Press, 1989.

Gay, Peter. *The Bridge of Criticism: Dialogues among Lucian, Erasmus, and Voltaire on the Enlightenment*. New York: Harper and Row, 1970.

Gilman, Stephen. "Bernal Díaz del Castillo and *Amadís de Gaula*." In *Studia Philologica, Homenaje a Dámaso Alonso*, vol. 2, pp. 99–114. Madrid: Gredos, 1961.

Gómez-Tabanera, José M. "En el bicentenario de Alonso Carrió de Lavandera, *Concolorcorvo*, autor de *El lazarillo de ciegos caminantes*." *Boletín del Instituto de Estudios Asturianos* 108 (1983): 3–36.

————. "Nueva luz sobre el gijonés don Alonso Carrió de Lavandera, *Concolorcorvo*: Su estirpe, hidalguía, nacimiento y relaciones." *Boletín del Instituto de Estudios Asturianos* (1984): 227–236.

González Echevarría, Roberto. "Humanism and Rhetoric in *Comentarios reales* and *El Carnero*." In *In Retrospect: Essays on Latin American Literature*, edited by Elizabeth S. Rogers and Timothy J. Rogers, pp. 8–23. York, S.C.: Spanish Literature Publications, 1987.

————. *Myth and Archive: A Theory of Latin American Narrative.* Cambridge: Cambridge University Press, 1990.

————. *The Voice of the Masters: Writing and Authority in Latin American Literature.* Austin: University of Texas Press, 1985.

González Suárez, Federico, ed. *Escritos del doctor Francisco Javier Eugenio Santa Cruz y Espejo.* 2 vols. Quito: Imprenta Municipal, 1912.

Greenleaf, Richard E. *The Mexican Inquisition of the Sixteenth Century.* Albuquerque: University of New Mexico Press, 1969.

Guillén, Claudio. *Literature as System.* Princeton: Princeton University Press, 1971.

Henríquez Ureña, Max. *Panorama histórico de la literatura dominicana.* Rio de Janeiro: Artes Gráficas, 1945.

Henríquez Ureña, Pedro. *La cultura y las letras coloniales en Santo Domingo.* Buenos Aires: Instituto de Filología de la Universidad de Buenos Aires, 1936.

Herman, Susan. "Conquest and Discovery: Subversion of the Fall in *El Carnero.*" Session on "Texts and Contexts: Critical Rereadings of Spanish American Literature to 1900." Modern Language Association Convention, New Orleans, Dec. 1988.

————. "Conquista y descubrimiento del Nuevo Reino de Granada." *Boletín Cultural y Bibliográfico* 20.1 (1983): 77–85.

Humphreys, R. A., and John Lynch, eds. *The Origins of the Latin American Revolutions, 1808–1826.* New York: Alfred A. Knopf, 1965.

Icaza, Francisco A. "Cristóbal de Llerena y los orígenes del teatro en la América española." *Revista de Filología Española* 8.2 (1921): 121–130.

Iffland, James. *Quevedo and the Grotesque.* 2 vols. London: Tamesis, 1982.

Jara, René, and Nicholas Spadaccini, eds. *1492–1992: Re-Discovering Colonial Writing.* Minneapolis: Prisma Institute, 1989.

Johnson, Julie Greer. *The Book in the Americas: The Role of Books and Printing in the Development of Culture and Society in Colonial Latin America.* Providence: John Carter Brown Library, 1988.

————. "A Comical Lesson in Creativity from Sor Juana Inés de la Cruz." *Hispania* 71.2 (1988): 442–444.

————. "Cristóbal de Llerena and His Satiric *Entremés.*" *Latin American Theatre Review* (Fall 1988): 39–45.

————. "Feminine Satire in Concolorcorvo's *El lazarillo de ciegos caminantes.*" *South Atlantic Bulletin* 45.1 (1980): 11–20.

————. "Lo grotesco en Terralla y Landa." *Revista de Crítica Literaria Latinoamericana* 14.28 (1988): 317–325.

————. "New World Chronicles: A Self-Evaluation." *Ideas '92,* no. 6 (January–April 1990); 7–16.

————. "*El Nuevo Luciano* and the Satiric Art of Eugenio Espejo." *Revista de Estudios Hispánicos* 23.3 (1989): 67–85.

————. "La obra satírica de sor Juana Inés de la Cruz." To appear in *Relecturas del barroco de Indias,* edited by Mabel Moraña. Madrid: Ediciones del Norte, 1992.

————. "La risa como medicina en el Perú del siglo XVII: El remedio de Juan del Valle y Caviedes." To appear in *Literatura latinoamericana del período colonial*, edited by Lúcia Helena Costigan and Beatriz González Stephan. Caracas: Ministerio de la Cultura de Venezuela, 1992.

————. "Rosas de Oquendo and *La victoria naval peruntina*." In *Studies in Honor of Merle E. Simmons*, edited by Heitor Martins and Darlene J. Sadlier, pp. 233–247. Bloomington: Hispanic Literary Studies of the Department of Spanish and Portuguese, Indiana University, 1990.

————. "Satire and Eighteenth-Century Colonial Spanish American Society." To appear in *Coded Encounters: Race, Gender, and Ethnicity in Colonial Latin America*, edited by Francisco Javier Cevallos, Jeffrey A. Cole, Nina M. Scott, and Nicomedes Suárez-Arauz. Amherst: University of Massachusetts Press, forthcoming.

————. "A Satiric View of Colonization: Rodríguez Freile's History of New Granada." *North Dakota Quarterly* 55.3 (1987): 166–174.

————. "Three Celestinesque Figures of Colonial Spanish American Literature." *Celestinesca* 5.1 (1981): 41–46.

————. "Three Dramatic Works by Juan del Valle y Caviedes." *Hispanic Journal* 3.1 (1981): 59–71.

————. "Traveling in Eighteenth-Century Spanish America: The Evaluation of a Disgruntled Spaniard." *SECOLAS Annals* 20 (March 1989): 40–47.

————. *Women in Colonial Spanish American Literature: Literary Images.* Westport, Conn., Greenwood, 1983.

Kolb, Glen L. *Juan del Valle y Caviedes: A Study of the Life, Times, and Poetry of a Spanish Colonial Satirist.* New London: Connecticut College, 1959.

Lanning, John Tate. "The Reception of the Enlightenment in Latin America." In *Latin America and the Enlightenment*, edited by Arthur P. Whitaker. Ithaca, N.Y.: Great Seal Books, 1961.

Lasarte, Pedro. "Apuntes bio-bibliográficos y tres inéditos de Mateo Rosas de Oquendo." *Revista de Crítica Literaria Latinoamericana* 14.28 (1988): 85–99.

————. "El retrato y la alegoría satírico-burlesca en Rosas de Oquendo." *Lexis* 10.1 (1986): 77–93.

Lastra, Pedro. "Sobre Juan Rodríguez Freyle (Notas de lectura)." *University of Dayton Review* 16.2 (1983): 35–41.

Lastra Espín, Alfonso. "Biblioteca General de la Universidad Central: Sección de libros coloniales que pertenecen a la Universidad de San Gregorio Magno y luego a la biblioteca del doctor Eugenio Espejo." *Cuadernos de Arte y Poesía* (Quito) 9 (1960): 107–147.

Lea, Henry Charles. *The Inquisition in the Spanish Dependencies.* New York: Macmillan, 1908.

Leal, Luis. "Picaresca hispanoamericana: De Oquendo a Lizardi." In *Estudios de literatura hispanoamericana en honor a José J. Arrom*, edited by Andrew P. Debicki and Enrique Pupo-Walker, pp. 47–58. Chapel Hill: University of North Carolina Press, 1974.

Leonard, Irving A. *Baroque Times in Old Mexico.* Ann Arbor: University of Michigan Press, 1966.

——. *Books of the Brave.* Cambridge: Harvard University Press, 1949.

Levin, Harry. *The Myth of the Golden Age in the Renaissance.* Bloomington: Indiana University Press, 1969.

Lohmann Villena, Guillermo. *El arte dramático en Lima durante el virreinato.* Madrid: Estades, Artes Gráficas, 1945.

——. "Un poeta virreinal del Perú: Juan del Valle y Caviedes." *Revista de Indias* 33–34 (1948): 771–794.

Lord, George de Forest. *Heroic Mockery.* Newark: University of Delaware Press, 1977.

Luciani, Frederick. "El amor desfigurado: El ovillejo de Sor Juana Inés de la Cruz." *Texto Crítico* 34–35 (1986): 11–48.

——. "The Burlesque Sonnets of Sor Juana Inés de la Cruz." *Hispanic Journal* 8.1 (1986): 85–95.

——. "Juan del Valle y Caviedes: *El amor médico.*" *Bulletin of Hispanic Studies* 64 (1987): 337–348.

Luzuriaga, Gerardo. "Sigüenza y Góngora y Sor Juana: Disidentes de la cultura oficial." *Cuadernos Americanos* 242.3 (1982): 140–162.

Manuel, Frank E., ed. *Utopias and Utopian Thought.* Boston: Houghton Mifflin, 1966.

Martinengo, Alessandro. "La cultura literaria de Juan Rodríguez Freyle." *Thesaurus* 19.2 (1964): 274–299.

Mazzara, Richard A. "Some Picaresque Elements in Concolorcorvo's *El lazarillo de ciegos caminantes.*" *Hispania* 46.2 (1963): 323–327.

Means, Philip Ainsworth. *Fall of the Inca Empire and the Spanish Rule in Peru, 1530–1780.* New York and London: Charles Scribner's Sons, 1932.

Merrim, Stephanie, ed. *Feminist Perspectives on Sor Juana Inés de la Cruz.* Detroit: Wayne State University Press, 1991.

Miller, Stuart. *The Picaresque Novel.* Cleveland: The Press of Case Western Reserve University, 1969.

Mohler, Stephen C. "Publishing in Colonial Spanish America: An Overview." *Inter-American Review of Bibliography* 28.3 (1978): 259–273.

Montross, Constance M. *Virtue or Vice? Sor Juana's Use of Thomistic Thought.* Washington, D.C.: University Press of America, 1981.

Moraña, Mabel. "Barroco y conciencia criolla en Hispanoamérica." *Revista de Crítica Literaria Latinoamericana* 14.28 (1988): 229–251.

Myers, Kathleen A. "Sor Juana's *Respuesta*: Rewriting the *Vitae.*" *Revista Canadiense de Estudios Hispánicos* 14.3 (1990): 459–471.

Nolting-Hauff, Ilse. *Visión, sátira, y agudeza en los "Suenos" de Quevedo.* Translated by Ana Pérez de Linares. Madrid: Gredos, 1968.

O'Gorman, Edmundo. *La invención de América.* Mexico City: Fondo de Cultura Económica, 1958. Translation: *The Invention of America.* Bloomington: Indiana University Press, 1961.

Oña, Pedro de. *Arauco domado.* Santiago, Chile: Imprenta Universitaria, 1917.

Ortega, Julio. *Poetics of Change: The New Spanish American Narrative.* Translated by Galen D. Greaser. Austin: University of Texas Press, 1984.

Palma, Ricardo. "Las cuatro PPPP de Lima." In *Tradiciones peruanas completas*, edited by Edith Palma, pp. 558–559. Madrid: Aguilar, 1957.

———. "El poeta de las adivinanzas." In *Tradiciones peruanas completas*, edited by Edith Palma, pp. 711–724. Madrid: Aguilar, 1957.

Parr, James A. *Don Quixote: An Anatomy of Subversive Discourse.* Newark, Del.: Juan de la Cuesta, 1988.

Pasquariello, Anthony M. "The *Entremés* in Sixteenth-Century Spanish America." *Hispanic American Historical Review* 32.1 (1952): 44–58.

———. "The Seventeenth-Century Interlude in the New World Secular Theater." In *Homage to Irving A. Leonard*, edited by Raquel Chang-Rodríguez and Donald A. Yates, pp. 105–113. East Lansing: Latin American Studies Center of Michigan State University, 1977.

Pavletich, Esteban. "El código del honor de Juan Rodríguez Freyle." *Boletín Cultural y Bibliográfico* 10.7 (1967): 1508–1520.

Paz, Octavio. *Sor Juana; or, The Traps of Faith.* Translated by Margaret Sayers Peden. Cambridge: Harvard University Press, 1988.

Penha, Evaristo de Souza. *La función ideológica de la ironía en "El lazarillo de ciegos caminantes."* Ann Arbor: University Microfilms, 1986. 7820762.

Peralta Barnuevo, Pedro de. *Obras dramáticas.* Santiago, Chile: Imprenta Universitaria, 1937.

Perelmuter Pérez, Rosa. "La estructura retórica de la *Respuesta a Sor Filotea.*" *Hispanic Review* 51.2 (1983): 147–158.

———. "El paisaje idealizado en *La Araucana.*" *Hispanic Review* 54.2 (1986): 129–146.

Pupo-Walker, Enrique. *La vocación literaria del pensamiento histórico en América, desarrollo de la prosa de ficción: siglos XVI, XVII, XVIII y XIX.* Madrid: Gredos, 1982.

Quevedo y Villegas, Francisco de. *Obras completas.* 2 vols. Madrid: Aguilar, 1958.

Real Díaz, José. "Estudio preliminar." In *El lazarillo de ciegos caminantes*, by Concolorcorvo, edited by Juan Pérez de Tudela. Biblioteca de Autores Españoles, vol. 122. Madrid: Ediciones, 1959.

Reedy, Daniel R. *The Poetic Art of Juan del Valle Caviedes.* Chapel Hill: University of North Carolina Press, 1964.

Reyes, Alfonso. "Rosas de Oquendo en América." In *Obras completas* 6:25–53. Mexico City: Fondo de Cultura Económica, 1957.

Rubio Orbe, Gonzalo. *Francisco Eugenio Javier de Santa Cruz y Espejo, biografía.* Quito: Talleres Gráficos Nacionales, 1950.

Sabat de Rivers, Georgina. "Sor Juana: Diálogo de retratos." *Revista Iberoamericana* 120–121 (1982): 703–713.

———, ed. *Proceedings of the Symposium on "Sor Juana Inés de la Cruz y la cultural virreinal."* *University of Dayton Review* 16.2 (1983).

Sánchez, Luis Alberto. "Dos palabras." In *Lima por dentro y fuera*, by Simón Ayanque (pseud.), pp. 5–6. Paris: A. Rueff, 1924.

———. *Los poetas de la colonia y de la revolución.* Lima: Editorial Universo, 1974.

Santamaría, Francisco J. *Diccionario general de americanismos.* 3 vols. Mexico City: Editorial Pedro Robredo, 1942.

Schöns, Dorothy. *Book Censorship in New Spain.* Austin: New World Studies, 1949.

———. "Some Obscure Points in the Life of Sor Juana Inés de la Cruz." *Modern Philology* 24.2 (1926): 151–159.

Sola, Sabino. *El diablo y lo diabólico en las letras americanas (1550–1750).* Bilbao, Spain: Universidad de Deusto, 1973.

Sontag, Susan. *Illness as Metaphor.* New York: Vintage, 1979.

Soons, Alan. "An Idearium and Its Literary Presentation in *El lazarillo de ciegos caminantes.*" *Romanische Forschungen* 92 (1979): 92–95.

Stern, Steve J. "The Age of Andean Insurrection, 1742–1782: A Reappraisal." In *Resistance, Rebellion, and Consciousness in the Andean Peasant World: Eighteenth to Twentieth Centuries,* edited by Steve J. Stern. Madison: University of Wisconsin Press, 1987.

Stolley, Karen A. *"El lazarillo de ciegos caminantes": Un itinerario crítico.* Hanover, N.H.: Ediciones del Norte, forthcoming.

Tanner, Roy L. *The Humor of Irony and Satire in the Tradiciones peruanas.* Columbia: University of Missouri Press, 1986.

Taylor, Mark C., ed. *Deconstruction in Context: Literature and Philosophy.* Chicago: University of Chicago Press, 1986.

Todorov, Tzvetan. *The Conquest of America: The Question of the Other.* Translated by Richard Howard. New York: Harper and Row, 1985.

———. *Mikhail Bakhtin: The Dialogical Principle.* Translated by Wlad Godzich. Minneapolis: University of Minnesota Press, 1984.

Vargas, José María. *Biografía del Dr. Eugenio Espejo.* Quito: Editorial Santo Domingo, 1968.

Vogeley, Nancy. "Defining the 'Colonial Reader': *El Periquillo Sarniento.*" *Publications of the Modern Language Association* 102 (1987): 784–800.

Weckman, Luis. "The Middle Ages in the Conquest of America." *Speculum* 26.1 (1951) 130–141.

White, Hayden. *Tropics of Discourse: Essays in Cultural Criticism.* Baltimore: Johns Hopkins University Press, 1978.

Wiesen, David S. *St. Jerome as a Satirist.* Ithaca: Cornell University Press, 1964.

Zamora, Margarita. *Language, Authority, and Indigenous History in the "Comentarios Reales de los Incas."* Cambridge: Cambridge University Press, 1988.

Ziomek, Henryk. *Lo grotesco en la literatura española del siglo de oro.* Madrid: Ediciones Alcalá, 1983.

General Works on Satire and Related Topics

Bakhtin, Mikhail. *Problems of Dostoevsky's Poetics.* Translated by R. W. Rotsel. Ann Arbor: Ardis, 1973.

————. *Rabelais and His World.* Translated by Helene Iswolsky. Cambridge: Massachusetts Institute of Technology Press, 1968.

Barasch, Frances K. *The Grotesque: A Study in Meanings.* The Hague: Mouton, 1971.

Bloom, Edward Alan. *Satire's Persuasive Voice.* Ithaca: Cornell University Press, 1979.

Booth, Wayne C. *A Rhetoric of Irony.* Chicago: University of Chicago Press, 1974.

Clayborough, Arthur. *The Grotesque in English Literature.* Oxford: Clarendon, 1965.

Elliott, Robert C. *The Power of Satire: Magic, Ritual, Art.* Princeton: Princeton University Press, 1960.

Feinberg, Leonard. *Introduction to Satire.* Ames: Iowa State University Press, 1967.

————. *The Satirist: His Temperament, Motivation, and Influence.* Ames: Iowa State University Press, 1963.

Frye, Northrop. *Anatomy of Criticism: Four Essays.* Princeton: Princeton University Press, 1957.

Hernández, Guillermo E. *Chicano Satire: A Study in Literary Culture.* Austin: University of Texas Press, 1991.

Highet, Gilbert. *The Anatomy of Satire.* Princeton: Princeton University Press, 1962.

Hodgart, Matthew. *Satire.* New York: McGraw Hill, 1969.

Hutcheon, Linda. *A Theory of Parody: The Teachings of Twentieth-Century Art Forms.* New York: Methuen, 1985.

Kayser, Wolfgang. *The Grotesque in Art and Literature.* Translated by U. Weisstein. Bloomington: Indiana University Press, 1963.

Kernan, Alvin B. *The Cankered Muse.* New Haven: Yale University Press, 1959.

————. *The Plot of Satire.* New Haven: Yale University Press, 1965.

MacAdam, Alfred. *Modern Latin American Narratives: The Dreams of Reason.* Chicago: University of Chicago Press, 1977.

Mack, Maynard. "The Muse of Satire." In *Satire: Modern Essays in Criticism,* edited by Ronald Paulson, pp. 190–201. Englewood Cliffs, N.J.: Prentice Hall, 1971.

Nelson, Ardis. *Cabrera Infante in the Menippean Tradition.* Newark, Del.: Juan de la Cuesta, 1983.

Palmeri, Frank. *Satire in Narrative.* Austin: University of Texas Press, 1990.

Paulson, Ronald. *The Fictions of Satire.* Baltimore: Johns Hopkins University Press, 1967.

Petro, Peter. *Modern Satire.* Berlin, New York, and Amsterdam: Mouton Publishers, 1982.

Randolph, Mary Claire. "The Medical Concept in English Renaissance Satiric Theory." In *Satire: Modern Essays in Criticism,* edited by Ronald Paulson, pp. 135–170. Englewood Cliffs, N.J.: Prentice-Hall, 1971.

Rodríguez Monegal, Emir. "Carnaval/antropofagia/parodia." *Revista Iberoamericana* 108–109 (1979): 401–412.

Rose, Margaret A. *Parody/Meta-fiction: An Analysis of Parody as a Critical Mirror to the Writing and Reception of Fiction.* London: Croom Helm, 1979.

Scholberg, Kenneth R. *Algunos aspectos de la sátira en el siglo XVI.* Berne, Frankfurt am Main, and Las Vegas: Peter Lang, 1979.

———. *Sátira e invectiva en la España medieval.* Madrid: Gredos, 1971.

Seidel, Michael. *Satiric Inheritance: Rabelais to Sterne.* Princeton: Princeton University Press, 1979.

Skłodowska, Elżbieta. *La parodia en la nueva novela hispanoamericana (1960–1985).* Amsterdam and Philadelphia: Purdue University Monographs in Romance Languages, John Benjamins, 1991.

Tittler, Jonathan. *Narrative Irony in the Contemporary Spanish-American Novel.* Ithaca: Cornell University Press, 1984.

Valle-Killeen, Suzanne Dolores. *The Satiric Perspective: A Structural Analysis of Late Medieval, Early Renaissance Satiric Treatises.* New York: Senda Nueva de Ediciones, 1980.

Worcester, David. *The Art of Satire.* New York: Russell and Russell, 1960.

Index

WIDENER UNIVERSITY
WOLFGRAM
LIBRARY
CHESTER, PA.